Towards the Third Generation University

Towards the Third Generation University

Managing the University in Transition

J.G. Wissema

Managing Director of J.G. Wissema Associates bv and Professor Emeritus of Innovation and Entrepreneurship at Delft University of Technology, the Netherlands

With contributions from Jan Verloop, author of *Insight in Innovation*

Edward Elgar

Cheltenham, UK • Northampton, MA, USA

Published by
Edward Elgar Publishing Limited
The Lypiatts
15 Lansdown Road
Cheltenham
Glos GL50 2JA
UK

Edward Elgar Publishing, Inc.
William Pratt House
9 Dewey Court
Northampton
Massachusetts 01060
USA

Reprinted 2010, 2015

A catalogue record for this book
is available from the British Library

Library of Congress Control Number: 2008939738

ISBN 978 1 84844 216 0

Printed and bound in Great Britain by the CPI Group (UK) Ltd

Acknowledgements

The development of this book was greatly stimulated by a series of lectures in Central and Eastern Europe, Latin America and Asia, visits to universities with know-how commercialisation activities (notably the universities of Cambridge, Leuven, Wageningen, Bandung and Rousse), and a seminar for European lecturers on entrepreneurship at Harvard Business School, sponsored by Dr B. Twaalfhoven and his European Foundation for Entrepreneurship Research (EFER). Preliminary versions of the book were published in Polish in March 2006 by the Polish Agency for Enterprise Development (PARP), and in Bulgaria by Ecorys South East Europe in September 2006. I would like to thank more than 100 colleagues who have been kind enough to enter into discussions with me and from whom I have learned a great deal. Special thanks go to Shell Global Solutions for making case material available and to Dr Bert Twaalfhoven for his ceaseless endeavours to stimulate entrepreneurship and for sponsoring this book. In addition, I would like to thank Jack Lang and Peter Hiscocks of the University of Cambridge and Leo Deuzeman for commenting on the text. Thanks also go to the co-authors of the cases of the Technical University of Bandung and the University of Rousse. I would like to thank Dr Jan Verloop with whom I collaborated on his book *Insight in Innovation*, and who took on the role of partner in discussing and challenging my drafts and co-authoring Chapter 4. Finally, I would like to thank my wife, Dr Julia Djarova of Ecorys International, for the many discussions we had on the contents of this book, at home or while carrying out projects in this field.

J.G. Wissema

Introduction and summary

Universities are changing in a fundamental way, moving from the model of the science-based university that emerged after the Napoleonic period into what we will call the 'third generation university' or 3GU for short. Several forces propel this change. The first is that top universities that want to continue carrying out cutting-edge scientific research are seeking alternative funding as the cost of such research has risen above the budgets that governments can provide. As a result, leading universities across the world are seeking collaboration with technology-driven enterprises. This coincides with a trend that such enterprises discontinue carrying out fundamental research themselves, seeking instead collaboration with universities of a high standard to work jointly on basic research projects that they consider of vital importance for their future competitive power. As a result, the once separated worlds of academic and industrial research increasingly intertwine.

The second trend is globalisation, which does not stop at the gates of universities. Most universities used to have a de facto regional monopoly concerning the intake of students. With the improved opportunities to study abroad, universities are now actively competing for the best students. Academics have likewise become a subject of competition and the research contracts of corporations also address a global market. The result of this threefold competition is a rapidly increasing gap between top and lesser universities. The winners of this race are those universities that manage to become the nucleus of an international know-how hub, a site of international excellence where academic institutions mix with institutions of industrial and other research, a place that no one in the field of interest can miss: students, academics, corporations. Second generation universities (2GU) focused on pure science and did not regard the application of their know-how as their task. In contrast, third generation universities actively pursue the exploitation or commercialisation of the knowledge they create, making it their third objective, equal in importance to the objectives of scientific research and education. Know-how exploitation includes an active involvement in stimulating technostarters – students or academics who start their own technology-based firm. Leading US universities such as Massachusetts Institute of Technology (MIT), Stanford University and Harvard University as well as European role models such as the University of Cambridge and the Catholic University of Leuven show the way.

Commercial activities, the third trend, have their roots in a changing perspective of national governments. In the epoch of the science-based or second generation universities, governments were content with universities carrying out scientific research and providing scientific education. Now they see universities as incubators of new science- or technology-based commercial activities, whether by existing firms or start-ups. Hence, governments demand that universities take an active role in the exploitation of their knowledge, and they make funds available to support such activities. Thus, universities have become explicit instruments of economic growth in the knowledge economy.

There is a fourth trend of a quite different nature. Research in the second generation university era was mainly monodisciplinary. Nowadays, the vast majority of scientists work in interdisciplinary teams that focus on specific research areas; Master's courses are often connected to such research teams. In the monodisciplinary epoch, faculties were the perfect organisational form. For interdisciplinary teams, faculties are often an obstacle and new organisational forms have to be sought. The same applies to university management, which has to create responsibilities for the task of know-how exploitation and has to adapt in order to remain effective in a time of increasing size and complexity.

A fifth driver is a reaction to the massive increase in the number of students, that began during the 1960s and led to increased government spending and controls. This made universities bureaucratic and they had to find ways to ensure effective management.

The explosion in student numbers led to mass education, which diluted the scientific element in academic education. Universities are now experimenting with special courses for the best and brightest, bringing scientific education back to the ideals of the Renaissance and the Enlightenment. This can be considered as the sixth driver for change. Universities became challenged by the new and independent research institutions outside their borders: first the institutes for applied research and later top institutes like the National Aeronautics and Space Administration (NASA), the European Organisation for Nuclear Research (CERN) and the European Space Agency (ESA) and many others. At the same time, the opening up of corporate research started to offer challenging options for collaboration while the rise of IT companies from universities offered a new and exciting opportunity for universities in commercialising their know-how.

In conclusion, one may say that the external and the internal landscapes of universities as well as their ambitions are changing in a fundamental way. Universities used to accommodate new developments by adding, say, a new faculty for a scientific subject on the rise. The present field of developments however calls for a new perspective, a new paradigm for universities, rather than just adding say a department for technology transfer or an incubator for technostarters. For readers of Alvin Toffler's *Third Wave*, it will come as no surprise that the three generations of universities coincide with the three 'waves' of human development he describes. Like his book, ours is not strictly a scientific book but rather a motivated view of what is likely to happen, and a consultant's guide for getting there. A number of universities have adopted the 3GU principles as guidelines for their development, although they may deviate in details from the descriptions presented in this book.

At this point, we need to clarify the authors' position on the third generation university. It is our opinion that the 3GU is both inevitable and desirable. It is inevitable because the trends that are destroying the 2GU model cannot be ignored:

1. The pressures on quality that are the result of a massive influx of students since the 1960s.
2. The impossibility to govern universities in the traditional way as a result of the increase in student numbers and the resulting strong intertwining with government departments.
3. Globalisation, which also affects universities and leads to competition on three fronts: students, academics and research contracts.
4. The rise of interdisciplinary research and the resulting frictions with the faculty organisation.
5. The increased cost of cutting-edge research.
6. The challenges offered by the establishment of specialised top research institutes outside the universities.
7. Government demands that universities play a role in technology-based economic growth in the knowledge economy.
8. The opening up of corporate research and the opportunities offered by collaboration with industry as a consequence.
9. The rise of academic entrepreneurship, kicked off by the university-driven IT companies in the US.

Although the 2GU had its charms and has brought us unprecedented wealth, it must not be remembered as a rosier picture ('free academic research') than it was; even Nobel laureates had to fight constantly for adequate budgets. In the 2GU epoch, the role of universities was limited to scientific research and education; it was considered wise not to bother them with the application of what they invented. This originated in nineteenth-century thinking in terms of specialisation: universities would generate the basic knowledge while companies and institutes for applied know-how would 'translate' this into practical solutions. That was the time that was;

now, a new model must be found that copes with the trends. The 3GU model gives the university more freedom to choose its own way. As we shall see, it has seven fundamental characteristics that offer challenges:

1. Exploitation of know-how becomes the third university objective as universities are seen as the cradle of new entrepreneurial activity in addition to the traditional tasks of research and education.
2. 3GUs operate in an internationally competitive market. They actively compete for the best academics, students and research contracts from industry.
3. 3GUs are network universities, collaborating with industry, private research and development (R&D), financiers, professional service providers and other universities via their knowledge carousel.
4. Research is largely interdisciplinary. 3GUs embrace the concept of consilience and creativity as a driving force of similar importance to the rational scientific method.
5. 3GU's are multicultural organisations with a wide and diverse range of staff and students; in this respect, they are close to the medieval universities. As they also want to play a leading role, they create special facilities for the best and brightest students and academics.
6. 3GUs are cosmopolitan; they operate in an international setting. They employ the English language for all courses as the new lingua franca.
7. 3GUs will become less dependent on state regulation.

The last point does not mean that the state can stop supporting universities. Fundamental research can only be pursued at the top level if both state and industry contribute. The 3GU is not a commercial enterprise in which everything is geared to profit maximisation. It is not a kind of engineering bureau with some enhanced educational facilities. Rather, it continues to be true to its mission: to create new knowledge and to make education part of the knowledge-creating process. This mission has to be carried out in today's context. Doing that, as we shall see, is very rewarding, and that makes the 3GU desirable.

This book sets out, first of all, to explore the historic development of universities (Chapter 1) which leads to a description of the contours of the university-to-come (Chapter 2). The University of Paris very much served as the role model for the medieval or first generation university while the Humboldt university of Berlin did this for the science-based or second generation university. We have chosen the University of Cambridge in the UK as the role model for the third generation university, the legislative and cultural environment of this university being closer to the majority of the world's universities than US universities such as MIT and Stanford that were earlier in adopting elements of the third generation university. In order to show that not only top universities can adopt third generation university principles, two universities that are working their way towards the 3GU model have been described as case studies; these are Institut Teknologi Bandung in Indonesia and the University of Rousse in Bulgaria (Chapter 3). These three chapters constitute Part I of the book; this part aims to outline the new paradigm for universities, in the historic context.

Part II of the book addresses the main partners of the third generation university: technology-based enterprises, technostarters and financiers for start-ups and young enterprises. Chapter 4 discusses developments in the way technology-based enterprises manage their research and development activities, using Shell Global Solutions as a case study. In the management of R&D a number of regimes can be distinguished that have been used in successive phases of the development of such enterprises. The latest regime incorporates the concepts of Open Innovation and this matches the development in universities. Technostarters are the subject of Chapter 5, which describes their motivation and shows their impact on economic developments. The role of financiers has been essential in creating the successes of MIT's know-how hub, Silicon Valley, the 'Cambridge Phenomenon' and many other examples of spinning out university knowledge through new ventures, whether at the initiative of enterprising students or staff members or the university itself. Chapter 6 describes the different kinds of financiers and the way in which they operate and make deals. For many university leaders this is new material. However, a university that does not understand angel and venture capital financing is like a farmer who does not understand rain.

Part III discusses the way in which changes in the university's mission should be reflected in organisational changes. This is the 'how-to' part of the book; it may be of great interest to university leaders and policy-makers who face the implementation problems of universities during the transition stage. The changing emphasis on what we call interdisciplinary research has organisational consequences: a shift from the faculty structure to a unit management structure in the form of relatively independent university institutes. Such institutes will become the main organisational elements of a university, with faculties eventually disappearing. A five-member board of management creates clear responsibilities for the three university objectives as well as general leadership and the responsibility for finances. Many countries are attempting to replace the input-based financing system by output-based financing. Such a change is mandatory for universities to become less intertwined with the ministries of education and science and hence become more governable. This concept has tremendous consequences, the possibility for universities to go bankrupt being one of them.

Chapter 7 ends with a discussion on university management. Like professional service firms, many universities are managed by the principles of the management of industrial organisations. This does not fit the academic context and causes unnecessary loss of motivation and effectiveness. We need a new understanding of how to manage (or, rather, not manage) professional service firms including universities. Chapter 8 focuses on the organisation of the know-how commercialisation function. This represents a new element in universities, which often lack even a marketing department. Even in the top universities in the US and the UK, this function is badly organised. Management of know-how exploitation requires first of all an overview of the many ways in which a university can dissipate its know-how while maintaining its academic integrity. The structure and the respective tasks of the know-how commercialisation function follow this overview. Finally, the chapter focuses on the support activities for technostarters. Chapter 9 addresses the issue of change management, starting with some observations on attitudes towards change and possible strategies. The chapter then proceeds by outlining an intervention model according to the step-by-step method, working at three levels: overall strategy, structure and culture, academic education and non-academic support. This model was used successfully to help migrating universities from the 2GU to the 3GU model. A description of the Triple Six Model, by which progress can be monitored, concludes the chapter and Part III. Appendix 1 describes basic mechanisms of technological development and innovation while Appendix 2 discusses models for education in entrepreneurship and the creation of awareness based on the 'funnel model' for educational activities and the concept of 'synchronised education'. A Bibliography and an extensive Glossary complete the book.

This book was written for university leaders to help them find the route to the future and offer practical advice on implementing the necessary changes. It was equally written for the university's partners – technology-based enterprises, technostarters and financiers – to help them see their role in the context of the changing university. Academics that are in charge of courses in entrepreneurship can benefit, and so can those in charge of know-how commercialisation and services for technostarters. We hope the book will also find its way to governmental departments and advisory committees on education as many countries are drafting new policies on innovation in which universities play a pivotal role. May it lead to challenging discussions and ultimately to change, because whether one likes it or not, change is inevitable and it is always wise to think and act proactively rather than to be taken by surprise.

PART I

Towards the Third Generation University

Part I explores the historic development of universities which leads to a motivated speculation of the contours of the university-to-come. Chapter 1 describes in major lines the historic development of universities starting with the medieval or first generation universities that developed, via the first transition period, to the science-based or second generation universities in the nineteenth century. New developments challenge this type of university which leads to experimentation and the conclusion that we now find ourselves in the second period of transition. Chapter 2 explores the university-to-come, using the University of Cambridge as a case, moving on to the characteristics of the third generation university by drawing from many trends that converge towards this model. To illustrate this, two cases of universities that are on their way to becoming third generation universities are given in Chapter 3.

1. From the medieval and Humboldt university to the third generation university

1.1 THREE PHASES OF UNIVERSITY DEVELOPMENT

To understand the changes universities go through under this time-frame, we need to take a look at their history. We distinguish three generations of universities: the medieval or first generation university, the Humboldt or second generation university and the third generation university (3GU). The last of these is still in the future; universities are currently in a transition phase and we can see advanced universities moving towards the 3GU model. A similar transition phase in the era between the Renaissance and the Enlightenment led to the second generation model (Figure 1.1; the dates are indicative).

In this chapter, we will describe the first and second generation university models and the transition periods. We will then discuss the forces that are pushing the Humboldt-type university beyond its limits. The next chapter will outline the contours of the third generation university.

1.2 THE MEDIEVAL UNIVERSITY

The first universities stem from the Latin schools, the personalities of famous lecturers and the inheritance of Plato's Academia and Aristotle's Lyceum.[1] When Christianity was adopted by European countries in the early Middle Ages, schools were started in which all lectures were given in Latin, hence the name Latin schools. Such schools were often located near an important church or a monastery. The Quartier Latin of Paris, still so named today, owes its name to the many Latin schools located there. These schools focused on the preservation of the sacred body of letters and sciences from antiquity in an age of barbarism. Although they did not intend to challenge this body of knowledge, the famous schools of places such as Reims, Tours, Angers, Laon and many others can definitely be seen as forerunners of the universities established later.

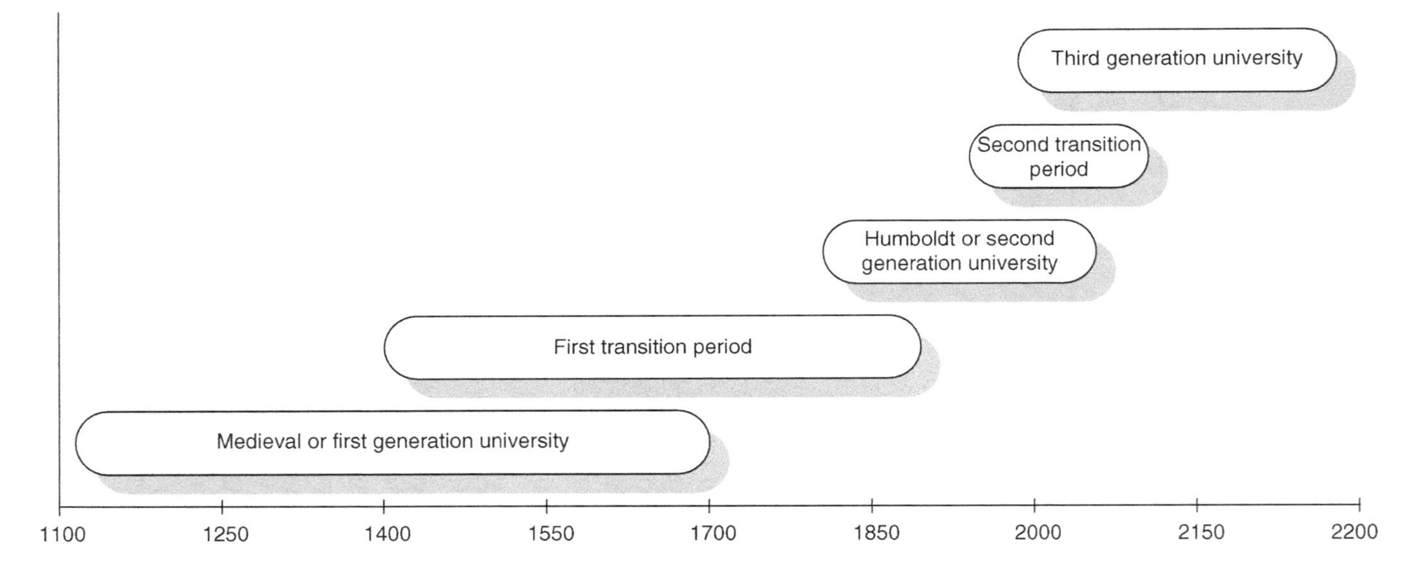

Figure 1.1 History of universities

The early universities however were not formed by transformations of the Latin schools. They arose because individual lecturers were given a licence by the city magistrates and the Church authorities to give public lectures. Such lecturers could attain fame throughout Europe, attracting students from every corner of the Continent. One such lecturer was Pierre Abelard (1079–1142) often seen as the ancestor of the University of Paris which was created 60 years after his death in 1200.[2] As Père Denifle, editor of the history of the University of Paris, wrote in 1889: 'Although Abelard taught long before the constitution of the University of Paris, his method of instruction for the sciences, and above all for theology and the liberal arts, nevertheless remained the model which the future university was to follow.'[3]

Abelard was a renewer, attacking (at the age of 20) the doctrines of his master, William of Champeaux. He was a great orator, drawing audiences of thousands of students, and producing an enormous effect on his listeners by the sheer force and logic of his arguments. He was also a man of great erudition, with an incredible memory and a wide-ranging interest; he left not only the dialectic tool of reasoning and a body of learned works, but also a collection of love poems (in common language) that became very popular. He was brought to court a number of times for heresy until he found his final enemy in St Bernard of Clairveaux who eventually brought him down. He developed what might be called Christian rationalism, which consists, above all, in the application of reason to theology; in other words, the right of an individual to consult reason rather than just following official doctrine. In doing so his method proclaimed the sovereignty of dialectics, emancipating reason by giving it confidence in its own forces, authorised by a process of argumentation. This excited the curiosity of other minds. Abelard's method became the soul of scholastic philosophy that lasted five centuries, up to and beyond the Renaissance.[4]

When Abelard was at the peak of his powers, and master of the prestigious School of Notre Dame in Paris, he fell in love with a student, Heloise. When she became pregnant, he sent her to his parents in the province and married her secretly, as an open marriage would have meant him being removed from his position. This would have jeopardised his role as a philosopher, which he saw as his duty and ambition. When he later moved her to a convent, Fulbert, one of the canons (Church authorities) in Paris and uncle and educator of Heloise, had Abelard castrated by his kinsmen. Abelard died in 1142, with Heloise outliving him by 21 years and becoming one of the Church's great abbesses. Their bones now rest at Père Lachaise and tourists and Parisians still place flowers there every day.[5]

The universities were not established at a stroke. They emerged step by step, 'by a concurrence of able men who had something they wished to teach and youths who desired to learn'.[6] Such an 'able man' would attract other doctors who, in turn, would attract students and in this way a *studium* (school) was founded. A *studium* was eventually sanctioned by civil or church authorities who then became its patrons and protectors. Many establishments had only one or two schools; the University of Paris, for instance, started with schools in philosophy and theology only. Such a group of schools was first called a *studium generale*, designated later a university. In the Middle Ages, the term *universitas*, literally 'the totality' or 'the whole', was used for a range of cooperative associations. The term had therefore to be supplemented in order to delineate what was meant, and the expressions *universitas magistrorum et scholarium* (society of masters and students) or *universitas studii* (society of studies) were used originally.[7] Italian universities tended to specialise in law, Spanish in medicine. This can be explained by the Roman traditions in law and the Spanish knowledge of medicine from Arab physicians. The word 'university' was chosen to indicate an association or corporation of teachers and students, *doctores et docendi*. Such associations could not have lasted without the blessing of the pope and approval of the civil authorities; both would give considerable privileges. The popes favoured the development and diffusion of learning because they believed this to be to the glory of God and the good of the Church. Moreover, they considered learning and teaching the best weapons against heresy. Universities were an instrument for maintaining the faith; they taught obedience to God and his servants: the Church and the emperor. The popes thus favoured universities for three reasons:

> they wished to strengthen the position of . . . doctrine amidst the diverse and mutually contradictory beliefs of the various religious orders and scholars, concerned to carry on a battle against the expanding heresies. They were furthermore desirous to . . . strengthen the central papal powers against the aspirations of the earthly powers.

They were also concerned with the recruitment of staff for their offices. Hence scholars became cardinals. Popes Celestine II (1143–44), Celestine III (1198–1208) and Alexander III (1159–81) were all pupils of Abelard.[8]

The civil authorities supported universities because of the status it added to their lands and the wealth brought in by foreign students. Universities helped consolidate the existing powers; studies in law could bring stability to the state just as studies in theology could bring stability to the Church. Universities were of great interest to the powers, and the powers endowed them with many privileges. In 1158, the Holy Roman Emperor Frederic Barbarossa wrote to the masters and students of Bologna: 'We will that the students, and above all, the professors of divine and sacred laws, may be able to establish themselves and dwell in entire security in the cities where the study of letters is practised. It is fitting that we should shelter them from all harm.'[9] As a consequence of this, students could be tried only by their own professors or the bishop of their city. In addition, students and university staff were usually exempt from taxes and duties (as were the nobility and the clergy). Finally, students and staff had the right to go on strike if, for any reason, they were dissatisfied. This proved to be a powerful weapon as there have been many instances where the university got its way in a conflict with the ecclesiastical and civil authorities. The students formed a class apart in the city, completely distinct from the other inhabitants. In the fifteenth century they could number up to 15 000 (4000 was more common); indeed a 'state within the state'.

Students favoured universities not so much because of their *amor sciendi*, the love of science, as for their desire to gain privileges and to acquire a more regular status rather than being mere listeners to famous teachers. They formed a sort of guild. The university's courses were public and open to foreigners as well as natives. Students organised themselves into so-called *nationes*, representing their country or language of origin. The students from different *nationes* had different gowns and berets, thereby preserving the customs of their countries. Students of the same *nationes* often lived in the same houses. *Nationes* could also include the professors. They became true corporations, each with their relative autonomy and leaders, and constituting self-governing societies within the universities.

Less organised than the *nationes* were the faculties, the second organisational building block of the university. Faculties corresponded to different branches of knowledge, taught by specialised professors. The subdivision in faculties followed Aristotle's guidelines that lasted until the nineteenth century. There were four basic faculties: theology (the most important faculty), law, medicine and arts (arts being the least important; in most universities students had to graduate in arts before they could enter the other faculties). Arts were a mixture of subjects, seven in total, divided in the *trivium* (grammar, rhetoric and dialectics (logic)) and the *quadrivium* (arithmetic, geometrics, astronomy and music). Our current faculties of science and arts are derived from the original arts faculties; the faculties of theology, law and medicine survived. Faculties were created spontaneously, with professors of each branch of study grouping themselves together in order to regulate all that was related to their specific field of study. Only in the second half of the thirteenth century did faculties become more institutionalised, with their own charters, ordinances and seals. They gradually won power and influence. In Italy, the word 'faculty' was hardly used. Professors organised themselves into bodies that would often be called a university. They can be regarded as single-faculty universities and we still know many of these today.

The universities, being almost independent republics, comprised *nationes*, faculties and colleges (see below), had great power to organise themselves; officers for most positions were elected. Such offices were held only for short periods, probably to prevent any group or person from gaining too much power despite the trouble associated with frequent changes of leadership. In Paris, up to 1266, the rector was elected for only four to six weeks, three months being exceptionally long. Later, this was extended to one or two years. The officers could only execute the will of their constituents; they did not have real power. The chief duty of the rector was to parade at front rank in ceremonies. The rector was initially often a student, elected from the wealthier students as his expenses were quite considerable. He could not be a member of any religious order and usually had to be celibate. Hence, he was often no older than 25. Rectors would walk in the first rank; indeed at a ceremony in Spain, King Ferdinand had the rector of the University of Alcala sit between him and Cardinal Ximenes. It is not surprising then to see that the installation of a rector constituted one of the most imposing ceremonies of the Middle Ages. Despite the pomp and circumstance, the real power of the rectors was limited; the procurators (secretaries) of the university and the *nationes* wielded greater power than the rector. More powerful were the chancellors, appointed by the Church, and alien to the other members of the university with whom they were often at odds: 'Our enemy is our master' was a common expression. The chancellors could grant and withdraw the right to teach, approve the acts of the university, excommunicate students and put them in jail. But over time chancellors lost power while the rectors gained in power; in conflicts, the popes often sided with the university staff rather than the chancellors they had appointed themselves. Gradually, most universities became completely independent bodies, with the chancellors having a symbolic function relating to the ecclesiastical origin of the universities; this is still the case in the UK.

The *nationes* and faculties together comprised the university. In Paris, there were seven organisational bodies, the three superior faculties and four *nationes*. In Bologna, the *nationes* were organised into two groups, the Ultramontanes (literally: from over the mountains; foreigners, 18 *nationes*) and the Citramontanes (from this side of the mountain, Italians, 17 *nationes*). Students from the city of Bologna did not participate in a *natione* because it was assumed they did not need protection. In this city, professors had their own corporation, the *Collegium Doctorum*, which was completely separate from the students' corporations.[10] There were two universities (which would have been called faculties in other places): in law, and in arts and medicine. Degrees were awarded by the *collegium*, an academic committee, with the degrees being the *licentia docendi* (literally the 'right to teach', in theory throughout the entire realm of Christendom) and the (higher) doctorate. Awarding degrees required collegial responsibility from the masters.

Universities spread rapidly over Europe. The University of Bologna received its charter in 1158 and is considered the world's oldest university.[11] In 1200, the University of Paris was established, followed by Oxford, Cambridge, Arrezo, Palencia, Padua, Napoli and others. At the end of the thirteenth century there were about 20 universities and in the fourteenth century another 25 were established, including the first German university, the University of Prague, in 1347 (Prague at the time was part of the German empire). The sixteenth century saw the founding of many new universities, stimulated by the Reformation and Counter-Reformation (the Jesuit universities). Gradually, the universities became more than instruments of obedience. In the fifteenth century, the University of Salamanca made great strides in navigation, which eventually enabled Columbus to make his trip to discover America. It taught the Copernican system while Galileo was in prison.

Basically, there were two models of universities. Bologna could be labelled a 'student university' where basically the students hired the professors. Paris was a 'professor's university', where the academics were the dominating force. Bologna and Paris are often regarded as the two archetypes of the medieval universities. In addition to the *nationes* and the faculties, a third organisational element appeared in the twelfth century in Paris, at the Sorbonne (1257): the university college (called at first *domus scholarium*). More university colleges followed: Harcourt (1280), Merton College (1263), Balliol (1261) and University College (1280) in Oxford, and Peterhouse (1284) at Cambridge. In 1300, there were 19 university colleges in Paris, six at Oxford and one at Cambridge; these numbers expanded rapidly during the fourteenth century. It was rare for a medieval university not to have colleges. At first, the colleges were nothing more than foundations serving to house (poor) students. In the fourteenth and fifteenth centuries, the colleges developed from simple lodging houses into privileged institutions, serving to guarantee their members the best conditions for work and study; in other words, to constitute a student elite. Thanks to generous donations, the colleges had their own teachers; they established libraries and adopted progressive pedagogic methods. They developed into genuine centres of intellectual life, far more dynamic than the rest of the university. Colleges were in a way competing with the faculties, the role of which tended to be reduced to the awarding of degrees.[12] The role of the colleges became less pronounced over time, but the system is still dominant in the universities of Oxford, Cambridge and Durham.

New universities usually drew heavily on doctors from existing universities; they copied their model from archetypes, mostly from the University of Paris. The scattering of science was enhanced by the almost nomadic life of the scientists and students of the time. Latin, as the common language, facilitated these transfers and so did the spirit of the universities that almost formed an unofficial league: 'A current stronger than national rivalry reunited all the universities of Europe in a sort of federation', helped by the fact that 'universities were the daughters of the University of Paris'.[13]

In summary we can say that the medieval universities were strong organisations in their own right and in the protection they enjoyed from state and Church alike. They were 'states within the state', having many privileges including their own law and jurisdiction, indeed similar to the monasteries. Thanks to Latin as the lingua franca, they formed an unofficial league. Collegiality was stronger than competition and this spirit has survived. Thanks to their 'academic freedom' and their independent minds, professors were often at odds with the official teachings of the Church, but this did not hinder universities from exploring new pathways into science and humanism. The main objective of the medieval university, however, was not the pursuit of new knowledge but 'the protection of the wisdom of the past and the teaching of obedience to the doctrines of the church'.[14]

Universities were democratic institutions with elected dignitaries (except for the chancellors). They yielded great influence in all matters; they intervened in politics and were confidants as well as critics of royalty, pressing them to perfection, educating the future princes of Church and state alike. But: 'They were not armed for the conquest of science, born as they were in an epoch when the only question was to preserve the deposit of traditional beliefs' and, we may add, the need for bringing discipline into Church and political affairs in times of great turbulence. 'They commented and discussed, they invented nothing. They wore themselves out in subtleties, in fine distinctions, in quibbling. But they laid the ground for the great harvests of the sixteenth and following centuries.'

Le Goff points out that:

> It should be noted that nothing could become an object of conscious reflection in the Middle Ages except by way of religion. It would almost be possible to define the medieval mentality by its inability to express itself apart from religious references. This remains as late as the sixteenth century. Craft guilds would make the tools of their trade attributes of a saint, integrated in a hagiographic legend . . . During the Middle Ages technical progress was perceived as a miracle, as a domination of nature which could have no origin than divine grace.[15]

1.3 THE FIRST TRANSITION PERIOD

In the fifteenth century, the feeling that the world was on the brink of a new era was widely shared. Book printing became widespread and the end of the century witnessed great geographical discoveries, triggered by the fall of Constantinople in 1453. The economy was booming after a century of plague. Around 1500, the map of the European universities became dense, yet the character of the universities did not change fundamentally. Increasingly, professors were paid by secular rather than Church authorities and universities were increasingly subjected to the civil authorities of city or state.

Universities experienced considerable change when the Renaissance and Humanism set in. A new intellectual movement, Humanism was set in motion by Petrarch (1304–74); the period of 1350–1550 is regarded as the period of Humanism. Humanism was an intellectual movement that emphasised human dignity, freedom and the value of the individual. The belief in a personal god was no prerequisite. In the medieval *studium*, there had always been a strict difference between the *auctoritates*, the doctors who knew, and the students who did not.[16] That relationship was to be replaced by a common quest for learning, the *studia humaniora* (humane studies) by professional researchers and amateurs together, *virtuosi et dilettanti*. A new term – of Greek origin – came into use in the early fifteenth century: *academia*.[17]

The sixteenth century was the century that saw great revisions of the foundations of theology, with dominating roles for Desiderius Erasmus, Martin Luther and John Calvin. The proliferation of new ideas was very much enhanced by the invention of the printing press (Columbus's description of his first expedition to America in 1492 appeared in print only a year later). A century later, the factor that dominated university development was the emergence of eminent mathematicians, such as Copernicus, Ramus, Galileo, Descartes, Huygens and many others.

The seventeenth century was dominated by exact observations about nature; with Bacon, Boyle, Newton and Boerhaave the experimental method became a firm basis for scientific work that complemented reasoning. Not all scientists taught at universities; many men of learning lived by their own means or on a stipend, sometimes through choice but also because they were forced to do so as universities were often hostile to the new learning. The great revival of science largely bypassed the universities as these correctly saw that the new learning threatened the established order of their disciplines. The result was that the emergence of applied sciences, such as engineering, forestry and veterinary sciences led to the foundation of specialised schools outside the university. This coincided with the slow but irrevocable decline of the influence of the Church over the universities. The University of Bonn was the first Catholic university established without a papal decree (1818).

Near the end of the eighteenth century, even the traditional structure of faculties for arts and philosophy, law, medicine and theology was gradually exchanged for more specialised faculties. In France, the Revolution established the *hautes écoles* as replacements for the universities it abolished. Polytechnics emerged and military sciences were introduced in new faculties. All these changes meant a fundamental shift away from the system of the medieval universities. Religious dissidents created their own universities, such as the University of Leiden, which was a product of the Reformation and a political statement by the rebellious Dutch. For a long time this university was not recognised by the German emperor as it was not based on a deed of foundation from the official authority, King Philip II of Spain.[18] Nonconformists established private schools in England and in 1527, Count Philip of Hesse founded a Lutherian studium without papal privilege or imperial approval (which came later in 1541). The Calvinist academies in Germany (Hochschule) and Geneva were not allowed to confer degrees.

The modernisation of the universities was further hampered by the attempts of the established universities to prevent the institution of new ones. The University of Cracow, one of the older universities in Europe, prevented later foundations from becoming full-fledged universities and the schools at Chelmno, Poznan and many other Polish cities were initially nothing more than outposts of Cracow University. In England, Oxford and Cambridge successfully prevented the establishment of universities in Manchester, York and Durham. The exact sciences had to overcome a bitter battle before they were recognised as disciplines taught in universities. Specialised chairs and institutes remained outside the university before true faculties of science were founded.

On the eve of the French Revolution, there was a dense network of specialised schools in France. Jarausch has characterised the development of universities in the eighteenth century with the keywords 'expansion', 'differentiation' and 'professionalisation'.[19] In the period of Humanism, Renaissance, Reformation, Counter-Reformation and Enlightenment, the universities were challenged. They fought back to maintain the status quo by not accepting new disciplines and methods of research and by preventing new universities from being established. This caused the emergence of real competition in the form of specialised institutions and university-imitations or universities not recognised by the traditional authorities: pope and king. Gradually, the traditional universities started to incorporate the new disciplines and scientific methods. Out of this convergence the Humboldt university emerged, not in France, Italy or Spain, but in Germany (Prussia), the then nascent power in Europe.

1.4 THE HUMBOLDT UNIVERSITY

Although we have seen that the modern scientific method has its origins in the Renaissance, it did not become central to the core of universities until the end of the eighteenth century. Researchers started drawing conclusions from objective, systematic and reproducible experimentation and, as in the Middle Ages, transparent argumentation, together becoming the 'modern scientific method'. Such conclusions could be condensed into 'laws' and the laws could be used to predict the behaviour of systems. Thus, modern science and, subsequently, technology were born. The resulting university could be called the Enlightenment university but we have followed the general use of the term 'Humboldt university',[20] after Wilhelm von Humboldt, the Prussian diplomat, founder of modern linguistics, Enlightenment philosopher, minister of education in the post-Napoleonic Prussian government, and founder of the University of Berlin in 1810 which was later named after him. He was an exceptional figure whose influence lasts right up to the present day. Humboldt persuaded the Prussian king to found the university on the basis of the liberal ideas of the philosopher Schleiermacher, who stated that:

> the function of the university was not to pass on recognised and directly usable knowledge such as the schools and colleges did, but rather to demonstrate how this knowledge is discovered, in order to stimulate the idea of science in the minds of the students, to encourage them to take account of the fundamental laws of science in all their thinking.[21]

This contrasted with the other model that appeared after the French Revolution, the French model of specialised colleges where students learned under an almost military discipline; this model was to disappear in the course of the nineteenth century with the German model becoming generally accepted. At the same time, the French *école polytechnique* became the model for many such institutes in Europe in which engineers and artillery officers were trained. Universities became very popular; in the period 1850–1950 their number doubled from 98 to 200 (in 1815 there were 83 universities remaining of the 143 in 1789). These 200 universities had 600 000 students and 32 000 professors.[22]

The Humboldt university focused on research carried out according to the 'modern method'. Education was integrated with research, with students and assistants acquiring increasing responsibilities, following the medieval pattern of apprentice, fellow and master of the guilds. Research was based on rationality, experimentation, argumentation and transparency, the latter allowing for verification and expansion of results by others. Only what was observed in reality could be taken to be true rather than relying on authority as in the Middle Ages. Conclusions could only be drawn in a systematic and rational way. Results of research must be verifiable for everyone, and part of the public domain, published in specialised journals or books that could be obtained by anyone. Education was directed towards science although many graduates chose careers other than scientific careers. The Humboldt universities were sanctuaries for pure science, *la science pour la science*, with scientific progress being the objective. The eighteenth- and nineteenth-century innovations that changed the world, such as the steam engine, railways, telegraphy, electric light and electricity, radio, telephone, photography and so many others, were all developed in the realm of inventor-entrepreneurs and their financiers and not in the domain of universities.

Following the nineteenth-century trend of nationalism, Humboldt universities became national institutions where teaching was given in the national language. Universities became the pride of nations in a nationalistic epoch. Especially after the introduction of the Nobel Prizes in 1901, it was clear where the leading universities were located. The successes of German universities were noticed everywhere and foreigners would come to Germany to complete their education. Latin as the lingua franca was sacrificed and communication between scholars and mobility between universities became more difficult. German became the most important scientific language and many international scientific journals were written in that language. There was certainly competition between the universities for reaching status in the scientific world. Still, the spirit of altruism and tolerance was preserved. This changed after the outbreak of the First World War after which nationalism sharpened and many universities expelled members of enemy nations. The Conference of the International Academy of Science held in October 1918 in London resolved to exclude all Germans from international conferences for 20 years.[23] Although this resolution did not hold in practice, it shows how close the scientific world had moved to nationalistic policies and culture.

Specialisation was a characteristic feature of the Humboldt university, in line with the specialisation that was such a dominant element of the Industrial Revolution. Universities organised themselves into monodisciplinary faculties; the *nationes* disappeared or became border phenomena and only a few universities in England maintained the college structure with its tutors. These faculties, especially the arts and philosophy faculties were the cradles of many sub-specialisations that in due course became faculties on their own, for example natural philosophy (later to be split up into mathematics, physics, chemistry and biology), economics and the social sciences. Faculties in theology, medicine and law remained as such. Arts moved largely outside the universities to specialised academies. University-like academies were created for military technology; many of these later expanded into civil engineering and gradually became polytechnics. These polytechnics, still so named in many countries, often gained formal university status in the twentieth century and then named themselves technical universities or universities of technology. The twentieth century also saw the establishment of specialised universities for agriculture and food sciences. In the 1930s, there were some 200 universities in Europe and some 300 institutions of higher education in the military, polytechnic, commercial, medical, veterinary, agricultural, educational, political and musical fields.[24]

Faculties, now the dominating structure of the universities, were led by a dean, usually a professor of high standing. This job was part-time and on a temporary basis. Deanships were rotated amongst the senior professors, with a typical term being four years. Deans would still see their research and educational tasks as of primary importance; administration was a job on the side. The rector or *rector magnificus* became the highest authority in the university, except in England where a chancellor, a ceremonial function, was chosen from royalty or aristocracy and where the real leader was the vice-chancellor. The rector also would devote most of his time to science and education; only later did it become a full-time job. The Senate, the meeting of all professors, was usually the highest authority, with the rector as chairman. In Europe, the rector would report to some sort of civil or ecclesiastical (in the case of Roman Catholic and Protestant universities) board of trustees. Students would organise themselves in a widely varied range of societies based on sports, cultural subjects or regions, over which the university had no authority. The university and the students initially had, in part, their own legislature; over time, this disappeared and members of the university lost their privileges and were treated just like other citizens.[25] Some universities switched to this model in the early nineteenth century; others followed later in that century.

Universities had primarily a local function; they would draw students from their direct neighbourhood. Exchange of students between universities became an oddity; diplomas were not recognised by other universities and students who wanted to spend time in a university other than their own had to pursue a range of permissions and recognition of subjects passed in the other university. There were either no or very limited funds to finance such exchanges. Academics would often make a lifelong career in their own university or move to another university in the same country in order to gain a doctorate. Exchange of academics across borders was an exception, although universities would invite foreign academics for short stays. Academics from different countries communicated via the printed media and sometimes by mail. Such communication could be quite lively, provided the scholars had mastered each other's language. Because of the regional function of universities, there was little competition between them; the collegial spirit of the Middle Ages prevailed.

Universities were increasingly financed from the national budget and thus became dependent on the goodwill of the autocratic kings of the nineteenth century and, later, on political priorities. The income from tuition became an ever-smaller percentage of their budgets, as governments wanted to keep the fees low to encourage students from the lower income groups. Indeed, the Enlightenment taught that education should have the highest priority as a tool for national as well as for individual development and well-being.[26] The universities were sanctuaries again, not for enlightenment and obedience as in the Middle Ages, but as instruments of understanding nature in all its forms. The distribution of the national budget for scientific institutions was always a matter of controversy, with the dilemmas often being solved by advisory committees made up of the academics themselves. Most ministers for science and education were former university professors. As a result, university financing was almost a closed system, given the prevailing belief that universities were paramount to the development of society; one could recognise a civilised country by its universities and their achievements.[27] Although in the later nineteenth century contacts with industry gained importance, especially for the science and technology faculties, in general there was a sharp border between universities and industry. The main inventors and entrepreneurs of the industrial revolution, such as Watt, Edison, Bell,[28] Ford and Eastman, operated outside universities although they benefited to a certain extent from their work.

The model of the Humboldt university was still largely intact when the author started his studies in 1960. He registered with the Chemistry Department of the Faculty of Mathematics and Physics of a Dutch university, where he could choose between two Bachelor's courses (with or without biology; the biology version gave access to a Master's course in pharmaceutics). These courses had no electives; in addition to subjects covering various aspects of chemistry there were a few courses in mathematics and physics. After graduation, he could choose from six courses for his Master's degree: biochemistry and inorganic, organic, theoretical, physical, and technical chemistry (chemical engineering). In the Master's course, there was a small space for electives. When he took a second Master's course in the UK, only about half the subjects there were recognised by his home university. He had to organise and finance this detour himself, helped by a stipend he procured from an oil company. Telephone communication was prohibitively expensive and travel was facilitated by a coaster line that was kind enough to offer him free passage (except for a tip for the cook!)

This story, although only 40 years old, will sound very strange to today's students and this is a consequence of a number of developments that fundamentally changed the Humboldt model, as we shall see in the next section.

1.5 LIMITS TO THE HUMBOLDT UNIVERSITY AND NEW OPPORTUNITIES

The Humboldt model has been extremely successful as the basis of a major part of our modern prosperity and our 'enlightened' way of thinking. It came under pressure for at least nine reasons.[29]

1 and 2: Explosion in Student Numbers with Two Important Consequences

The first two reasons were the result of the explosion in the number of students from the 1960s. Many universities quadrupled in size within a decade. This increase was very much in line with the ideas of the Enlightenment (liberalism and socialism alike), which wanted equal opportunities for everyone. Many countries abolished entrance exams, as suitable secondary education was considered sufficient as an entrance criterion. A lavish system of government grants for students was introduced, and as academic freedom was still very much honoured, little was asked in return. In addition to students pursuing a scientific career, this system brought masses of young people to universities who just wanted to obtain a diploma that would open up opportunities for good employment. This was encouraged by politicians. In the UK, the 1963 Robbins report declared that: 'higher education was for instruction in the skills suitable to play a part in the general division of labour'.[30]

The first effect of the explosion in student numbers was that education became a commodity, with fewer contact hours with academics and with multiple-choice exams. The average period to graduation increased and so did the percentage of students that did not graduate at all. Although quality came under severe pressure, universities remained successful in turning out graduates of very high quality, even when average quality took a downturn. Intelligent students managed to get extra time from their professors, especially in the later study years.

The second effect of the explosion in student numbers was that, since government spending on universities and other institutions of higher learning had rocketed, universities became increasingly subjected to government regulation and continued rounds of budget-tightening programmes. The demands for higher efficiency and effectiveness heralded the end of academic freedom, a cornerstone of the Enlightenment. Academic freedom meant that at least the professors could choose the areas of research they considered most relevant. The academic objective was to increase the body of knowledge. Subsequently, governments started to channel budgets for research through agencies which would assess research proposals and only fund the better ones.

The increased governmental involvement led to an increase in bureaucracy in universities. This, together with their increased size and complexity, heralded the end of university management as a part-time assignment for academics. Full-time managers were needed to cope with the increased complexity and bureaucracy, and not all professors were good at this – or were motivated to give up their academic life for a job as manager. The lack of academics with managerial talents and ambitions led to the introduction of so-called professional managers, for instance former civil servants, politicians or corporate managers. An odd side-effect was that when these managers were appointed as deans, they also became professors, as deans were traditionally professors and, by reversing the logic, managers appointed as deans should also be professors. This led to a devaluation of the authority of professors and universities in society. Some professional managers did a good job but they could not provide scientific leadership. Others just messed things up. According to Lucy Kellaway: 'Universities import third rate management fads the private sector has already junked and implement them badly.'[31] Universities started looking like factories, boasting about their increase in 'research productivity', as measured by the number of publications and citations. In short, the explosion in student numbers with the increases in government involvement, bureaucracy, management time and complexity, and the need for efficiency savings, put severe strains on the 2GU model as it existed before the 1960s.

3: Globalisation

A third new trend is globalisation, which has had as profound an impact on universities as it has on other sectors of society. Partly due to the Internet, English has become the new universal language, the lingua franca, which greatly facilitates communication and the sourcing of information. Because of the sharply decreased costs of travel and communication, mobility has increased and studying in universities outside one's homeland is becoming mainstream. The ICEF Moscow workshop (International Consultants for Education and Fairs), a meeting opportunity between universities and potential students, for instance, drew 3573 students and 113 providers of education from 19 countries and four continents. University staff have also become more mobile. All this leads to increased competition between universities. Perhaps they are still recruiting undergraduates from their own region, but older students as well as staff members are looking around to select the best opportunities. As a result, universities have been forced to deliver courses in English and this again enhances competition. In Europe, the competition is further increased as the universities recognise and accept Bachelor's and Master's degrees from establishments other than their own. This is known as the Bologna process and it greatly facilitates mobility[32] as do the many funds for financing international study and research.

4: Interdisciplinary Research

The fourth challenge to the 2GU model resulted from the rise of multi- and interdisciplinary research, which emerged in the 1960s. Originally, science was carried out as monodisciplinary research, that is, involving only one scientific discipline. In multidisciplinary research and development (R&D), two or more scientific, technological or design disciplines work together in complementary but separated ways. Transdisciplinary R&D is comprised of integrated scientific, technological and/or design disciplines; in this case, the various disciplines sit around the table from the start of the project. Finally, in interdisciplinary research and development, scientists, engineers and designers of many disciplines work together, while the disciplines are no longer one-to-one related to individuals. Interdisciplinary R&D signals the return of the 'Renaissance Man' who perished in the age of specialisation and the mainly monodisciplinary research of the Humboldt period.[33] To enable interdisciplinary research, cross-faculty teams were established but these were often at odds with the faculties, which were still all-powerful. In short, the structure of the Humboldt university was not geared for this type of research and new organisational forms had to be sought.

5: Rising Cost of Cutting Edge Research

In hindsight, research up to say the 1960s was relatively cheap. It is amazing to see how little equipment was needed for top scientists in say the 1930s to gain a Nobel Prize. When interdisciplinary research became necessary, the size of the teams increased from a handful of assistants to a larger team of highly qualified specialists. As we will see in the next chapter, this caused top universities such as the University of Cambridge to look for other funding than that by the state. This collaboration then brought new opportunities as enterprises were willing to share their resources.

6: Emergence of Special Research Institutes

A sixth challenge came from the competition that arose from the emergence of specialised institutes for applied R&D such as the Fraunhofer Gesellschaft in Germany. Departments of Defence, Agriculture, Health, Transport and others initiated their own institutes for applied research. Industrial corporations started R&D activities on a massive scale, conducting fundamental research as well as applied research and even collecting Nobel Prizes. These trends started around 1900 and became very strong after the Second World War. Universities were not interested in playing a role in applied science and technology, immersed as they were in pure, purpose-free science. Closed borders were maintained between this academic work and the applied research carried out by enterprises and government-sponsored institutes. The competition from new institutes for top research that were created after the Second World War, such as NASA, CERN and the European Space Agency, was even more serious. Top research took place outside universities, although the universities often acted as subcontractors. This development resembles the wave of new institutions in the eighteenth century when universities resisted the trend of the renewal of sciences that was spreading over the world.

Taken together:

> Europe's universities, taken as a group, are failing to provide the intellectual and creative energy that is required to improve the continent's poor economic performance. Too few of them are international centres of research excellence, attracting the best talent from around the world. Their efforts in both teaching and research are limited by a serious, and in many cases desperate, lack of resources.

These are the conclusions of a recent report of the Centre for European Reform, a UK-based think-tank.[34] The reasons that European universities are slipping away, are, according to this report:

- They are seriously underfunded, leading to an exodus of academic talent (the US spends 2.6 per cent of its gross domestic product (GDP) on universities; Europe spends half that figure).
- Most European universities have limited autonomy and poor systems of governance.
- Europe does not create top universities. The available resources are spread too thinly over nearly 2000 universities in Europe against fewer than 100 recognised research-intensive universities in the US (there are 3000 universities in the US if colleges are included).

The report points out that European universities do not cooperate sufficiently with companies in comparison with universities elsewhere. It calls for different government and EU policies.

The Humboldt type of university is starting to change under the weight of an explosion in numbers, bureaucracy and governmental policies on education, the rise of interdisciplinary research and the increasing competition from specialised research institutions. At the same time, a number of new trends, that offer challenges as well as opportunities, are emerging:

7: Universities as Cradles of New Economic Activity

The emergence of new information technology (IT) companies from American universities such as the Massachusetts Institute of Technology (MIT) and Stanford University is the first trend that offers opportunities to universities. It shows that universities can become cradles of new technology-based clusters of enterprises, some of which have grown to be amongst the largest companies in the world. Such companies farm out contract research to the universities and offer challenging jobs for graduates. The trend brought a new and different life to the already dynamic universities, and European universities are trying to imitate this trend with the support of governments that have discovered the large economic and employment benefits of market-oriented academic institutions. Today, almost any European and Asian government has the establishment of an IT, life sciences or other 'valley' in its programme. This trend is rapidly gaining strength and momentum; society wants universities to deliver good employees for industry and government as well as new technology-based firms, preferably with high growth potential. Many governments have investigated how to improve the innovation infrastructure, the totality of institutions and agencies linking pure basic research with the ultimate applications. Such analyses are the foundation of the innovation policies that just about every government in the world has initiated.

8: Collaboration with Industry

Many industrial R&D organisations have cancelled their programmes for fundamental research. Science-based corporations used to carry out fundamental research, partly value-free, partly because they needed to understand phenomena at a basic level in order to maintain and expand their market positions. When corporations started to skip the 'free' part of their fundamental research, they found that the scale to carry out the required part of their fundamental research had become too small and they had to find other solutions. This made cooperation with academic institutions essential. Such corporations will only collaborate with universities that have a significant and deep level of fundamental research. In addition, these and 'lesser' universities increasingly act as development bureaus for smaller companies. Those universities that have the expertise and know-how to play the acquisition game receive tremendous benefits from access to corporate resources and knowledge.

9: The Rise of Entrepreneurship

Today's global cultural climate favours entrepreneurship. Entrepreneurship is no longer seen as a means of enriching yourself at the expense of others – which it isn't! Many young people, although certainly not all or even a majority, want to create their own life, rather than being a cog in the wheel of a large enterprise. As a result, in addition to seeking industrial employment, students are active in creating new, technology-based firms of their own, and such firms can be very successful. Asian countries are not to be underestimated. There is a new and entrepreneurial spirit; Choon Fong, the President of the National University of Singapore, calls it a paradigm shift.[35] A participant of the 32nd International Geological Congress in Florence in 2004 wrote in a letter to the *Financial Times*:[36] 'There was curiosity, there was fun and it was coming from China. In contrast, the glossy presentations from the US and Europe were beautifully polished but few. Much of it was what geologists call SOS – same old stuff.'

1.6 SUMMARY: THE SECOND TRANSITION PERIOD

With the trends of the previous section pushing the 2GU into change, one may conclude that universities are now in a state of transition, the 'second transition period'. They are experimenting with models for the commercialisation or exploitation of know-how, new organisational structures, marketing activities in order to attract more and better students and staff, and new ways of financing (acquiring endowments and others). Some call themselves 'entrepreneurial universities', giving different meanings to this statement. Know-how exploitation is still seen as a sideline to the main functions of research and education. We would postulate, however, that the trends are converging and that a new model for universities is in the making, just as it was during the first transition period. Then the Humboldt university emerged as a powerful model that would bring unprecedented benefits to society and that lasted for two centuries. At this point, we can only speculate what the new model that is emerging out of the crisis of the Humboldt

Table 1.1 Characteristics of the three generations of universities

	Characteristics of the:		
	First generation university	Second generation university	Third generation university
Objective	Education	Education plus research	Education and research plus know-how exploitation
Role	Defending the truth	Discovering nature	Creating value
Method	Scholastic	Modern science, monodisciplinary	Modern science, interdisciplinary
Creating	Professionals	Professionals plus scientists	Professionals and scientists plus entrepreneurs
Orientation	Universal	National	Global
Language	Latin	National languages	English
Organisation	Nationes, faculties, colleges	Faculties	University institutes
Management	Chancellor	(Part-time) academics	Professional management

model will look like. However, as many trends can be observed and as many examples of successful universities are available, an intelligent speculation of the emerging model can be made, which we will attempt in the next chapter.

Table 1.1 summarises the characteristics of the three generations of universities, with key words by way of summary.

2. Contours of the third generation university

2.1 THE CAMBRIDGE PHENOMENON

As a starting point of our speculations on the role and shape of the third generation university or 3GU, let us take a look at the developments in Cambridgeshire, UK. Thanks to the emergence of a substantial high-tech industry, this county has been transformed from one of England's poorest areas into its second-richest. This extraordinary change occurred as a result of a strong interactive process with the University of Cambridge that was itself subjected to a modernisation process aimed at keeping this university amongst the world's top. The two transformations together are named the Cambridge Phenomenon, and although universities like MIT (Massachusetts Institute of Technology) and Stanford University in the USA saw similar developments earlier than Cambridge, we will take Cambridge as an example because the Cambridge Phenomenon was more explicitly part of a wider social and political development.

The emergence of a high-tech industry stems from spinout activities of the university, and entrepreneurs who were drawn to the scientific and increasingly dynamic environment. Cambridge can trace its spinout activities back to companies such as Cambridge Instruments, established in 1881 by Horace Darwin (Charles Darwin's son) and Pye Radio, founded in 1896 with links to Cambridge's Cavendish Laboratory (taken over by Philips Electronics in 1960). Just after the Second World War other firms started to exploit the developments in electronics that occurred during the war. Cambridge then was a rural place with no other industry. In 1970 there were some 20 firms located there. Shortly after that, a new wave of enterprises emerged with ARC, Sinclair, Acorn Computers and others. In 1983, Cambridge was one of the three clusters of new industrial activity in the UK, the others being west of London and in central Scotland:

> Several hundred small, high-technology firms around Cambridge have thrived on inventive people and ideas, many from the university. Cambridge was the first university in Britain – as Stanford was in America – to attract high-technology firms to a science park. Most recruits were from the mathematics and computer departments and from a government-funded computer-aided design centre

> where engineers, tired of wrangling about money, left to found their own firms . . . In Cambridge, the electronics manufacturer Pye was the local version of Silicon Valley's Fairchild: it had plenty of clever, disgruntled engineers who left for smaller firms. Commercial research laboratories also bred entrepreneurs: more than 20 companies having been formed by people leaving Cambridge Consultants, founded in 1960 by three alumni who returned to Cambridge after having served in World War II. Among its spin-offs was a second contract research laboratory set up with management consultant firm PA, which also became a nursery for entrepreneurs.[37]

This quotation from an editorial in *The Economist*, anonymous but no doubt written by its then deputy editor Norman McCrae, is from 1983.[38] In 1987 there were some 360 companies operating in Cambridge, many of them created by or from the consultancies that were founded in the 1960s with the objective of 'putting the brains of Cambridge University at the disposal of the problems of British industry'. The consultancies included Cambridge Consultants, PA Technology, Scientific Generics, Analysys and TTP. Cambridge is a networking place and that network of personal relationships provides a safety net for start-ups that fail.[39] Some people call it the innovation and entrepreneurial ecosystem.[40] The Cambridge experience shows that it is the serial entrepreneur who has the great impact.[41] Right now, there are some 3000 high-tech industries in the 'Cambridge Technopole' (the area around Cambridge and the name of an informally organised network). These have created direct employment for about 60 000 people (indirect employment is about twice that); 98 per cent of these new companies are there because of the university, although only 10 per cent have been initiated by the university itself. In addition, many large international firms have operations or research and development (R&D) activities in the area, including Philips, Microsoft, Motorola, Nokia, Novartis and many others.

The University of Cambridge as an institution was not involved in these activities. Cambridge was and still is a typical research university, collecting selected academics and students from all over the world. It has the highest number of Nobel laureates (83, as of 2008) in the world and it has an incredible history. Newton and Darwin pioneered their theories in Cambridge; Rutherford split the first atom there (in the Cavendish Laboratory, still there, and amazingly small); Crick and Watson discovered the DNA double helix structure. It is not surprising that commerce was anathema to such a university. Quoting from the same article:[42]

> Sir Clive Sinclair, whose company does much of its research in Cambridge, says attitudes towards business could not be more different than when he arrived in 1967. British prejudice against wealth creation lives on, even in Cambridge. The lack of a single business management course at the university (in 1983) is absolutely pathetic.

Despite being a medium-sized university with 11 500 undergraduate and 6000 graduate students, 5000 academic and research staff, and 3500 support staff (figures from 2006), Cambridge covers a full range of faculties and specialisations in the arts and sciences, including academic hospital facilities with Addenbrooke's hospital.[43] The University of Cambridge has preserved its medieval structure, meaning that most students and staff members are incorporated in independent colleges through which the students get extra tuition in addition to housing and catering facilities. Colleges sometimes act as initiators of new scientific and other programmes financed by endowments. They also act as a link between the university staff and industrial researchers who work in the region. High-flying researchers from Microsoft's Cambridge team were, for instance, invited to be fellows of the colleges and thereby drawn into the academic community.[44]

In the 1990s, the university started its modernisation programme. In 1991, it appointed its first full-time vice-chancellor, that is, the president of the university; previously the position was filled by the master of one of the colleges on a part-time basis for a period of two years. The second full-time vice-chancellor, Sir Alec Broers (vice-chancellor from 1996 to 2003; now Lord Broers) began collaborating with industry on a large scale. Concerns about academic freedom were replaced by the view that cooperation with industry was an essential part of the development strategy of the university, both for scientific reasons as well as financial reasons. Maintaining a leading role in research required far more funding than the government was willing to provide:

> funding from the UK research councils was felt by some of the leading scientists to be insufficiently strategic, overly egalitarian, risk aversive and short term. They will seldom, if ever, fund even eminent researchers outside their established fields, whereas industry may well be prepared to do so and, equally importantly, reach a quick decision.[45]

The collaboration with industry was favoured by the fact that high-technology enterprises started farming out their fundamental research activities in order to reduce their in-house research efforts. Indeed, the 1990s saw a sharp decline in such in-house research activities. A typical outcome was so-called embedded research in which a team of researchers from an industrial firm co-locate with researchers from the university; this is often accompanied by a donation of the corporation to the university. The University of Cambridge has embedded research agreements with Microsoft, Glaxo, Rolls-Royce, Hoechst, Hitachi, Toshiba, SmithKline Beecham, Unilever, BP Amoco, Seiko and others. Interdisciplinary research became more important, for instance in a new chair in medical materials in which the

Medical School, the Veterinary School, the Department of Engineering and the Institute of Biotechnology cooperate.

While the collaboration with industry gained speed, the university successfully bid for a host of new government grants, benefiting from its experience and reputation. (The system did not hand out money proportionally to all universities, but was based on competitive bids and letting the best bids win. One fund gave ten universities £100 million and the other 121 universities £10 million between them.)

When Gordon Brown became Chancellor of the Exchequer (minister of finance) in 1997, he initiated a government White Paper[46] stating that: 'the ability to turn scientific discoveries into successful commercial products and processes is vital in the knowledge-driven economy'. This statement is of historic significance, because it made 'transfer of technology to the community' the third formal objective of institutes of higher education, next to research and education.

The White Paper also announced a range of measures including the creation of the Higher Education Innovation Fund (HEIF) and later the Higher Education Reach-Out to Business and the Community Fund (HEROBC) to enhance the links between higher education with business – all financed by the Treasury. With these funds, eight Entrepreneurship Centres were created, one at the University of Cambridge. In addition, money was allocated to establish seed funds (University Challenge Funds) and Technology Transfer Offices. In 1999, Cambridge merged its Entrepreneurship Centre, Challenge Fund, Corporate Liaison Office and Technology Transfer Office into a new entity: Cambridge Enterprise. Cambridge Enterprise provides incubation, seed funding and teaching. It administers the intellectual property rights (IPR) of the university through Cambridge University Technical Services Ltd and acts as the vehicle for commercial activities related to IP. As such, it concludes licensing agreements and helps create new enterprises, whether based on the university's IP or otherwise. The establishment of Cambridge Enterprise followed earlier activities such as the establishment of Cambridge Science Park by Trinity College in 1970.[47] Cambridge Science Park was the first science park in the UK and now houses some 71 high-tech enterprises which employ some 5000 people. Cambridge Science Park also began to accommodate spinouts from tenant companies such as Cambridge Consultants. The initiative was followed by the establishment of private technology parks such as Babraham Bioincubator, Granta Park, Melbourn Science Park, Peterhouse Technology Park and Cambridge Research Park.[48]

The first business incubator was established by St John's College in 1987 for early-stage knowledge-based companies. St John's Innovation Centre offers accommodation, and shared facilities such as conference rooms and a restaurant. Advice on business issues is free. The centre organises programmes with university departments and government bodies and gives assistance in gaining access to funding through the business angel network and venture capital funds. The centre houses some 65 companies employing over 500 people (2006). Over a five-year period the survival rate for companies is close to 90 per cent, compared to about 50 per cent for other similar businesses in the Cambridge area, and 45 per cent for businesses generally in the UK. In and around Cambridge there are now well-established groups of business angels such as Cambridge Angels, Cambridge Capital Group and the Choir of Angels, meeting platforms such as Great Eastern Investment Forum, and research and data service companies such as Library House.

In 1990 the Judge Management School was established, following an initial donation and expanding as further donations were received. A successful bid for government funding helped create the Centre for Entrepreneurial Learning in 2003; in 2006 it gave some 30 courses on entrepreneurship, including a course that helps technostarters write their business plan and establish their company. With government support, the management school established collaboration with MIT on education, research, faculty exchange and post-experience programmes, including programmes in innovation and entrepreneurship. Another major event in the context of this book was the establishment of the Institute for Manufacturing with research and educational activities at the engineering–management interface.

The Cambridge Technopole Group acts as an informal network of business support organisations with the aim of improving the range and quality of such organisations with a focus on technology-based firms. The success of the Cambridge Phenomenon is not so much a top-down, centralised approach, but rather a 'constructive chaos and a sense of community and collaboration'.[49] An essential element is the fact that the university leaves much of the intellectual property rights (IPR) to academics and students. This stimulates academics to set up new enterprises – one professor is said to have made £250 million – from which the university benefits in return.[50] The idea of entrepreneurship is very much supported by students who established Cambridge University Entrepreneurs (CUE) as: 'A passionate student organisation created to inspire and educate, and to facilitate the creation of real businesses from the university. This is mainly achieved through the organisation and running of various Business Plan Competitions (BPC).'[51]

In conclusion, we can say that the Cambridge Phenomenon was not designed, it emerged; only at a later stage was it deliberately supported by the university, the colleges and the local administrations. There were three interacting developments: the establishment of a community of high-tech enterprises; the process of modernisation of the university; and the creation of technostarter facilities.

The development of a community of high-tech enterprises was the spontaneous creation of new technology-based firms that benefit from proximity to the university. They were created either by academics and (former) students or by companies that moved in from other areas, including international enterprises. Their emergence or arrival provided a dynamic environment, common to the early stages of the era of the Industrial Revolution, in which employees left their companies in order to start their own.[52]

The modernisation of the university started from the realisation that traditional ways of financing would be insufficient to stay at the leading edge of science and technology. The ambition to stay in the premier league, combined with a strong vision and leadership, could move the university beyond the age-old tradition of value-free, pure science into an era where the university creates value to society and starts cooperating with industry.

Finally, the development of technostarter facilities was initiated by some of the university's colleges, later supported by government grants. Private capital moved in as business angels and venture capital funds. The result is a rich and varied range of incubators, shared accommodation facilities, financiers, and all kinds of professional support. The three streams together have created a sustainable cluster for innovation and entrepreneurship and an entrepreneurial culture – the critical success factors of which were summed up by Jack Lang, entrepreneur in residence at the Centre for Entrepreneurial Learning, and business angel:[53]

1. You need exemplars, local heroes who have pioneered the way and shown it can be done without losing your soul (or your house), people the starter can associate with.
2. It must be OK to fail. Many US venture capitalists will not invest unless the founders of the company have failed before. It is part of their education as an entrepreneur. Sometimes one can have a soft start – using, for example, a sabbatical break or a period of part time work to test starting a company, and if it doesn't work returning to the academic treadmill. It is also easier to spin out in a growing economy and high skill employment demand, since if it doesn't work it's easier to get another job.
3. The job of setting up a company should be within the reach of what an individual or small team can do. That means for example that local support of all kinds should be available that truly understand and are sympathetic to new companies. The starter needs to be able to get whatever is needed to get his or her enterprise going: funding, broadband connectivity, people, liquid helium or whatever, with a minimum of fuss and delay so that she can concentrate on the core business problems like tech development and sales.

4. Starting a business must be compatible with one's lifestyle. The starter should not need to lose her soul or put her family at risk. Part of this is societal acceptance but there are also more practical things such as loan guarantee schemes, mortgage and rates holidays, childcare facilities, late night shopping etcetera.
5. The rewards need to be there. Measures here include suitable tax incentives and sensible IPR policies, either from an employer or academia. If the university insists on a major cut of any exploitation of her research she did at the university, the incentive for her to work her socks off and spin out a company is much reduced. The game has to be worthwhile.

Note that it took Cambridge 30 years to establish the cluster and many people have made a lot of effort to get it going. The driving forces were the university's outspoken desire to remain a top establishment for the development of science and technology and many private (and college) initiatives to create high-tech enterprises linked to the university's rich sources of science and technology.

2.2 THE SEVEN CHARACTERISTICS OF THE THIRD GENERATION UNIVERSITY

Generalising, second generation universities (2GUs) can be characterised by the following features:

1. 2GUs have two objectives: research and education. Research is pursued in the interest of the advancement of science. Scientific results are public, allowing each and everyone to benefit equally. Efforts to apply the knowledge created are considered counterproductive to the objectives; this is left to the initiative of others. Education is pursued to create future scientists and scientifically trained professionals.
2. 2GUs are informally ranked according to the number of scientific breakthroughs and authoritative publications. Although there is a certain amount of migration of academics from low- to high-status universities, 2GUs see each other as colleagues, not competitors. Students are recruited from the immediate neighbourhood; there is little competition for students.
3. 2GUs are stand-alone institutions. They exchange information with the scientific world but they have no formal links with other organisations.
4. Research and education are monodisciplinary. The monodisciplinary faculty organisation is dominant. Faculties hardly interact with each other; the 2GU is a conglomerate of faculties.

5. Education is open only to bright students who satisfy the entrance criteria. Most of these are from a well-to-do background, while there are provisions for highly qualified students of lesser means.
6. 2GUs are institutions of national pride. The national tongue is used for the written and spoken word.
7. 2GUs are financed by the state, with possibly relatively small donations from individuals or other organisations. The state finances universities in good confidence; it asks little in return. This allows 'academic freedom', the right of academics to choose their own fields of research and to educate as they think best.[54]

From the case of the University of Cambridge and other examples of front-running universities, we can see that these characteristics have been reversed or supplemented with other elements. With again a good deal of generalisation, the 3GU can be characterised by the following features:

1. Exploitation of know-how becomes the third university objective as universities are seen as the cradle of new entrepreneurial activity in addition to the traditional tasks of research and education. Knowledge generated at a university can be public or proprietary. Education is pursued to create scientists, scientifically educated professionals and entrepreneurs.
2. 3GUs operate in an internationally competitive market. They actively compete for the best academics, students and research contracts from industry.
3. 3GUs are network universities, collaborating with industry, private R&D, financiers, professional service providers and other universities via their knowledge carousel (see below).
4. Research is largely transdisciplinary or interdisciplinary. 3GUs embrace the concept of consilience (see below) and creativity as a driving force of similar importance as the rational scientific method. University institutes, transdisciplinary units that focus on a particular field of interest, are essential structural elements of the university. University institutes have an entrepreneurial nature; they employ their own personnel and they report directly to the board of management. Faculties are responsible for basic education. As personnel move to university institutes, faculties reduce in size and importance and may eventually disappear.
5. 3GU's are multicultural organisations with a diverse range of students; in this respect, they are close to the medieval universities. Most 3GUs cannot avoid being mass universities as politicians pursue 'equal opportunity' policies. As they also want to play a leading role, they

Table 2.1 Characteristics of the 2GU and 3GU

Characteristics of:	
Second generation university	Third generation university
1. Two objectives: research and education. No interest in the use of the knowledge created.	1. Exploitation of knowledge is core business and becomes the third objective.
2. Operate on the local market.Other universities are seen as colleagues.	2. Operate on an international, competitive market.
3. Stand-alone institutions with no formal links with other organisations.	3. Open universities, collaborating with many partners.
4. Monodisciplinary research and dominance of faculties.	4. Transdisciplinary research and rise of university institutes.
5. Mainly elite education for well to do students.	5. Multicultural organisations; mass and elite education.
6. National university.	6. Cosmopolitan university.
7. Important role of state financing and state interference.	7. No direct state financing. No state interference.

create special facilities for the best and brightest students and teachers. 3GUs therefore will be two-track universities, catering for top scientists in one way while supplying mass education in other programmes. The idea of the two-track university also applies to the domain of research where 'incremental research' exists next to cutting-edge scientific work.

6. 3GUs are cosmopolitan; they operate in an international setting. They employ the English language for all courses as the new lingua franca.
7. 3GUs will become less dependent on state regulation and in the extreme could be completely disconnected from the state if direct financing is replaced by indirect financing and if the state ceases to influence curricula and diplomas. This will not reinstate 'academic freedom' however, as research grants are given under politically established conditions.

These characteristics are summarised in Table 2.1 We will now discuss the characteristics in more detail.

Characteristic 1: The Third Objective

3GUs adopt the transfer of the value of their generated knowledge to society as their third objective, the first and second objectives being research and education. In Finland, such a third objective ('to serve society') is incorporated in the 2004 Universities Act.[55] In Indonesia, it was already incorporated in 1961 in the Basic Law of Higher Education. This law is based on the Tri Darma philosophy that defines three tasks for a university: research, education and community service; the careers of academics depend on achievements in each of these areas. Societal or community services of a university will be based on its scientific and technological achievements as this is the only way it can contribute. The translation of the third objective is therefore 'exploitation of know-how'.

The adoption of the third objective and the need for a university to become the centre of a know-how hub are closely linked. 2GUs, and to a certain extent 1GUs (first generation universities), have of course also sold or given know-how (advice, patents or other) to industry and the public sector. 2GUs often have an incubator and other facilities to support technostarters. The difference between the commercialisation activities of 2GUs and 3GUs is that 2GUs see commercialisation as a private matter for its academics, an interesting spin-off at most, an activity that is tolerated as long as it does not conflict with the core activities of research and education. 3GUs, on the other hand, see the commercialisation of know-how as the third core activity, as part of their license to operate. A 3GU has the obligation to generate value from the knowledge it creates.

A small enterprise can buy know-how from a 2GU if it manages to find its way to the department or professor concerned. After that, the deal is basically between the SME and the individual researcher, while the university simply allows the researcher to make some money on the side. 3GUs have a more active approach, with university institutes being responsible not only for research and education but also for the commercialisation of know-how.

Characteristics 2 and 3: International Competition, Open Universities and the Know-how Carousel

Recently, MIT's Sloan School of Management and the Harvard–MIT Division of Health Sciences and Technology started a two-year MBA Biomedical Enterprise Programme. The programme hopes to create 'business leaders' for the 150 or so life science companies in its area; these include Biogen, Amgen and Genzyme. There is an intense interaction between the Sloan management school, the science and technology faculties of MIT and Harvard, the biotech companies and the academic hospitals in the area (such as those of Tufts, Harvard and Boston University). These alliances attracted research contracts worth $3.9 billion in the period 1996–2005. Harvard alone invested $1.5 million in a number of courses related to hospital management, including a five-year MD/MBA course aimed at management in the pharmaceutical industry and medical services.[56]

We would argue that a leading 3GU needs to develop itself as the hub of a group of know-how institutions. We will call this the know-how carousel or know-how hub, defined as: 'a group of institutions, in and around the university, and preferably on the university's premises, that collaborate with the university, its academics and research teams and each other'. Such a centre can acquire international standing as a front-runner in knowledge creation in specific fields; a centre no researcher and no enterprise active in the field can ignore, a centre highly attractive for students as well as academics. In other words, it is a place where it is happening, where you have to be present if you want to be in the front line of developments, whether you are an enterprise, a technostarter, a researcher or a student. Stanford University with its Silicon Valley and the Massachusetts Institute of Technology[57] in the US serve as role models, and so do the University of Cambridge (with its subsidiary Cambridge Enterprise), the Catholic University of Leuven (K.U.Leuven, with its entrepreneurial subsidiary Leuven R&D and its IT science park IMEC), the National University of Singapore (with its NUS Enterprise), Wageningen University in the Netherlands with its renowned 'Food Valley', and many other universities.

In addition to the university's research and education, an international know-how carousel (see Figure 2.1) includes the R&D institutes of enterprises, independent (often specialised) R&D institutes, facilities for technostarters, financiers and professional services of many kinds, such as accountants, lawyers, management consultants, marketing consultants, and IP specialists. The more elements are present, and the more interactive they are, the stronger the hub will be. The underlying concept of the know-how carousel is that world-class performance in academic research will be possible only if there is a strong interaction between existing and new enterprises and with other kinds of R&D institutions: no Nobel Prize without cooperation with industry and other research centres. The competitive advantage of a university will depend on the extent to which it is capable of positioning itself as the centre of a know-how hub, an open network with other researchers, enterprises and government or non-governmental institutions. This is in sharp contrast to the closed societies of the medieval and Humboldt types of universities. K.U.Leuven has established itself as a 'must-be-there' location for the development of advanced information technology (hardware and software), with virtually all major international IT corporations participating. It is now planning to establish a similar site for biotechnology and this site will benefit from the financial and professional expertise already present. Thus, in the development of know-how hubs, the law of evolution applies; more complex systems are based on more efficient information transfer mechanisms.[58]

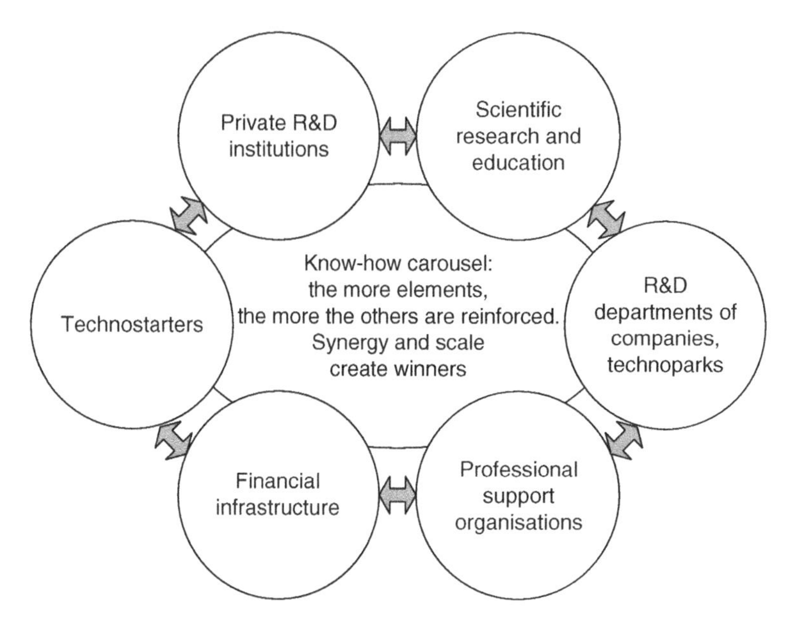

Figure 2.1 The know-how carousel

One may wonder whether it is necessary to have all these institutions in one location. Indeed, with the advance of the Internet and other global means of communication, many argue that location no longer matters. We would argue that it does. With all elements of a know-how carousel within walking distance, it is easy say for professors to become advisors of enterprises and start-ups, and for a company or non-academic institution to hire students on a temporary basis or give them an assignment. With all institutions in one location, people can move in and out of each other's buildings and thus create synergy and opportunities. The Internet is good for gathering information and for communication in a project that has already been set in motion and that is well structured. It is not good for serendipity, developing complex ideas, speculation, or using on-the-job experience in situations where a project has not yet been defined.

Universities that do not manage to create successfully a know-how carousel around them will not necessarily disappear, but will reduce to regional research and education centres. Most universities recruit their undergraduates from an area of, say, 100 kilometres around them, as school leavers tend to choose to study at the university nearest to where they live. Only a minority make a well-reasoned decision as to which subject they are going to study or which university is best suited for their purpose. However, once they have made it to Bachelor's status and have to make a choice for

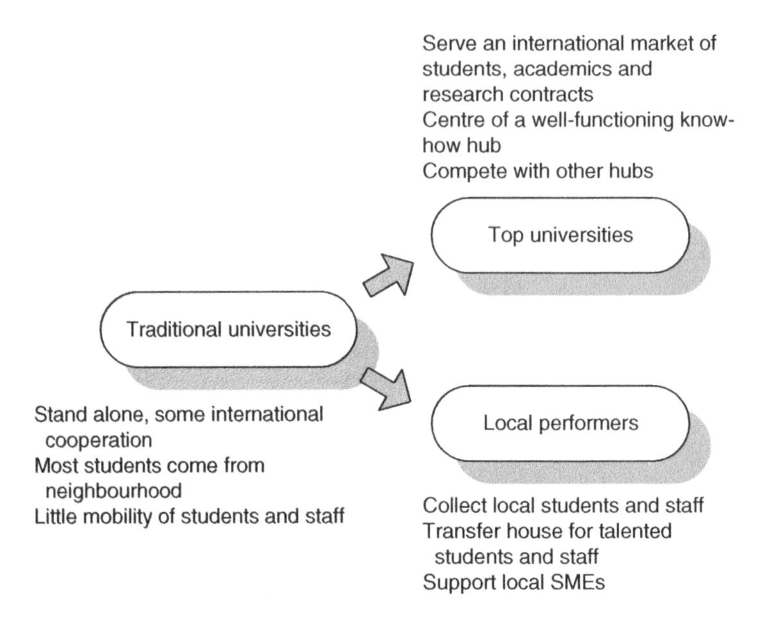

Figure 2.2 The bifurcation of traditional universities

a Master's course, they know very well what they want and they know very well where they can best get it, courtesy of Internet information and email communications with friends. In Europe and the US, universities stimulate mobility by accepting each other's Bachelor's degrees as entrance criteria for their Master's courses. Travelling and communication have become cheap, and studying in another country is no longer a major obstacle, in contrast to the situation up to the middle of the twentieth century. Universities that do not develop themselves as centres of a knowledge hub can still act as 'vacuum cleaners' for local talent and support for local small and medium-sized enterprises, while becoming transfer houses for the best and brightest (Figure 2.2).

Not only universities are developing into know-how hubs; corporations are doing the same. Philips Electronics, for example, built a 'high-tech campus' on the site of its R&D facilities in Eindhoven, the Netherlands. The campus invites start-ups – and even competitors – to join it.[59] An agreement was reached with US venture capital firm New Ventures Partners to bring bits of know-how belonging to Philips to the market. Thus, the once sacred and closed R&D departments of big business are opening up, in the belief that collaboration in the early phases of R&D and an open structure for buying and selling know-how benefits all. Companies can cooperate in pre-competitive research, that is, in developing the basic know-how that still leaves enough room for competition when it comes to the development of specific applications. This belief, plus the fact that in most branches the development of basic know-how has become quite expensive, explains the drive towards know-how hubs, whether university-based or corporation-based.

Characteristic 4: Transdisciplinary Research, Consilience, Creativity and Design

Transdisciplinary research need not be confined to combinations of sciences and technology. In a groundbreaking work, E.O. Wilson reintroduced the term 'consilience', the unity of knowledge, the 'bringing together' of knowledge of different disciplines.[60] This term, in his words:

> roots in the ancient Greek concept of an intrinsic orderliness that governs our cosmos, inherently comprehensible by logical processes, a vision at odds with mystical views in many cultures that surrounded the Hellenes. The rational view was recovered during the high Middle Ages, separated from theology during the Renaissance and found its apogee in the Age of Enlightenment. Then, with the rise of modern sciences, the sense of unity gradually was lost in the increasing fragmentation and specialisation of knowledge in the last two centuries. The converse of consilience in this way was Reductionism.[61]

From this principle, Wilson argues that there is no fundamental fault line between the exact sciences on the one hand, and the humanities on the other. Cognitive psychology and biological anthropology show a growing consilience with biology. Such consilience (Wilson avoids such words as 'coherence' or 'interconnectedness' as they have acquired different meanings) opens the way towards a more precise characterisation of human nature. Intuitive understanding of human nature is the core of the creative arts as well as the foundation of the social sciences. According to Wilson: 'Understanding the human nature objectively, studying it scientifically and understanding it in all its manifestations, would be to find the Holy Grail, a fulfilment of the dreams of the Enlightenment'.

Universities are instruments of Reductionism; 'arts' such as architecture and industrial design are tolerated in our universities of technology, although we do not regard them as 'scientific'. In the university of the future the synthesis (or, better, consilience) between the reductionistic process and creativity will have to be restored. An interesting approach is used in David Kelley's d.school (of the Institute of Design at Stanford; d stands for design) where: 'difficult messy problems that demand interdisciplinary solutions are solved by teams of students of several disciplines. These students, together with experts from industry, work in radical collaboration.'[62] The underlying belief is that this way, not only top designers are being educated but also top decision-makers in other fields. The approach is being used in Europe as well, for instance in the team of Professor Alex Vahčic of the University of Ljubljana.

Consilience is a difficult concept for second generation universities. One recently appointed rector of a technical university asked a colleague what to do with the design faculties. Should they not be farmed out, as they did not fit the pattern of scientific analysis and development of technology? When the deans of the corresponding faculties heard about this, they protested heavily: did their faculties not turn out famous designers and architects? Were they not known the world over? This defence was understandable but beside the point. The question is: what do we consider science to be?

Design is not an art like painting, sculpting or composing music; it is based on solid engineering. According to James Dyson, the British inventor cum entrepreneur: 'If you want to make real progress, it is not enough to be a designer. You should be an engineer as well.'[63] Design schools are fertile ground for new enterprises, not only for high-tech innovations but also for replacements of common household items; Dyson for instance reinvented the wheelbarrow by replacing the wheel with a ball. He also reinvented the vacuum cleaner. Douwe Egberts together with Philips Electronics reinvented the preparation of coffee using coffee patches. A group of students from Delft reinvented the umbrella, making it storm-resistant using aerodynamic concepts. All these examples are the result of the combination of creativity, design, ergonomics and solid engineering. We would therefore argue that a 3GU is not complete without a design faculty. In a 2GU a design faculty may not fit so easily, because it does not produce papers in ISI journals (Intercollegiate Studies Institute) and thereby lacks not only academic status but also income, as universities receive bonuses for such publications.

Transdisciplinary research involves members of several faculties. When asked, most researchers state that they spend more time with colleagues from other faculties than with members of their own faculty. In many universities, cross-faculty teams or university institutes are emerging. As their staff is subordinated to the faculties, their work is hampered by the faculty structure. This applies not only to research but also to teaching as many Master's courses are given by cross-faculty teams or university institutes. We will discuss this further in Chapter 7.

Characteristic 5: The Two-Track University

In 2001, City University of New York (CUNY) initiated a programme for diligent and clever students, allowing them to study without paying a fee and even giving them an annual stipend of $7500 and a personal computer (PC). Most of these students are from poor backgrounds. Out of 60 000 students, some 1100 benefit from this scheme. Testing shows that the group is in the top 7 per cent of students of the US. The history of CUNY is interesting:[64]

> Founded in 1847 as City College in Harlem, it produced nine Nobel Laureates (twelve if subsidiaries are included), thanks to high admission standards. Then, under pressure from its students, CUNY scrapped the admission standards in 1969. This – and the lack of tuition fees – brought an explosion in the number of students. Quality collapsed. The city then reinstated tuition funding (CUNY is financed by the city of New York) while input standards were raised, particularly for its honours programme. Counterintuitively, this resulted in the highest enrolment ever and the university is picking up the brighter students. The approach attracts endowments; half of the target $1.2 billion has already been raised.

The Humboldt university was designed to educate future scientists and practitioners who would utilise scientific approaches in their professional life. It was an elite university in the intellectual sense. In the 1960s a new paradigm emerged, the result of a happy convergence of conservative ideas ('education is the basis for future prosperity') and socialistic ideas ('equal opportunities for all'). The result was a sharp increase in the number of universities ('every region its own') and an explosion in the number of students. The result was huge classes (up to 1600 students), and multiple-choice exams, with personal interaction reserved for only the last stages of the education – the thesis work. The task of educating future scientists became hampered by the large number of students who had to be prepared for professional work. For most students only lip service was paid to the original idea of scientific education. While universities came under pressure by maintaining, as far as possible, the academic nature of their education[65] and while institutes of higher vocational education put more emphasis on scientific education rather than just applied problem-solving, the gap between the two types of organisation narrowed. In many countries, institutes of higher education won the right to call themselves universities (for example the UK) or are contemplating laws to do so. In Europe, institutes of higher education can issue BA and BSc degrees that give access to universities' Master's courses while many such institutes offer their own Master's courses, sometimes in cooperation with an old-style university. In order to safeguard the education of future scientists, City University of New York introduced what it calls the 'three-barrel approach', that is:

1. Raise admission standards.
2. Create specific facilities for bright students.

3. Acquire endowments to finance bright students and cutting-edge research.

Raising input standards may work nicely in the US and some other countries: in many other countries, however, admittance exams are banned by law. This means that for most universities there is no alternative to being a mass university. In order to serve the education of future scientists, most third generation universities will have to be two-track universities, meaning that they will offer standard courses with a good deal of academic education to the majority of students, while offering science-oriented academic courses to the best and brightest. Such *grandes écoles* within the universities resemble the university colleges of the Middle Ages and many universities now adopt the name 'University College' for their special courses. Students are willing to pay for good education. The ten-month MBA course at Insead, Fontainebleau, France, costs €45 000, while the IESE Business School in Barcelona, Spain, charges €61 900 for its two-year MBA.[66] Other tools are the creation of Honours classes, again for selected students with a higher level of education than those of the regular classes. The Humboldt-Universität in Berlin has initiated Honours classes for students selected by the university. The subject is still controversial however.[67] Delft University of Technology can invite successful students to follow Honours Master's classes. This requires a tuition-free extra half-year of study, on top of the regular two years. In addition, students get more 'contact time' than they would receive otherwise. Students welcome this initiative and often complete the extra work within the two years anyway.

Medieval universities also had a double track. On the one hand, they passed on the insights of the 'fathers', whether ancient or Church fathers, uncritically to the next generations. On the other hand, they asked challenging questions – mostly philosophical and religious ones – and tried to solve them by logical and transparent reasoning; logical because one argument followed the other, and transparent because the reasoning would be open and could be challenged by anyone – courtesy of Socrates, Plato, Aristotle and others. Yet the medieval way of thinking contained a good deal of the irrational. Everything derived from God; God cannot be known and so one can only speculate about Him. The modern scientific method was based on observation of, and experimentation with, natural phenomena. Objective observation and transparent experimentation were added to logical reasoning. The rise of Cartesian rationality pushed the irrational into a corner of irrelevance as far as universities were concerned. Education in arts and music, normal components of the *Artes* faculties of the Middle Ages, mostly disappeared from the curriculum of the second generation universities and found their way to specialised, non-scientific, academies.

Characteristic 6: The Cosmopolitan University

Third generation universities will adopt English as their daily language. All lectures and tutorials will be given in English as well as all written documentation; even administrative documentation will be written in English, as staff will increasingly be drawn from international sources. The national languages will still have a role, such as in clubs formed by students who come from the same home country. Such clubs do not bear any relationship to the powerful *nationes* of the medieval universities; rather, they will be occasions for diversion.

Whether one likes it or not, English has become the new lingua franca. It has become the language of international corporations and business as well as of international diplomacy; it will also be the language of universities.

Teams in which the members have a different background enhance creativity. 3GUs are multicultural universities; university managers and in fact all staff and students will have to learn to work with diversity. Moreover, they need to exploit it. The catering department of KLM Airlines employs staff from 54 countries. According to the managing director: 'Every conflict in the world can be found on our work floor.' The company set up an elaborate programme to enhance mutual understanding and mutual respect. The original target was to create peace in the workplace but it soon became more than that, an exercise in mutual understanding. Diversity was a major element of the medieval universities that got lost in the nationalistic nineteenth century when the 2GU matured. It will be back in the 3GUs.

Characteristic 7: Financing the 3GU

In the Middle Ages, universities were financed mainly by Church and kings. In addition, they would generate income from property and students' fees. In the nineteenth century, the national states took over as the main suppliers of finance of universities. With the mass education that started in the 1960s, university education became a major item of the national budgets and the control of the state over universities grew to grim proportions. Control over research budgets was delegated in many countries to independent foundations that selected research projects by peer evaluation. Even with this provision, the majority of the funds of universities still come directly from the state. A 3GU cannot flourish with state controls. Funds for education will therefore be transferred to independent intermediaries. This does not mean that the state will stop financing academic research and education, it means that the direct financing will be substituted by financing through intermediaries. We will work this out in section 7.3.

The trend to liberalise universities from state bureaucracies is worldwide. In October 2006, the German state of North Rhine-Westphalia freed the hands of its 33 universities to decide what courses to offer and which professors to appoint.[68] Other (German) states have adopted similar, but less radical, changes, allowing for greater autonomy. Several states are for the first time charging students a tuition fee (€500 per six-month semester); such fees were banned in Germany before. Fees are common in most countries (they average €4500 a year in the UK), Germany being a notable exception. Another move from the egalitarian culture in which politicians kept universities is the assignment of three universities as 'elite universities', meaning they get extra research funds worth €21 million per year for a period of five years, part of a €1.9 billion scheme launched in 2004 aimed at creating competitors for the international top universities. Germany will name more elite universities later. French president Mr Sarkozy has announced that his minister of education will present a bill to parliament that will give universities more autonomy. They will be able to offer jobs themselves and set remuneration individually. Universities will be able to own and manage their own property and raise private money. Students will be able to enrol anywhere they wish, but universities will not be allowed to select students through entrance exams.[69]

Finally, a note on endowments, the 'fourth flow of finance'. Cambridge has its William B. Gates Building (guess who sponsored it?)[70] and US universities seem to be made up entirely of sponsored buildings. Alfred Mann, a serial entrepreneur of Los Angeles and founder of enterprises that pioneered solar energy, pacemakers, neuro-simulation and other high-tech subjects, donated US$200 million to the University of California, Los Angeles (UCLA) and the University of Southern California (USC). His aim is 'to build biomedical institutes that will act as bridges between industry and the ivory tower'. They will be large, each employing more than 100 people. They will license their know-how to a range of companies, not just Mr Mann's own. This way, a stream of income will be generated for the universities concerned.[71] Harvard University alone has a fund of $29 billion (and made 16.7 per cent on it in 2006, net of expenses and fees)[72] coming from endowments; Yale has $12 billion.

In continental Europe, such sponsoring is rare and universities blame the mentality of the rich and wealthy.[73] But universities should blame themselves and make a greater effort. People often wonder what they can give to 'the man who has it all'. The answer is that universities are in the position to give that ultimate reward and rare commodity that is called immortality. We do so by creating Nobel laureates and lesser distinctions such as honorary doctorates and we sometimes name buildings after successful professors. The establishment of a building that bears your name will last forever and will support generations of young people in their personal and professional development. This is a deeply felt desire by many of the very rich and they are willing to spend vast amounts of money for it, given proper guarantees. A good example is Mr Klaus Jacobs who donated €200 million to the International University of Bremen in Germany. This university, with 30 programmes and 1000 students from 86 countries, would have gone bankrupt otherwise. Mr Jacobs does not just give the money away. He will donate €15 million annually for the period 2006–10 and then donate the remaining €125 million only if there is sufficient progress. The university has changed its name to Jacobs University.[74] Hopefully, the habit of endowing[75] will spread in Europe.

Most endowments come from alumni. The motto of Dr Bert Twaalfhoven, successful Harvard Business School alumnus, entrepreneur, business angel and sponsor of academic entrepreneurship through his European Foundation for Entrepreneurship Research (EFER), is: 'Learn, earn and return'. That is, learning at the university, earning as an entrepreneur and returning money to the alma mater. We would add that the success of a university is proportional to the way it deals with its alumni.

2.3 SUMMARY: 3GU AS A SEVEN-POINTED STAR

The main features of the 3GU can now be summarised as shown in Figure 2.3.

In the previous chapter, we saw how each era gets the university it deserves. The Middle Ages had its scholastic university where consolidation of the universal truths and their teaching to the future leaders of society were the prime objective. The University of Paris was a role model.

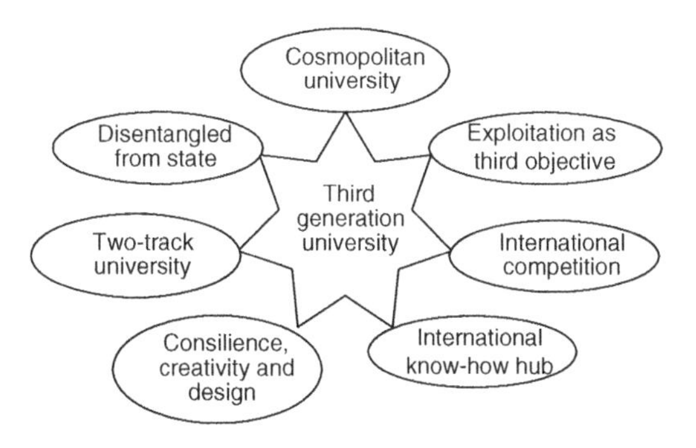

Figure 2.3 The third generation as a seven-pointed star

In the Rational Ages, the creation of knowledge became the second objective and research scientists became the new elite. Reductionism reduced the universal truths to experimental and logical verification of specific theories and hypothesis, and the world to a collection of competing nations. We used the Humboldt university of Berlin as a role model.

We are now entering a new era that we will tentatively call the Digital Era, where certain developments of the Rational Era are brought to their logical conclusion – all that we know and sense can be reduced to digits – but other trends swing back to earlier sources such as a more holistic view and globalisation.

This new era will need a third generation university. The contours of this 3GU are still under development, but using the University of Cambridge as a role model, certain characteristics are emerging:

1. The third objective of the 3GU is 'transfer of capabilities to society'. This has several major implications: the university no longer serves an elite but society at large; the university is no longer an independent 'state in the state' only subject to the laws of science; and the university has to create value to society with the knowledge it generates. The 3GU is tripolar – its teaching objective is directed to educate the new mass market of professionals and this is executed by the traditional faculties, and its research is cutting edge by establishing multi- and transdisciplinary institutes in cooperation with industry and as a means to attract new income streams.
2. The 3GU is entrepreneurial – it actively supports the creation of value to society (the third university objective) by supporting technostarters and making money from IPR.
3. The 3GU is global, rather than national – it is the centre of an international know-how carousel, attracting staff and students from all over the world, and uses English as the lingua franca. The 3GU is a hub – the centre of a knowledge and innovation network, collaborating with industry, spinout companies, research institutes and universities abroad. The 3GU reverses the reductionistic trends of the Rational Age and reaches back to Renaissance values such as consilience and transdisciplinary research.
4. The 3GU needs a new organisational format to meet the three objectives; this will mean a reduction of the role of the faculties, a new approach to channel and prioritise research funds, a new way of teaching and mass education, and so on.

3. Two case studies

3.1 A CLASSIFICATION OF UNIVERSITIES

At this point, we would like to introduce a classification of universities by plotting quality in research and education against progress towards the third generation university (3GU) model (Figure 3.1). Types 1, 2 and 3 are basically first, second and third generation universities while Types 4 and 5 are excellent versions of second and third generation universities.

Type 1 universities are mainly or only teaching institutes. The research activities of these universities are limited in size and scope or they are not present at all. Quite a few of such universities teach on the level of higher professional education. They may form the majority of the world's 30 000 institutes for higher education. If a Type 1 university wants to develop itself, the first thing it has to do is to create a thorough research base. Without it, it cannot develop a know-how carousel and hence it cannot develop into a 3GU.

Type 2 universities have a solid scientific base, having some outstanding scientists amongst their staff. Education is linked to the research efforts. Type 2 universities are 'true' universities, not higher professional schools that are only universities in name. When these universities collaborate actively with industry and other partners in the commercialisation of know-how and when they have extensive educational and operational facilities for technostarters, they become Type 3 universities. Alternatively, they can strengthen their research base and become a Type 4 university. The transfer to a world-class university however is quite costly; the European Union (EU) for instance estimates that the cost of a new European Institute of Technology, comparable to Massachusetts Institute of Technology (MIT), would cost €35 billion.

The few leading universities that create cutting-edge science are Type 4 universities and the best collect the Nobel Prizes. But the Type 4 model is inherently unstable, as these universities have to migrate to Type 5 universities in order to maintain their scientific front position in the future. If they do not, Type 4 universities will fall back to Type 2 universities.

Most universities that are on their way to become 3GUs are Type 2 universities that move to become Type 3 universities. The examples of the Type 5 universities are inspiring for them but they are exceptional examples. We

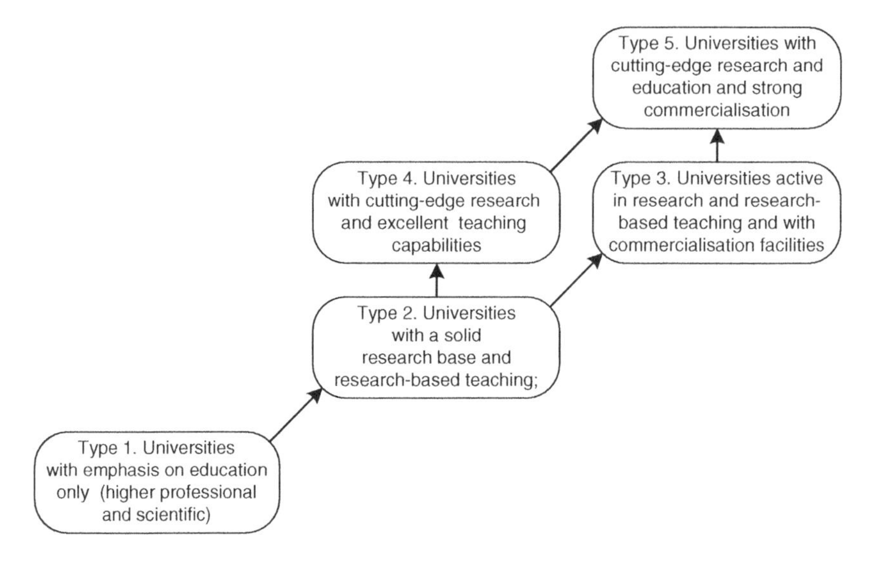

Figure 3.1 A classification of universities

will therefore describe two Type 2 universities that are on their way to become Type 3 universities. We include these cases in order to show that you do not have to be a Stanford, MIT, Cambridge or Oxford to become a third generation university. On the contrary, the 3GU position is very much in reach for the Type 2 universities.

3.2 CASE 1: INSTITUT TEKNOLOGI BANDUNG

Founded in 1920, Institut Teknologi Bandung (Bandung University of Technology, ITB) is the oldest university in Indonesia. It can boast of many successful alumni including the first president of the country, President Sukarno. Unlike most Indonesian universities, ITB has a strong research base. It has excellent international contacts and a strong alumni network. It is one of Asia's leading universities of technology. ITB realises that Indonesia's economy has to become more innovative if it is to avoid the role of just being a market for international enterprises; in this respect it sees its task in the exploitation of its know-how as one of national duty.

ITB is governed by a board of trustees that appoints the rector and has to approve major management decisions concerning the university. The rector is the highest manager in the university; the Academic Unit (SA), the Endowment Unit (SKD) and the Unit for Innovation and Enterprise Development (SUK) report to him. The latter two are relatively indepen-

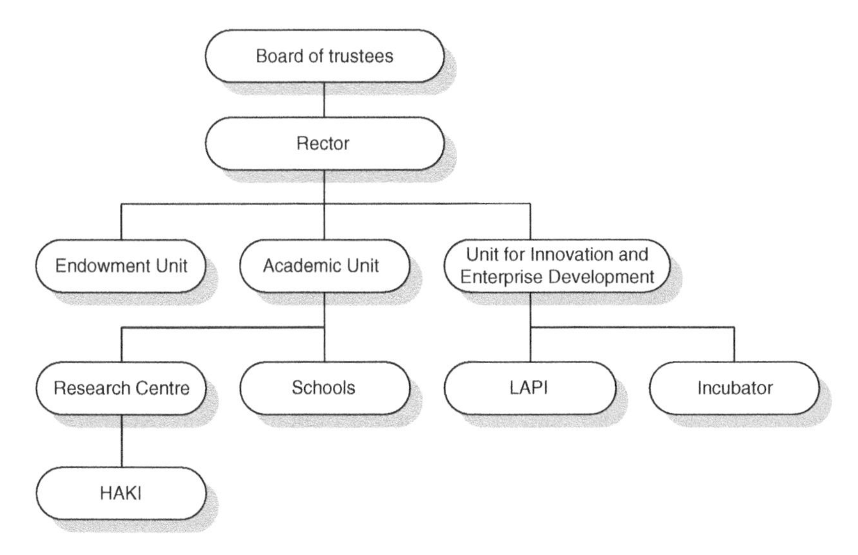

Figure 3.2 Organisational structure of Institut Teknologi Bandung

dent bodies; their managers are proposed by the rector but appointed by the board of trustees. The Academic Unit consists of two parts: the Research Centre (LPPM) and the faculties, headed by deans and called schools.

The Research Centre has an IPR unit (intellectual property rights) called HAKI that licenses technology to third parties. The Unit for Innovation and Enterprise Development has an incubator (IPB) that supports technostarters and young enterprises that have emerged from its efforts. It also has a facilities unit called LAPI. The organisation is presented in Figure 3.2.

Altogether ITB has 15 000 full-time students in graduate, undergraduate and doctoral programmes and a staff of 2100, of which 1200 are academics.

Know-how Commercialisation and Technostarters

ITB takes the need to create enterprises seriously. In its *General Development Policy 2001 – 2006* it states that it wants to: 'Perform research to develop applicable technology, to build national economic strength. ITB is expected to create technopreneurs who have capabilities to develop competitiveness of local industries in the global economy.' This statement clearly shows the commitment of the university to help create Indonesian technology-based enterprises that can compete in the global economy. The statement can be regarded as the third objective of the university, next to its other objectives of research and education. The three objectives can be recognised in the organisational diagram. ITB has three objectives:

- enrichment of the academic environment;
- technology transfer and commercialisation;
- regional economic development.

In practice the commitment takes shape in a number of academic and non-academic support functions.

Activities concerning technopreneurship started early at ITB when the then rector, Professor Iskander Alisyahbana, initiated Radio Frequency Communication plc in 1973, a company fully owned by the university and engaged in research and sales of modern telecommunications. After some time, this company was absorbed by the Ministry of Defence as its know-how was considered of military importance. Another reason for this transition was that at the time, a university could not own an enterprise in Indonesia. After the transition, many people left to start their own companies. One company was Control Communications that subsequently was split up into a number of other companies, such as Hariff.

Hariff started in 1982 with 20 people and today it employs 500 people in offices and warehouses all over Indonesia. Hariff develops and delivers custom-made telecommunication systems and energy backup systems for companies and other clients. It also develops and partly manufactures hardware that becomes part of the turnkey projects it delivers. After installation, Hariff services its systems. Here, Hariff guarantees an impressive MTTR (maintenance time to repair) of two hours on Java and four hours in the rest of Indonesia. The growth of Hariff was entirely financed by bank loans on projects. This is a relatively expensive way of financing, but the founders and managers decided upon this course as inviting an external party to invest in the share capital was considered too risky. The research of Hariff has the nature of customer-driven development. Hariff maintains its good name by networking rather than advertising; this leads to the acquisition of new projects. Hariff is a good example of an early university spinout. It has the potential to become a major export company and it could add products and services to its portfolio if it could finance the research to design them.

The School of Business and Management and the Centre for Innovation, Entrepreneurship and Leadership

The School of Business and Management was founded in 1990 when ITB started offering a two-year MBA course (then called 'Magister in

Management'); ITB was one of four pilot universities to offer such a course in Indonesia. The MBA course and the establishment of the school were preceded by lengthy debates as to whether such an activity fits within a university of technology. The MBA course became quite successful and in 1996 the school started a three-year BA degree course in management. This course is given in English (the first year is bilingual) and has maximum classes of 100 students per year.

The School of Business and Management has a relatively independent position in the university as it can take many decisions autonomously (for example hiring and firing of staff). The school receives all revenues of external activities of its staff, in contrast to the usual practice where academics themselves cash the proceeds of consulting activities. The school is sponsored by the Putrasamporo Fund and it is engaged in international projects of cooperation, for instance with the University of Sankt Gallen in Switzerland, the National University of Singapore (NUS), the Malaysian University in Kuala Lumpur, Malaysia and the University of Groningen in the Netherlands. The school has a campus in Jakarta where it plans to organise an executive MBA course. This campus is very strategically located on the Jakarta industrial site, and only two hours driving from Bandung.

An important educational tool of ITB is the course in 'Innovation Management and Entrepreneurship' that is given for all faculties (albeit under different names and with different details), given by the School of Business and Management. This course is obligatory for all undergraduate students.

The Incubator (PIB)

The incubator (Pulsat Inkubator Bisnis, PIB) has the mission: 'to create entrepreneurs and enterprises by providing assistance and facility services, as needed by the potential entrepreneur'.

PIB has a research inventory that contains items of research results that could be commercialised. It extracts this information from the Research Centre and from HAKI. This way, PIB has a good insight in the know-how position of ITB. The other activity is to scout potential entrepreneurs from the student population, fresh graduates, alumni and others outside ITB. PIB also negotiates financial support. Indonesian state-owned companies are obliged by law to transfer 2 per cent of their profits into a venture capital (VC) fund. Such a fund can be owned and administered by the company itself, or the contribution may go to a VC fund created for this purpose. The resources of the funds may also be used for other purposes such as community building, so not everything goes to technopreneurs. The

Indonesian telecommunication giant Telkom has a fund that has financed some of PIB's start-ups. Other sources of finance are private investors, companies and investment funds.

The basic plan for technopreneurs consists of three phases:

1. During the pre-incubation phase the entrepreneurs have to commit themselves, prepare a sound business plan, create a team, carry out market research and pre-operational activities. This phase lasts six months.
2. The incubation phase, when the enterprises are housed in the incubator, lasts 24 months. During this time, there is a regular evaluation of performance and all kinds of services are delivered.
3. During the post-incubation phase (another six months) the companies have to relocate. This does not mean the end of the involvement of PIB as it continues to provide services. Many enterprises relocate to a private industrial park in the surroundings of Jakarta.

The total involvement of PIB lasts three years.

We investigated three technopreneurs who were at PIB, the incubator, in August 2006 – Fermentech, Natural Resource Foundation and Lorco Multimedia – which we will summarise below.

Fermentech

The original company was founded by Zaki Rahman Nur, a biology student at ITB since 1999, in 2004. Fermentech produces and sells iced yoghurt-based soft drinks in proprietary counters under the brand name Ciko; the name refers to Cikomeng, a milk-producing region in West Java. The outlets consist of a counter, where customers can buy the products, and a mini-restaurant. They are a nice break from work or studies. The products now include a wide range of soft drinks and different kinds of coffee, but yoghurt-based drinks are still the core of the business. The Ciko outlets have an attractive and recognisable design; they can be spotted immediately, very much like the McDonald's and Starbucks outlets. Ciko is already well known in Bandung and surroundings and Zaki is preparing to make his business a franchise. This way, Ciko could spread very rapidly. Fermentech rents factory space near Bandung. This factory produces the ingredients of the yoghurt drinks. The drinks are freshly made at the counters with a mixer. Zaki realises that hygiene is of utmost importance; a mistake could give negative publicity and be very harmful to all counters. He therefore trains his staff carefully with much attention to hygiene, and he only hires staff when they have completed the training successfully.

When setting up his business, Zaki's studies hardly played a role; he invented everything in his own time. He got much support from the incubator staff who coached him and gave him much useful advice in addition to giving him cheap office space. Without the incubator, it would have been much more difficult. Zaki especially had to learn a lot about marketing, and only when he had mastered this did the company take off.

He designed his yoghurt-based drinks and set up the company while a student at ITB. This took him so much time that his studies were severely delayed. However, he persisted and he graduated in the autumn of 2006, having spent seven years to do his Bachelor's degree. But that he considers a small price for realising his dream: having his own company.

Ciko now has two counters with a staff of two people each. The factory has also two employees. Zaki works with three partners who work for the company on a part-time basis. Zaki is the chief executive officer (CEO) of the company. 'Expansion' is the first word he uses when asked about the future. It seems that he has found the right formula for expansion. Is he afraid of the competition? 'No', he says, 'the taste is all important and we have unique tastes, for instance a mango based yoghurt drink that I designed myself.' In addition, we may add that Ciko has a unique style that will help it find its place with Indonesian consumers.

Natural Resource Foundation (Yayasan Sumber Daya Hayati)

When Genti Setiyaningrum studied pharmacy, her attention was drawn to traditional medicines based on herbs. It emerged that she has not only a good taste for herbs ('You have to buy them in East Java, the herbs there taste better than the ones of West Java') but she could also relate herbs to specific diseases. So, in 2003 while studying she set up a company that produces the herb mixes. She develops her recipes herself. Having graduated in 2004, she works for a pharmacy and runs the company in her own time together with some friends. She works with one partner who is in charge of the purchasing of the herbs and the production process, while Genti focuses on product development and marketing.

The herbs are washed and boiled in water with the addition of some sugar, then filtered and bottled. There are several kinds of this medicine, each having a different function in relation to complaints or diseases, like diabetes, high cholesterol levels and so on. One batch produces ten bottles and at present the company produces one batch per day. The bottles are distributed via a distribution service. Genti has her own radio programme on health advice. In addition, she has opened a first health clinic where customers can detoxify using the natural medicines and massage. This clinic is called Ruma Herba, House of Herbs.

Genti got the idea of starting her own business in her second year when her professor urged students to create their own company in order to fight unemployment in Indonesia. She feels that she contributes to this problem by creating jobs rather than using an employment position herself. She was very much supported by her professor when setting up her business, and later by the incubator. The company took off after it was presented at an exhibition. It benefits from the current interest in health by the Indonesian public.

Talking about the future, Genti has many plans. First of all she wants to expand the number of medicines she produces. Then she wants to produce capsules of herb extracts, but she still has to master the technology. She also wants to expand the number of clinics and have her own radio programme. Does she ever sleep? 'Well, it is nice to be active and work on your dream. I feel I do a good job, not only for myself but also for my customers. And in creating employment, I give a little help to our national economy', she says.

Lorco Multimedia & Software Development

When he entered the last semester of his biology studies at ITB, Doni Tirtana realised that he had to choose what kind of employment he would seek after graduation. He was wondering what to do. Employment with a large firm or the government did not look attractive to him and he discovered that there was 'another way', meaning entrepreneurship. He decided he would start his own enterprise, and since multimedia was his hobby (he studied instrumentation and was an active member of the multimedia students' club) he decided to make multimedia his business. The first activity of his enterprise, Lorco, was to make an interactive CD for learning purposes for the consumer market using multimedia. Unfortunately, this turned out not to be a success as it was difficult to reach the mass market as a small enterprise. But Doni is persistent and he decided to switch to the business-to-business (B2B) market. For this market he designed three types of products:

- The core products are multimedia presentations, human resource management programmes and customer management programmes.
- His second product line is other communication tools.
- Advertising has become his third product.

Lorco sells mainly in a niche market, the market of safety, health and environmental companies and organisations. The focus on a niche and the subsequent specialisation give it a strong name in its market. Lorco sells mainly through the Internet, and also the video clips it makes for his customers. So the company has virtually no distribution costs – everything is made to measure and mailed over the Internet.

The switch from the B2C (business-to-consumer) to the B2B market was inspired by a similar switch of another company in the incubator. Doni says he learns much from the incubator staff and they remind him of his reporting duties – not the strongest point for most entrepreneurs. He also learns much from his colleagues. They exchange information, in meetings but especially in informal ways, when they happen to meet. Other than the incubator, Doni did not benefit really from his studies at ITB other than his membership of the multimedia club. His study subject has little to do with the portfolio of his company.

3.3 CASE 2: THE UNIVERSITY OF ROUSSE[76]

The University of Rousse 'Angel Kunchev'

Founded in 1945 as the Higher Technical School, the University of Rousse is one of the oldest Bulgarian universities; it was elevated to university status in 1995. In 1981 it was named after Angel Kunchev, a Bulgarian rebel and intellectual, who died for the liberation of Bulgaria from the Ottoman Empire when he was 22. In the 1980s, the University of Rousse won the national competition for the title of 'Research University' twice. During this period, the university received the majority of its budget from industrial contracts, giving it considerable experience in contract research.

After 1989, during the years of transition from a planned to a market economy, the university went through a period of stagnation, as did all universities in former communist countries. Despite the lack of funds, the university maintained a high quality of education; research however came virtually to a stop. The positive side of the opening up of the country was that it became possible to develop close cooperation with many universities in Europe and the USA.

In the transition years, the research budgets from industry dried up as state enterprises closed down or were privatised, with the new owners spending far less on research than the previous state enterprises. In this period universities abroad increased their commercial research output and began a process of systematic know-how commercialisation. The University of Rousse is following this example and wants to regain its eminence in contract research. The university has been working successfully towards its major strategic objective: 'to establish itself and develop as a leading and prestigious intellectual centre in the Rousse region and North-Eastern Bulgaria and perform educational, scientific, and various other cultural activities whose merits are recognised nationwide and internationally'.

Today, more than 9600 students are taught in modern laboratories and classrooms, distributed over seven faculties. In addition, the university has a number of specialised centres: the Studies Centre, Centre for Further Education; University Library; University Computing and Information Services Centre; Centre for International Cooperation and Mobility; Bulgarian–Romanian Interuniversity Centre; University Sports and Recreation Centre and a number of other institutes to be discussed below.

Each faculty is led by a dean. The deans report to the rector who is elected for four years. There are three vice-rectors, respectively of studies (education); of scientific and staff development (research); and of educational quality and accreditation; there is one deputy rector who acts as the chief financial officer (CFO). Altogether, the university employs over 800 staff of which about 490 are academics; half of them are full professors or associate professors ('docent') who hold doctoral degrees.

The University of Rousse participates in many international programmes with the aim of improving the teaching process. In addition, it participates in international research programmes, mainly sponsored by the European Union, and there are bilateral contracts with universities from the UK, Germany, Greece, Lithuania, Portugal, Romania, Russia, USA, Turkey, Ukraine and the ex-Yugoslavian states.

The University of Rousse today realises it must undertake serious actions in order to become a 3GU. Lacking this, it will have to accept the unattractive role of a secondary university, producing mostly Bachelor's degree graduates for local employers. The process of differentiation between first- and second-class universities has already begun. The University of Rousse traditionally plays an important role in the economic development of the region and it is picking up this role again. The university organised a number of workshops for its leaders. The conclusion of these workshops is that there is no way back. If a twenty-first-century university strives to be attractive to students and companies, it must undertake the transition to the third generation model by adding to education and research the third component – commercialisation of its know-how and cooperation with industry. In addition, technostarters should get adequate help when they establish their own science- or technology-based firms. The university counts the development and expansion of its Career Centre, its Entrepreneurship Centre and its Technology Transfer Centre amongst its main priorities. With the synergic effects of adding other elements, it is possible to fill in the contours of the 3GU and realise the desired change. 3GU is the way forward, although it will take time to implement it.

The Faculty of Business and Management

In the beginning of the 1990s the University of Rousse established its first graduate and undergraduate courses in the field of management. In 1994 the Faculty of Business and Management was established, uniting some earlier departments.

The faculty has four departments: Business and Management, Economics, Industrial Management and European Studies. The faculty collaborates with Cornell University (USA), the University of Central Lancashire (UK), Volgograd State University (Russia), the Bucharest Academy of Economics (Romania), Karel de Grote-Hogeschool (Belgium) and others. Many representatives of the academic staff have been lectured abroad through EU programmes. The faculty offers undergraduate and graduate courses in business administration, marketing, industrial management, international economic relations, European studies, financial management, regional development management and agrarian economics. Many of the students join the EU mobility programmes, studying in EU universities for one semester.

This Faculty of Business and Management has developed courses for technostarters such as 'How to Start and Run your own Business', 'Entrepreneurship and Intermediation', 'Small Business Management' and other courses in entrepreneurship. This has had an effect on the establishment of new technology-based firms, as we shall see later. The faculty has initiated the establishment of an Entrepreneurship Centre and a comprehensive educational programme. The following four-step approach has been adopted:

- Awareness programmes will be given to all students of engineering degree courses through the existing lectures in the field of economics and management. The purpose of the awareness programmes is to get students acquainted with the general idea of entrepreneurship.
- Elementary education. Students will be offered an elective course in entrepreneurship. This should give a deeper understanding of entrepreneurship while filtering out potential technostarters.
- Advanced functional education. Students of undergraduate and graduate courses in engineering have the option to participate in courses of other faculties (for example the faculties of business and management, law, and so on) in order to learn about subjects such as business plan development, marketing, financing, intellectual property rights, and so on.
- Advanced entrepreneurship education. Potential technostarters will be able to attend special seminars organised at the Entrepreneurship

Centre with external lecturers such as consultants, businessmen, and so on.

The latter two options should give students more practical knowledge and experience about entrepreneurship.

Activities Concerning Know-how Commercialisation and Collaboration with Industry

Over the years, the University of Rousse has developed a variety of activities, which will be of significant importance for the transition to a third generation university. First of all, the university has established, or participates in, specific institutions such as:

- The Management and Business Development Centre Ltd, Rousse, which was established under an EU Phare project as a joint venture company of the University of Rousse, the Rousse Chamber of Commerce and Industry and the Mid-Yorkshire Chamber of Commerce and Industry (UK). Each partner holds a third of the shares. The centre engages in business consulting and financial planning and has a relationship with the European Bank for Reconstruction and Development (EBRD) in London for acquiring finance for companies. Other areas of activity are human resource management and foreign investment. The centre is an important link between the university and domestic and international enterprises.
- The union of sponsors of the university, which is developing into a business angel club to finance young entrepreneurs. At present, it is a source of guest lecturers and business placements for end-of-term students.
- The Career Centre, which improves the link between students and business. It has been established in May 2005 with the support of the USAID, the Labour Market Project and Job-tiger. About 5 per cent of the students have registered at the Career Centre and this number keeps increasing. The Career Centre organises presentations on finding appropriate jobs, preparation of curriculam vitaes (CVs) and cover letters, and so on. It helps companies to find appropriate young staff. The Career Centre has been developed successfully in cooperation with companies from Rousse and the region, many of which are industrial and information technology (IT)-related.
- The Research & Development Sector (R&DS; the technology transfer centre), founded in 1965, which has as its main task the organisation of 'the research and production work, as well as student

internship'. At present the R&DS is the main unit for business contacts of the university with state and private organisations and firms. Within the framework of the R&DS, groups of selected scientists, doctoral students, students and technicians perform, on a contractual basis, fundamental scientific research, as well as development, implementation and consulting activities. The concrete results from the work of these scientific teams have found their application all over the country and in a number of other countries such as Germany, Hungary, the Czech Republic, Russia, Belarus and Latvia. Along with the creation of new scientific knowledge and products, the R&DS helps to increase the scientific potential of the university staff by modernising and updating the material and technical resources and the training process as a whole.

In addition to these institutions, there are many activities relevant to entrepreneurship, such as:

- The student competition, 'Writing a Business Plan', initiated in 2000 and managed by the Faculty of Business and Management. Between 2002 and 2007, 64 students from two faculties have participated.
- The 'Club meetings', conducted by the university and the Rousse Chamber of Commerce & Industry with the objective of getting the academics closer to small and medium-sized enterprises (SMEs). During these meetings, company managers and members of the academic community discuss topics of mutual interest.
- The training of lecturers as 'Business Link Advisors' under the Durham University Business School (UK) programme. This university is specialised in the field of small and medium-sized enterprise issues.

Future Plans

The University of Rousse has the vision that research, education, cooperation and commercialisation of know-how are of equal significance. A number of activities are being prepared.

The Entrepreneurship Centre will be the main organisational element for technostarters, together with the lectures of the Faculty of Business and Management. It will allow technostarters, other students, alumni and other interested individuals to commercialise their know-how. That Centre must have horizontal links with all faculties (departments) and vertical hierarchical links with the Rector Body, that is the meeting of

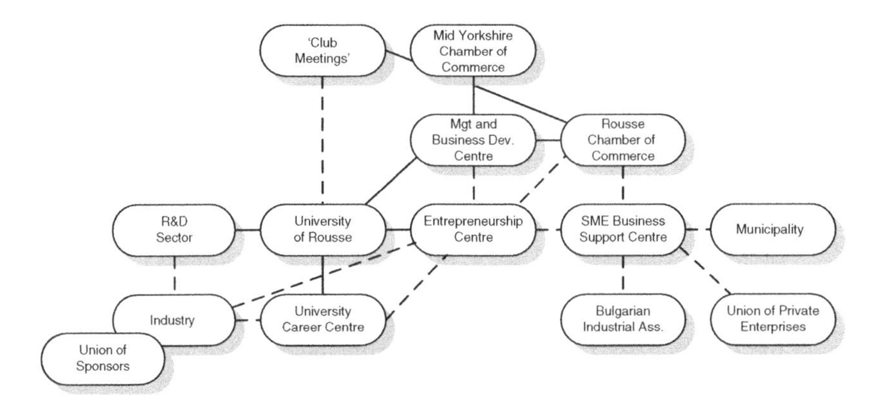

Figure 3.3 The network of the University of Rousse

rector and vice-rectors that acts as the governing body of the university. It is necessary to develop university rules on how to generate income from the know-how commercialisation, and to adopt a financial award system, stimulating the academic staff to encourage students to become technostarters. The more generous the reward system is towards (new) entrepreneurs, the more activities will be initiated at and around the university, thus making the university more interesting to students and staff. Generating income from technostarters is not a first priority. The Entrepreneurship Centre is a long-term initiative and it would effectively facilitate the university's efforts towards the adoption of know-how commercialisation. It would be a driving force and a coordination tool for all activities concerning technostart and even the know-how commercialisation.

The University Centre for Continued Education will offer special programmes in entrepreneurship for graduated technostarters.

The university has a small fund, called the Scientific Research Fund. Part of it could be used to finance the basic research for some of the technostarters. More funding has to be acquired from EU funds, the National Budget and the Bulgarian Innovation Fund.

Figure 3.3 illustrates the local network of the University of Rousse; international contacts have been omitted.

A number of companies have sprung from the University of Rousse. As there were few support activities in the past, these enterprises very much created themselves, benefiting from lectures in entrepreneurship and the general entrepreneurial climate of the university, meaning that much (tacit) support was given by individual lecturers. Below we present some of these companies.

Networx

When he started laying high-speed network cables in the dormitory of the University of Rousse in 2000, Svilen Maksimov could not have imagined that six years later he would be heading a significant Rousse company with over 60 employees. A student in informatics at the universities of Rousse and Linz (Austria), Svilen found that there was a need amongst students for fast Internet connections in their dormitories. In his final year as a student, he started laying cables and providing services, soon joined by two friends. They worked together for many years and the three of them are still the only shareholders of the company they named Networx. In hindsight Svilen says:

> Dormitories were a convenient place as students are willing to experiment and this way we learned a lot. We learned from the inventive type of students who brought us ideas and suggestions. We equally, albeit in a different way, learned from other students who acted as hackers, trying to steal our bandwidth and concepts. From them we learned security. Fortunately, there was a third category of students, the conscientious customers who paid their bills on time. If we had set it up in the centre of Rousse, it would not have worked.

They rented a small office at the campus, moving out as demand started to grow. The university was supportive but did not at that time have facilities to help them. There was however the lecture in entrepreneurship at the Business and Management Faculty that they found very useful: 'It was one of the few lectures that was practical, taken from the real life.' But Svilen sadly remembers that most students did not have a real interest in entrepreneurship. He adopted a saying while participating in a competition organised by Cisco Corporation: 'I learn as I go'. He takes this literally and listens to tapes about entrepreneurship while he travels in his car. He is always learning; he has a keen interest in everything.

Networx now has 107 kilometres of glass fibre cable in the ground in Rousse, replacing copper and aerial cables. With a speed of 100Mbps available for each and every customer, the company offers technology that is 20 years ahead of its time and that brings Internet and cable television to homes and offices. It will offer voice-over-Internet protocol (VoIP) telephone services as soon as there is a generally accepted standard and it expects a vast expansion of its business when this is the case. The company also offers video-on-demand and runs a citywide Wi-Fi service, making Rousse one of the few cities in the world where one can connect with the Internet literally anywhere. At present, this service is free of charge but the company will soon sell vouchers by which customers buy capacity, very much in the way of prepaid mobile telephones.

Networx farms out much of its work; the laying of the pipes in which the cables are drawn for instance is outsourced to construction firms. One cable contains 96 fibres, each capable of transmitting 10 Gb/second. Their only competitor in Rousse employs co-ax cables, which is the old technology. Networx used credit financing and this way the owners managed to avoid dilution of their stakes.

Svilen thinks that the attitude of students as well as teachers needs to change at the university, but, he says: 'Of course I am now five years out of the university and there have already been changes.' Most students enter the university just to get their diploma. They do not have a real learning attitude and hope to find employment in established companies. This is why education should be made more expensive – like in other countries. Education should be more Internet-based; Networx buys just about anything on the Internet.

Ecohumus

At weekends, you can often see Ivan Petkov helping his father on his farm. The farm is a high-tech industry with combine harvesters, tractors and all kinds of other equipment. Father and son also managed to start a transport company. This company has a large truck and they employ a driver. The company works all over Bulgaria and will soon also cover the EU. Ivan was very much interested in transport problems and decided to start studying transport technology at the University of Rousse. While a student, his interest was drawn to Humus (Biocompost). This is a natural fertiliser made from the manure of cows, pigs or chickens by Red Californian Worms. Biocompost is a black, dry, fibre-like powder with a light, spring-'forest-like' odour. It can be transported easily and it can be stored for long periods of time. The production of Biocompost is a natural process that brings two advantages. Firstly, it produces a natural fertiliser and secondly, it helps farmers to get rid of the manure from their animals, an increasingly severe problem as the legislation on the disposal of manure gets stricter every year. There is plenty of manure and the manufacturing process is relatively simple and not capital intensive.

Ivan is very much the entrepreneurial type. He wanted to do something new, something with great potential and something environmentally clean. He picked up the idea of using the Red Californian Worm and searched the Internet until he found that there was to be a lecture on the subject at the nearby Agricultural University of Plovdiv. This lecture proved to be the turning point. He got support from the lecturer and he started experimenting until he found he had a good grip over the process. He then established the enterprise with his father and named it Ecohumus IVP. In the meantime he found more documentation about Biocompost. It has a wide spectrum of applications in agriculture and horticulture where it increases the yields significantly (up to 40 and 50 per cent) in comparison with chemical fertilisers. Biocompost improves the structure of the soil; the time of application is not critical. Ripening of fruits is faster and more vitamin C is developed. Although all this is documented in scientific experiments, the market is developing slowly. 'Farmers are conservative', says Ivan. 'They do not like to experiment.'

Ivan and his father built a tank for the production of Biocompost, using manure from their own farm and the farms of others. Other farmers are happy to bring the manure; no money is exchanged. There is a storage space for the Biocompost as not everything produced can be sold at the time and the plant has to be run at a minimum capacity of 10 m^3/year. The maximum capacity is 40 m^3 in the first year, increasing to 160 m^3 over the coming years as the worms multiply.

Ivan is now finalising his MSc degree course at the Entrepreneurship section of the university. The marketing issue will receive his special interest. Ivan says he wants to start at the high end of the market; when he is successfully there, other market segments will follow. Biocompost is very well suited for intensive farming, as practiced in greenhouses. He expects more options now that Bulgaria has joined the EU, as legislation on the use of chemical fertilisers is strict in the EU and Biocompost might be a way out. There is much to do, but Ivan is still only 23 years old. That leaves enough time to bring the product to the market and then act as the vanguard for other farmers.

Dartek

As early as 1994, Asen Tasev and two partners decided to become entrepreneurs. They were good programmers, second-year students in informatics at the University of Rousse, when they started their software company. They wrote business programmes for inventory control and other applications, but much to their regret, they found that the market was not ready for this. There were successful software development companies in Rousse but these were working for foreign companies that wanted to benefit from the low labour cost in Bulgaria. But working as 'body shoppers' (acting as a temporary employment office without added value in technology) was not what the partners had in mind. They realised they had to try something else as they did not want to give up the idea of having their own enterprise. Instead of making software, they started to service computers and this proved to be the traditional gap in the market. They found increasingly more work and they set the next logical step: trading in computers. With this, they targeted middle-sized companies as large companies often have their headquarters in Sofia and this was too far away.

The sale of hardware expanded with the rapidly developing market. The key to their success is that they not only sell hardware, but they also service it. They found an additional niche for their service activities, performing warranty repairs for retailers that could not service defunct products themselves. They also started – experimentally – a service for the larger Rousse companies, dealing with spam and viruses, and giving emergency services. They could develop a preventive maintenance service but the market for this is not ripe: companies call them when their system is down and are not yet prepared to spend money on preventing breakdown.

Although the university was supportive when Tasev and his partners started their company, they did not get much practical support as the university itself still had no idea how to do that. Please keep in mind that this was 1994! At that time, the university had hardly any IT equipment itself; this came later from EU projects.

In 2007, the company employed 15 people, including the three partners. Most of the earnings still come from the trade in hardware but an increasing share comes from servicing. They provide warranty services (repairs for hardware under guarantee) not only for the large retailers but also for the computer manufacturers themselves, as it is cheaper for these companies to have the warranty work done by a local firm than to ship defunct hardware to Sofia. This way, they have companies like Dell, Siemens, Lenovo, Philips, Samsung, Acer and other well-known names as their customers. With trade and warranty services booming, they look to the future with confidence. After all, they have already been in business for more than eight years and during this period they have shown themselves to be flexible in their choice of activities. It took time to find their markets, but now that they are well established – witnessed by the size of their staff and a fleet of repair cars behind their office – they can work on expansion, more of the same, and who knows, one day also preventive maintenance.

3.4 CONCLUSIONS: THREE STAGES OF UNIVERSITY DEVELOPMENT

From the cases of the universities of Cambridge, Bandung and Rousse and the descriptions of other universities in Part III (notably the universities of Leuven, Delft and Wageningen), it appears that there is a certain pattern universities go through.

The first stage, with the university still operating in the traditional second generation university (2GU) model, consists of private initiatives to support technostarters and some academics carrying out research for industry on an individual basis. The initiatives come from individual academics and/or alumni and later financiers. Courses in entrepreneurship appear, initiated by enthusiastic academics and alumni rather than as the result of faculty or university policy. The university welcomes such lectures and activities as it has welcomed new subjects for hundreds of years. At this stage, foreign students arrive in small numbers, to do research rather than to follow courses, as courses are still given in the national language. At this stage, interdisciplinary teams may be formed from members of different faculties, although this is unrelated to the other events.

The second stage sets in when the board of management or the team of rector and vice-rectors adopts know-how commercialisation as an official task. Such decisions are often taken to benefit from government schemes aimed at financing the corresponding activities. It seems that the role of government is of paramount importance; if it does not make dedicated funds available, the university is likely to stay in the first stage. The second stage sees the creation of technology transfer centres, career centres to help students find jobs and internships, and an entrepreneurship centre that gives support to technostarters and that stimulates lectures in entrepreneurship in faculties. At this stage, we see the first courses in English – usually Master's courses to start with – and the establishment of formal university institutes, dedicated to a certain subject rather than discipline. When we asked universities whether they would continue the activities concerning commercialisation and technostarters if the government stopped funding them, the answer was usually: 'That is a very good question'.

The third stage is marked by what one could call the internalisation of the commercialisation efforts. This is often characterised by the appointment of a board member or vice-rector who is responsible for commercialisation, technostarters and collaboration with industry. The university creates a fully equipped centre for marketing and know-how commercialisation, and it adopts a patent policy. In other words, although government funding is still required for research and education, the university is now itself the driving force and the commercialisation efforts are professionalised. Collaboration with industry becomes a mainstream activity that is executed via university institutes rather than faculties. Gradually, all courses are given in English.

If we state that commercialisation activities depend on financial support from the government, we must make an exception for the case of the US, where universities themselves initiate commercialisation activities and fund them from their own sources, often from endowment funds. There is also a difference between universities where commercialisation activities result from bottom-up initiatives, such as Cambridge and the US universities, and universities such as Leuven where the activities are the result of deliberate university policy from the start. But, as we shall see in section 8.2, even the activities of Leuven have been strongly enhanced by individual academics, so the differences are perhaps not as large as they seem.

PART II

Know-how Creation and Exploitation

In the third generation university (3GU) model, universities cooperate with partners with whom they do not work traditionally. Good cooperation is conditional to good mutual understanding. For this reason, we will outline characteristics and developments of the main partners of the 3GU: technology-based enterprises, technostarters and the financiers of new firms. Of these three, universities have perhaps the best understanding of industrial corporations, if only because many of their professors and governors originate from such enterprises. However, as we shall see, the landscape of corporate innovation and R&D has changed dramatically over the last decade of the twentieth century and universities should be aware of this if they want to be good partners (Chapter 4). Technostarters are a relatively new phenomenon and traditional universities do not see it as their task to support them. However, technostarters contribute significantly to the know-how hub that ambitious universities try to create around them. Technostarters not only bring knowledge to the market, but they also collaborate intensively with large corporations and the faculties (Chapter 5). Finally, much know-how is being commercialised through the creation of new firms, be it through technostarters or university-initiated spinouts. New crops only emerge if there are good seeds and fertile ground, but they need water in addition. Likewise, new ventures need good know-how and a stimulating environment in order to emerge, but without a varied financial infrastructure they will remain a dream. Chapter 6 outlines the role and ambitions of financiers and the ways in which they make deals. Together, Part II is devoted to the main partners of universities in the collaborative knowledge generation and value-creation processes.

4. Creation of knowledge and value in industry

4.1 EVOLUTION IN INDUSTRIAL RESEARCH: THE FIRST FOUR REGIMES

Technology-based companies are engaged in research activities to make discoveries and subsequently develop them into inventions, and these inventions are then turned into innovations by bringing them to the market. This final stage has to create value for the company and recover the cost of the research and development (R&D) stages. This sequence of the stages from discovery via invention to innovation is intrinsic. Traditionally this sequence was also the basis for the way in which companies organised their product development and innovation effort. But over time this has changed and the sequential approach is no longer adequate and cost-effective. In response to an increasingly more challenging and complex business environment the organisation of research and innovation in industry evolved over time to an increasingly more complex and efficient system. Research developed from a relatively insular, technology-driven effort in laboratories to an open, collaborative, value-creation activity as a business in its own right. To appreciate the logic and necessity of this development, we will start by describing the five evolutionary regimes in industrial research and illustrate the transition to the final regime with a case study from industry.[77]

The First Regime: Trial and Error

The first regime concerns the experimental, largely pre-scientific search for the creation of new products and production processes by the great nineteenth-century inventors such as James Watt, Thomas Edison, Daniel Bell and so many others. Although these inventors worked with the scientific insights of the time, their achievements were mainly based on a trial-and-error approach rather than systematic scientific research. Edison understood the role of oxygen when he tried to extend the lifetime of the light bulb, but he needed to test thousands of filaments, not being aided by scientific insights into the qualities and properties of the materials. Henry Ford's invention of the production line was based on common sense and trial and error, not on a scientific analysis. In the early stages of the Industrial Revolution firms were organised around the manufacturing function. The development work was not carried out in dedicated laboratories but in separate rooms within the plant or just simply between the factory's machinery. In start-up companies or smaller enterprises in emerging economies we can still see this model today.

The Second Regime: Technology-Push

It was the nineteenth-century chemical industry that pioneered the use of scientific methods to find innovative dyestuffs. It was soon followed by the electrical and mechanical industries, and later by the man-made fibre industry. Companies started hiring scientists who would be working in university-like environments. They were given a free hand in the pursuit of knowledge because the main 'belief' of leading enterprises was that success depended on technological excellence and leadership. Such leadership was believed to result in innovative products that would make the company grow and compensate the costs of R&D many times over. Once the technology was there, the rest would follow based on the premise that a good product would sell itself, as it often did and still can do in emerging markets. This was a time of great technology-based entrepreneurship. It led to the idea that the best ways to run the R&D department was to run it like an academic institution. In the words of Professor Gilles Holst,[78] director of the Physics Laboratory of Philips Electronics from its start in 1914 till 1946, but sometimes attributed to his successor Professor Hendrik Casimir:

1. Hire highly intelligent researchers, preferably young but with experience in academic research.
2. Do not pay too much attention to the details of the work they are doing.
3. Give researchers much freedom and accept their peculiarities.
4. Encourage researchers to publish and to participate in national and international scientific activities.[79]
5. Avoid a too-strict organisation; let authority depend on scientific expertise.
6. Do not organise the laboratory according to scientific discipline, but form multidisciplinary teams.
7. Give researchers great freedom in choosing their work, but make especially the leading persons aware of their responsibility towards the firm.
8. Do not apply project budgeting in an industrial research laboratory and do not allow manufacturing departments to get budgetary control over research programmes.
9. Stimulate the transfer of successful senior researchers from the laboratory to development groups in manufacturing.
10. Choose the subjects of research partially by the state of the art of science.

In the Technology-Push regime, R&D was financed directly by the board of the company. Typically the annual R&D budget was established as a percentage of turnover vis-à-vis the level of that percentage of competitors. The spending of the budget was left to the vision and experience of the R&D director as the custodian of the company's science and technology capabilities. He usually established advisory boards with 'users' of the R&D efforts such as marketing and manufacturing, but it could also occur that the research director was more guided by the standing of the company research in the eyes of the academic world than by the needs of the company. The nature of the R&D was very much science-driven and the atmosphere of the R&D department was optimistic; R&D staff was proud of the growth it had initiated and of its standing in the scientific world. The disadvantage of the Technology-Push regime was that the R&D effort was very much a stand-alone activity, disconnected from the rest of the business. R&D did the technical development, kicked the ball over the fence to marketing or manufacturing, and hoped they would catch it and turn the technology into business. When things went right nobody complained, but when things went wrong, the marketing and R&D departments would accuse each other of 'creating solutions looking for a problem' on 'inability to bring a good product to the market'. Such 'sectoral wars' were the downside of the functional organisational model that most corporations had adopted at the time when the Technology-Push regime was used. This model provided for very effective functional capabilities, but it was poor in dealing with cross-functional problems such as innovation, because the functions only came together at the top, and at that stage it was difficult for the board to disentangle or resolve such internal conflicts.

The critical limitation of the Technology-Push regime was one of communication. The R&D organisation had difficulties in bringing its insights across to the other functions, and although research was fed by the needs from the business side, in the end the solutions were created by technology-driven minds. R&D would work on problems or market opportunities as it perceived them itself. These inefficiencies in communication were well known and management would go to great lengths to improve interfunctional communication without, however, fundamentally changing the model. After all, it was R&D that laid the basis for market leadership and business expansion.

The Third Regime: Market-Pull

The intrinsic limitation of the Technology-Push regime came to light when the markets became more mature and the customers more demanding.

Whereas Henry Ford could still satisfy his customers who wanted to buy a car with a single colour – 'any colour, as long as it is black' – in later stages of the product cycle customers demanded a genuine choice and companies needed to respond in order to maintain their competitive position. The typical response was to improve the functionalities of the product for meeting more customer demands. However, research was still functionally disconnected from the customer and the technology-driven improvements developed in the laboratories were not always the ones that the customer was willing to pay for.

Although the need for more marketing involvement became apparent in most organisations, it was often difficult to change the engrained practices that had been so successful, not to mention the established positions that came with it. The trigger to address the inefficiencies of the Technology-Push regime was created by the high inflation in the 1970s. Companies were faced with rapidly increasing costs that could only gradually be accommodated by price increases. The cost–price squeeze called for strong efficiency measures. Manufacturing could combat high inflation with efficiency measures such as automation and quality control, or reduce the cost in other parts of the production chain, for instance by better managing purchasing and logistics. Marketing and sales departments could reduce their cost by outsourcing the back-office activities and changing the customer interface.

R&D expenses were very much people-related and therefore sensitive to inflation. In addition, realising economies in R&D proved to be particularly difficult because efficiency had never featured prominently in research management. As a result, companies started to ask questions about the effectiveness of the R&D effort and the answers were not comforting: in a typical company, only two or three in ten projects would ultimately contribute to profit. One could argue that successful projects often stood on the shoulders of the less successful ones, but this argument did not impress company management. Getting rid of unsuccessful research projects became the key to cost reduction and the marketing function was charged with doing that. The new paradigm became: 'Let marketing tell what R&D should do because ultimately marketing is responsible for the commercial success'. This resulted in what can be called the Market-Pull regime for R&D management. Research managers, in the 1980s: 'encountered major changes including cross-functional teamwork, emphasis of R&D's contribution to profit, R&D's capability to quickly bring to market new products that customers value, efficient use of R&D resources, and R&D alliances'.[80]

A much-quoted article in *Chemical Week* set the new tone: 'Research gets the word: If it doesn't fit, forget it'.[81] In other words, R&D should support direct business goals or it should be shelved.

The Market-Pull regime introduced systematic management into the research function. The research departments used to be collections of curious minds without too much cohesion; within the context of a broad objective or science domain, the researchers very much did their own thing. This mode of operation was replaced by executing properly defined research projects with multidisciplinary and multifunctional teams. Good project management became the tool to keep research costs under control.

The Market-Pull model led to more R&D projects being turned into profit. However, radical innovations became rare; visionary researchers felt fenced in and fundamental research would have been abandoned if it had not been saved by a corporate research budget. The Market-Pull model also left another controversial aspect unresolved. The R&D budget would still be fixed by the top of the company, but the costs of the R&D activities were subsequently charged out to all the departments that were supposed to benefit, whether they had asked for the research or not. A manager of a well-managed department could see the result of his hard work on cost reduction being eaten up by R&D expenses over which he had no control.

With its emphasis on the short term and the top-down budgeting, the Market-Pull regime was not the ultimate answer to the shortcomings of the Technology-Push regime. Many companies adopted a hybrid model balancing Technology-Push and Market-Pull. Both research and marketing had their own responsibility for finding the right solution that was both cost-effective and meeting the customer needs. This approach had its merits as it involved the major stakeholders in product development, but it institutionalised rather than resolved the conflict between Technology-Push and Market-Pull. Thus companies continued searching for a methodology to combine the benefits of both models and eliminate their shortcomings.

The Fourth Regime: Strategy-Steer

The answer was found in the philosophy and techniques of strategic planning as introduced by Ansoff and others in the late 1960s. Strategic planning was created as an instrument to support top management in assessing investment opportunities in the era of diversification.[82] Strategic planning soon developed into strategic management,[83] an integrated, interfunctional approach that translated long-term objectives into short-term actions and targets, used by top as well as operational managers. Embodied in strategic planning and strategic management was the idea that a company can create its own future if it makes a rational analysis, takes a well-considered decision and sticks to the action plan to realise the objectives; the difference is that strategic planning was carried out by top management and experts in order to create a secret 'war plan', while strategic management incorporated line management, thus using the method as an instrument and a motivator for change.

It took until the 1980s for the new paradigm to emerge in the research domain: the Strategy-Steer regime, also called strategy-driven technology management. Technology was seen as a strategic asset that had to be developed and employed to serve the overall business strategy. Technology became a core asset in line with the then dominant corporate strategy for concentrating on core activities; activities in which the company had a competitive advantage.

The Strategy-Steer regime was more than a merger of the Technology-Push and Market-Pull regimes. It was in the first place a response to a change in the markets. With the markets maturing, the role of technology changed; with the competition shifting to cost, cosmetic features and brand, technology was no longer the prime source of competitive advantage. Minimising technology cost became a feasible strategic option.

The appearance of the book *Third Generation R&D* in 1991 marked this paradigm shift in the philosophy on R&D management.[84] In it, Roussel and colleagues – consultants with the then prominent consulting firm A.D. Little – argued that research management was moving to a new 'generation' which became known as third generation R&D or strategic R&D management. The first generation R&D management, according to Roussel, concerned creativity and technology-driven research efforts – what we have called the Technology-Push regime. The second generation R&D management brought the introduction of market-driven project selection and project management, the Marketing-Pull regime. In third generation R&D management the R&D activities are synchronised with the strategies of the corporation and its business units.[85]

The Strategy-Steer regime distinguished R&D activities in two ways[86] (Figure 4.1). The first breakdown is by research methodology:

1. Pure science: widening scientific knowledge by new descriptions of phenomena and forming and testing fundamentally new theories.
2. Applied science or technological development: using existing theory to develop original new technology and adding applied knowledge without developing new theories in the domain of pure science.
3. Development: applying existing science and technology to solve a problem without adding to the domains of pure science and technology.

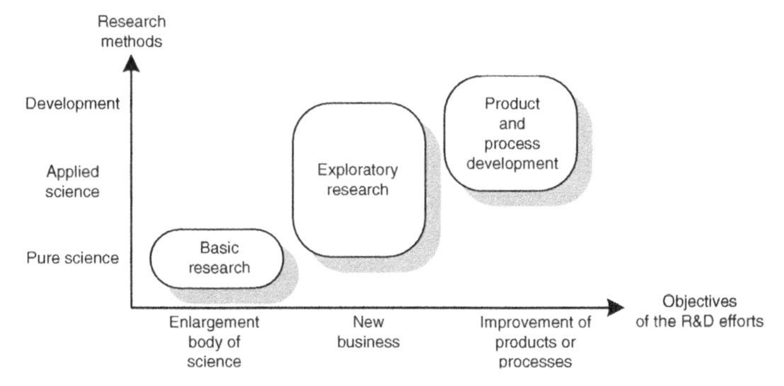

Figure 4.1 Breakdown of research activities in the Technology-Push regime

The second breakdown of R&D concerns its objectives, answering the question of what the research should lead to. Three objectives can be distinguished:

1. The enlargement of the body of scientific knowledge as a goal in itself; science for science. In hindsight, it may seem strange that companies were heavily involved in 'academic' research, but at the time it was considered necessary for firms to be engaged in pure science activities, in order to stay ahead of the competition, and to prevent a competitor finding new phenomena earlier.
2. The development of new business, either entirely new business activities, or products or processes stemming from technological substitution where the new product is based on new technology giving the resulting product a superior quality–cost ratio. This objective was reached by using the applied science methods with added development-type work. However, in many cases it involved activities in the field of pure science as well. Quite a few of the activities would emerge as a spin-off of the purely scientific activities.
3. Improvement of existing products or processes. This work was carried out mainly in the development domain with occasional activities in the applied science domain.

Combining the two breakdowns resulted in three types of R&D:

1. Basic or fundamental research: the search for new scientific discoveries using mainly purely scientific methods. Only the scientific disciplines are defined; the direction is indicated but without specific objectives or applications. Basic research was often defended by

saying: 'we have to stay up front, otherwise we may miss important developments'.

2. Exploratory research: the search for entirely new products and processes or superior new technologies that can substitute existing technologies by the process of technological substitution. In these cases, the technology domain and the business objectives are defined, but they can be adjusted depending on the emerging results of the research. In other words, there is a well-defined technological and business target but the road towards it is uncertain. Exploratory research stems from offensive corporate strategies; the work is optimistic in nature.
3. Development: the search for improvements to existing products and processes with the aim of improving the quality–cost ratio. This type of work involves mainly development work, hence the name. Both the target and the road are well defined. Although often viewed otherwise, development work has a mainly defensive nature as it can easily be copied by competitors and does not lead to lasting competitive advantage.

The characteristic feature of the Strategy-Steer regime is that research is no longer an independent activity, but part of the overall strategic effort of the company and as such is considered a core capability. The aim of R&D is to enhance the competitive power of the enterprise and its business units, supporting offensive as well as defensive strategies. The downside of this regime can be that in a business environment where competition is not based on cost or quality, the value of technology can be judged to be low and is no longer considered to be a core asset.

Some of the characteristics of the Strategy-Steer regime are similar to those of the Market-Pull regime, others are distinctly different:

- R&D projects are selected by combining technological opportunities and market needs, and prioritised on the basis of the strategic and tactical plans of the business units.
- The business units pay the costs of the business-related R&D projects. Corporate funding is restricted to exploratory research not related to the current business, and basic research to maintain or expand the company's long-term know-how position. It is thus reduced to a small amount of what it used to be under the previous regimes.
- Integrated project management is used, meaning that projects are run by multifunctional teams; marketing and manufacturing are involved in the selection of the R&D projects and the research function remains active during implementation.

- The R&D director, reporting to the board or being a member of it, is responsible for the basic research as well as the resources and the operational performance of the R&D function. He coordinates the research efforts sponsored by the various business units. He becomes a 'client' of the business units and – to a lesser degree – corporate management.
- Research remains an in-house activity. Although the R&D units may occasionally hire a university professor or consult other scientists, the R&D work is carried out by the company's own R&D staff in its own laboratories.

The Strategy-Steer regime was dominant in the period from 1980 to 2000 and it is still important. But at the end of the twentieth century another development emerged that triggered a fundamental change to the role of research. As with the previous regimes, this new regime came in response to a change in the business environment, and was created with a new look at the way research should be carried out and how it should create value. The case study below of how Shell responded to the change in the markets for R&D illustrates the complexity of the change.

4.2 RESEARCH AT ROYAL DUTCH SHELL

Royal Dutch Shell is a global group of energy and petrochemical companies, operating in 140 countries and employing some 109 000 people. Royal Dutch Shell is organised in four globally operating businesses:

- Exploration and Production (EP), the 'upstream' business that searches for and subsequently produces oil and gas.
- Oil Products (OP), the 'downstream' business engaged in transporting, refining, marketing and selling oil products such as lubricating oils, fuels, bitumen, base chemicals and biofuels.[87]
- Gas and Power (GP), the business for natural gas, engaged in the transport and trade of gases and in the manufacturing, transport and trade of liquefied gases. GP does not sell to the final consumer so it is sometimes called a 'midstream' business.
- Renewables (RN), the business for renewable energy sources, including hydrogen, wind and solar energies. Shell is a large producer of wind energy.

The global business structure was introduced in the 1990s to replace the earlier country organisation model in which local operating companies in different countries were the dominant organisational element and were responsible for managing the business. Functions, such as research, shipping, trading, manufacturing and marketing were organised in service companies at the corporate centre, and provided advice and services to the operating companies. The structure was tilted towards global businesses because it was felt that the business had to be managed on a global scale and the country structure in general was not geared to the global economy.

Research as a Business Opportunity

In the old organisation the research laboratories were part of the research function; the total research budget was agreed centrally and distributed across the laboratories by the research coordinator. The research costs, which included a significant share of fundamental research, were charged to the operating companies via a complex allocation system.

In the new structure, each global business became responsible for its own technology requirements and had to decide on the way in which R&D had to be carried out. Shell already had adopted the Strategy-Steer regime approach to make research management part of technology management, and the global businesses decided to continue this practice. As a consequence the decision was made to combine for each business the research and the technical services into one organisation called R&TS. The R&TS units were charged to ensure that the businesses had access to the technology they needed for their activities. The trigger that created the real changes was that the cost of R&D could no longer be charged out to the operating units, but the research programmes and projects had to be developed and agreed with the customers that paid for it. Research was no longer a cost centre, but had to generate its own income streams and this required a new business model. The obvious first response was to reduce cost in anticipation of reduced income streams, but that was not the essential change. The relevant consequences were:

- A drastic change in the research portfolio. All the research areas were assessed as to whether there was a competitive position, and those that had none were abandoned or outsourced. This latter result reflected an important shift. Traditionally the preferred position was to have all the essential technologies in-house, but now it was recognised that access to technology was sufficient and buying in could be more efficient. It also turned out that none of the business units was very interested in fundamental research, and this was either stopped or outsourced to universities. The third change was the introduction of exploratory research to develop outside-the-box ideas that were generated by the GameChanger initiative (see below).

- The customer entered the research domain. The focus of research had to shift from the delivery of technical data as such, to technical know-how that the customer understood and could use. The research effort had to change from a supply-driven to a demand-driven activity; customer intimacy became an objective in the laboratories.
- Research had to open up. The integration of the R&D function with the TS (technical support) function, the shift from proprietary technology to the best available technology and from in-house development to the most efficient way of getting access to technology, and the discovery of the customer, all stimulated research to open the windows to the world and adopt a new way of working.

Besides these internal, company-driven factors, there were also external factors that pushed the same way. Sustainable development became a global concern and research was required make a contribution. Shell had to shift from being 'part of the problem' to being 'part of the solution'. However, sustainable solutions can never be created in an insular, technology-driven environment, but need integral input from all stakeholders including society at large. This was the end of value-free research.

Research had to create value to the business. The research effort had to create revenue streams at least equal to the cost. Here EP-RT&S and OP-RT&S opted for different business models.

EP-RT&S maintained the traditional approach of serving only internal customers on a cost-related basis, although it also started a venture unit to monetise its intellectual property (IP) for generating additional income. OP-RT&S adopted a breakthrough business model and decided to serve both internal and external customers on a commercial basis at value-related rates. This approach not only avoided the possibility that the R&TS activities could reduce to a sub-critical level because of the deemed small internal demand, but it also created the correct business relationship with its internal customers. OP-RT&S became Shell Global Solutions International, a company fully owned by Shell, and working on a contract base with internal and external clients mainly, but not exclusively, in the oil, gas and chemical industry, and competing with other consultants in the same arena. Shell businesses have no obligation to contract their technology services to Shell Global Solutions and are free to use other technology consultants if they so desire.

Shell Global Solutions quickly developed into a profitable company, with profits from internal customers being refunded. The businesses are the owner of the IP they sponsored and Shell Global Solutions monetises the

IP on their behalf. Looking back, one may conclude that the fact that technology development has to compete with external providers has improved its quality. The new approach has also made clear in which way R&D created value and how much; this led to a revival of the interest in technology. After a phase of downsizing from about 2500 employees to 2000, Shell Global Solutions now employs over 5000 people, including in the manufacture and sales of catalysts.

In order to be able to develop new ideas away from the day-to-day business, all of the global businesses have set up GameChanger activities following the initiative at EP. There is also a corporate GameChanger unit which picks up innovative ideas that are cross- or intra-business. Ideas can be forwarded by anyone working at Shell. An idea is assessed by a panel comprising technological as well as marketing and financial experts, and if the idea is approved GameChanger will sponsor the first, conceptual phase of the development. The outcomes of GameChanger projects can be incorporated in a division or they can be outsourced. A good example of the latter is C-Fix, a thermoplastic binder for the construction industry based on very heavy residual oil mixed with aggregates, sand and filler materials, that combines the qualities and advantages of asphalt (flexibility) with cement concrete (strength). Using C-Fix rather than cement concrete reduces CO_2 emissions significantly. C-Fix can be recycled and not only outperforms cement concrete and asphalt in many applications, but also has lower costs compared to similar materials. The C-Fix product was developed and patented by Shell and is brought to the market by C-Fix B.V., a joint venture between Shell and UKM Ltd of the United Kingdom.[88]

Collaboration with Universities

Shell has concentrated its R&TS activities in three main Technology Centres in Amsterdam, Houston and Rijswijk, and nine other centres: Bangalore (India), Calgary (Canada), Doha (Qatar), Hamburg (Germany), Louvain la Neuve (Belgium), Muscat (Oman), Oslo (Norway), Seraya (Singapore) and Thornton in the UK. Today, there is a renewed interest in technology as a major competitive factor.[89] This interest in technology has resulted in new and increased research programmes, but not in open-ended programmes for fundamental research. Fundamental aspects of an R&D project are budgeted and contracted like any other R&D project; this can be done in-house, but usually it is done by universities. There is no central budget for fundamental research. However, Shell has a chief technology officer (CTO) who advises the CEO and the board on technological matters and who has a relatively small budget as seed money. The seed research projects are being administered by the Shell Research

Foundation, which takes custody of the money as agreed by a Shell business. Subjects sponsored include new energy (biomass, biotechnology, hydrogen, solar photovoltaic), deep science (catalysis, polymers, physics) and sustainable development (biodiversity).

Altogether, Shell spends over $1.2 billion per year on technology development, roughly 50/50 upstream and downstream. Licensing-in roughly equals licensing-out, the amount being less than 10 per cent of the R&D expenditure. About half the amount of funds that go to universities stem from the EP division, and the other half comes from Shell Global Solutions which acts on behalf of the downstream businesses.

Shell has appointed a number of chief scientists who spearhead collaboration with universities and the scientific world in general. The collaboration is two-way: universities can propose research which the corresponding chief scientist may decide to sponsor in cases in which there is a strong indication that the results will be useful for Shell's operations. On the other hand, chief scientists may take the initiative and start a project in a selected university if there is a need for fundamental backup of R&D projects. There are chief scientists for geophysics, chemistry and catalysis, physics and physical separations, well engineering and production, chemical engineering, materials and biotechnology.[90] The chief scientists are not only the interface with universities; they also encourage publications in scientific journals and act externally as ambassadors to the scientific world in general. They are also internal ambassadors who communicate the role of technology within the businesses.

Universities that carry out substantial and high-quality research are of interest to the chief scientists. Shell has established so-called 'selected partnerships' with 11 universities in the USA, the Russian Federation, the UK, China, Norway and the Netherlands. With these universities Shell has concluded framework contracts covering several fields of scientific investigation, with concrete projects being added as annexes to the framework contracts. In addition, there are ad hoc contracts with a host of other universities. The collaboration with universities enables Shell to benefit from the public funding of fundamental research, while the universities benefit from the broadened scope that comes with the additional funding from the enterprise. The chief scientists monitor progress; they are actively engaged in the research and they often participate in the promotion committees of the PhDs they sponsor. The basis of the collaboration is that the university can publish the results of the supported research while Shell retains the IP rights (IPR). Depending on the situation, there are however deviations from this principle, and Shell may not have the full IPR. In the case of contracted fundamental research, Shell has the IPR and the university is bound by a secrecy agreement, at least for some time.

The Learning Points

Shell had to change its technology effort in response to changes in the business environment. It moved away from the Technology-Steer regime and developed a new mode of research management based on integrating it into the value-creation process:

- The gist of the restructuring of the downstream research function was to turn it from a cost centre – with mandatory costs charged to operational companies – to a profit centre that works on a contract base for customers on a competitive, commercial basis. In order to enhance the customer base and keep its capabilities above the 'critical mass', the new company would serve the oil industry at large rather than Shell only.
- The change was facilitated by the low appreciation of the value of technology in the business at the time. Proprietary technology was not regarded as a significant source of competitive advantage for the oil industry. The adoption of the new business model and the integration of research and technology were instrumental in giving back to technology the high profile it traditionally had in Shell, and it is now a valuable part of the 'corporate identity'.
- Shell Global Solutions created a major competitive advantage from the integration of research and technical services. It could now service the oil industry with an integrated approach for the whole value chain, from selecting crude oil to product sales. No other company could offer a similar service with consultants who all had hands-on experience in their field of expertise. Looking back, one can conclude that open competition improved the quality of technology development.
- Open-ended, in-house fundamental research was replaced by collaboration with universities in fundamental aspects of specific R&D projects. This research has clearly defined business objectives and cannot be compared with the 'free' fundamental research of the past which is not likely to come back. The interest in a university depends on the quality of its research and good project management. The basic IPR arrangement is that the university is free to publish while the IPR remains with the sponsor, but individual cases may deviate from this model.

4.3 THE FIFTH REGIME: TECH-BUSINESS

The Strategy-Steer regime had brought research into the realm of technology management with the objective to ensure that the company had access to all the technological capabilities it required, whether generated in-house or supplied by third parties. This incorporation of externally sourced technology was a major shift in strategic thinking for most companies; the capability to develop all the core technology in-house had always been considered as one of the major strengths of large, vertically integrated companies.

This shift in strategy was triggered by the rapid developments in IT technology; most big companies had tried to cater for their own requirements, but in the end all big companies had to admit to failure and changed to outsourcing their IT requirements. The new corporate strategic paradigm became outsourcing, typically starting with the manufacturing units and back-office services, but gradually also drifting to what used to be untouchable core functions such as research and human resources. A few companies divested their research functions; others outsourced their R&D internally by creating a separate company. The R&D function lost its position as an independent function and became part of the technology business. Research had to create value and monetise its product directly and in its own right, and not only in the traditional indirect way via the products and services sold by the company. This is best done by making research and technology development a separate business that has to generate its own income. The switch from 'cost centre' to 'value-creating business' represents the transition to the fifth regime of research management. Several factors and circumstances in the business environment facilitated the emergence of this regime:

- The prime factor was the breaking-up of the traditional value chains. Vertically integrated companies were no longer more efficient in every stage of the chain and they had to create new, more complex value chains with suppliers and specialised companies that could do parts of the value chain better and more efficiently. This break-up of the value chain also applied to the research process and many tasks could better be outsourced. Research and technology could be outsourced, and developing all the technology in-house was not only impossible even for the largest companies, but also inefficient and more expensive.
- Because technology became a distinct, separable segment of the value chain, it was a small step to make it an independent activity. The requirement to earn its own money would also make it apparent how research and technology created value. But a change from a cost to a value-creation centre requires a complete reorientation on who

the real customer is and what the customer values and is willing to pay for. Creating value for the customer became the new driver for R&D, as is the case in every profitable business.

- Emphasis shifted from technology management to innovation management, and research became part of a value chain that clearly created value.

The factors that characterise the fifth regime of research are: outsourcing, open research, value creation, customer orientation and research as part of a value chain. The Tech-Business regime shares with the Technology-Push model the independent position of research and technology, but it is now subject to the laws of business rather than to the principle of 'science for science'.

The five regimes of research have been introduced as an evolutionary process in response to changes in the business environment, and whereby research management has to invent a more efficient system for operating in a more complex environment. This historic approach has its merits because the new research systems emerged over time just as in the evolution of mature new energy supply systems emerged for supporting increasingly complex life systems. In both evolutions, new mechanisms do not replace earlier ones but only put them in the background or at a lower level. This means that in different business environments, different research management models need to be applied. Thus in emergent markets it can still be the best approach to adopt the 'simple' Technology-Push model; trial and error always has its place in research as long as serendipity is an important success factor, and when research is still a cost factor there is no need to adopt a fifth regime of research management. Table 4.1 summarises the five research regimes and the characteristics that become prominent in a specific business environment.

Another way to represent the developments in research management is to consider the two axes of development as used in Figure 4.2; one is the value driver for the research and the other the way the research is managed. Along the first axis, the focus of research management developed from the use of scientific methods to including business methods, with the Trial and Error regime as the pre-management stage, and along the other axis the driving force changed from science to value, including the customer and company strategy.

Table 4.2 illustrates the relation between the research regime and the conditions in the markets and the business environment. In each change of regime research needed to become more complex in response to more complex challenges and requirements from the markets as represented by the additional external drivers. But at the same time each research

Table 4.1 The characteristics of the five research management regimes

Regime	External driver	Characteristics	Business environment
Trial and Error	Curiosity	One-person effort Absence of systems	No systematic links between research and markets
Technology-Push	Science	Independent function Academic environment	Emergent, supply-driven markets
Market-Pull	Market	Cost centre Multifunctional teams Project management	First generation products Growth, demand-driven markets
Strategy-Steer	Company	Cost centre Integrated research and technology management	Competition Mature markets Strategic positioning
Tech-Business	Value	Technology is strategic tool Creating customer value Research as a business Profit centre	Complex, multiparty value chains Outsourcing

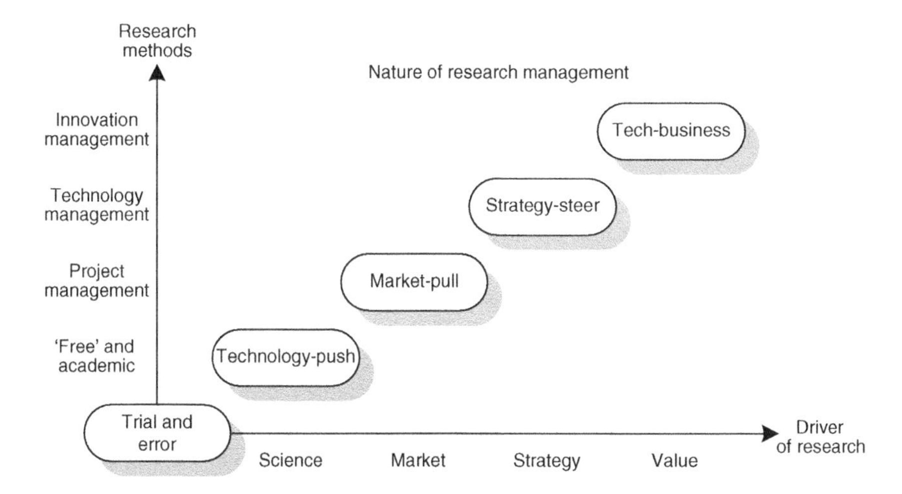

Figure 4.2 Evolution of the regimes of research management

Table 4.2 The triggers and efficiency measures of the research regimes

Transition to:	Cost trigger	Efficiency mechanism
Market-Pull regime	Inflation	Project management No 'free' research
Strategy-Steer regime	IT/Total development cost	Outsourcing Collaboration
Tech-Business regime	Cost charge out system	Servicing external markets Monetising research

management regime had to create a more efficient system to contain cost. The triggers that initiated the changes in regime are all cost-related, as are the associated changes in the way research was carried out, as illustrated in Table 4.2.

4.4 CREATING VALUE FROM KNOWLEDGE: OPEN INNOVATION

In principle, there are two modes for creating value from research: the first is the direct approach by selling the results of the research either as data sets or as an invention protected by IPR; and the second is the indirect approach via innovation, by bringing novel products and services successfully to the market. The unique characteristic of the fifth regime is that research is actively involved in creating value from the R&D effort. In the other regimes, it was done as well, but more or less in a passive mode. The research was carried out in-house for use elsewhere in the company and if the results were not used, they were left on the shelf for future purposes. Licensing-in and licensing-out were practised, but were often low-key and a side business. As a result, many companies had no idea what the real value of their IP portfolios was and when they did assess it, the results were usually surprising. But they all faced the simple truth that unused IP on the shelf is worth very little. In order to create more value from their IP, some enterprises made contracts with smaller technology firms that were allowed to commercialise unused technology. This hardly worked, as the commercialisation required the cooperation of the original R&D workers and their priority was to contribute to the corporate activities, not to support spin-offs. Other firms would actively seek to sell IP to third parties, whether to existing firms or spinouts. IBM today, for instance, makes about a quarter of its profit by selling know-how to third parties.

As we saw in the Shell case, integrating research into the business units makes value creation from research very effective because the research results can be used directly in the technical services that are sold to the customers. Selling technical know-how to the competition may seem odd at first sight and such a move would have been considered foolish in the Technology-Push era ('the last thing you want to share with your competitors is your know-how'), but it is inevitable if one considers the scale effects needed to maintain technological leadership.

These shifts in R&D practices were recently reviewed in an article in *The Economist*. The article illustrates that the R and the D components are no longer separated, research workers and development workers acting close together. This stands in contrast to the period that started after the Second World War when the recipe was to observe a strict separation between research and development, research being carried out in academic institutions or research laboratories like AT&T's Bell Labs, IBM's Zurich Laboratory or Xerox's Palo Alto Research Centre PARC. These laboratories made famous discoveries and even collected an impressive number of Nobel Prizes, but they made little money out of it. This is attributed to the distance between research and business.[91]

The counterpart of a profitable licensing-out business must be that buying technology is an attractive proposition for the user, and indeed many companies realised that open sourcing of technology is often cheaper and faster than in-house development. Many high-tech firms, especially in the IT sector, started buying successful young high-tech firms as an alternative to developing technology themselves. Firms like Intel have played this game very successfully, followed by the large pharmaceutical companies which have been buying start-ups in genetic engineering.

The rapid growth of multidisciplinary and interdisciplinary research made it unattractive for even large enterprises to recruit all the specialists themselves. In addition, firms came to the obvious conclusion that most of the world's talent lies outside the firm. Rather than doing everything themselves, it is advantageous even for large enterprises to engage in joint research and development projects with external partners. Collaboration is cheaper, more flexible, and it leads to results faster than when the company goes it alone. 'I think that the boat has left the dock. This is the way that airplanes will be developed in the future', said Jim McNerney, chairman and chief executive officer (CEO) of Boeing, after signing an agreement for cooperation with United Aircraft Corporation, the Russian state-owned aerospace group that includes Sukhoi, which adds one more partner to Boeing's worldwide network of partners.[92]

The apex of the philosophy of cooperation is the development of Linux, the software that is increasingly being used on network and other computers. The basic design of Linux was written by Linus Torvalds. By making the source code freely available, he enabled any programmer to write applications, improvements or additions, provided that their additions also become freely available. Torvalds calls this 'open source' software and claims that some 100 000 programmers are developing Linux-based software.[93] As the basic software is free, prices are low.

This open approach to R&D fits very well with the new approach to innovation. The new paradigm for innovation is 'Open Innovation', an essential extension of the Strategy-Steer regime in which research is integrated into the innovation process. Modern innovation literature emphasises that the right business process and management approach are key success factors for innovation.[94] Innovation is the outcome of a well-designed process aimed at realising pre-set goals rather than a matter of luck. Managing innovation depends on using dedicated business processes and this approach made innovation management a mature profession, undoing whatever was left of the mystique that surrounded the stage of Technology-Push.

Open Innovation is the term introduced by Henry Chesbrough with his influential book with the same title.[95] Chesbrough argues that traditionally the technological leaders with the highest R&D spending would be making the highest profits (for example companies like Dupont, IBM, Merck, General Electric, AT&T). In contrast, the new companies (Intel, MS, Sun, Cisco, Genentech, Amgen, Genzyme) conduct little or no research of their own, innovating with the discoveries of others. The old paradigm of Closed Innovation is based on the notion that successful innovation requires control. A company should do everything itself: 'If you want something done right, you've got to do it yourself'. The culture is internally focused; the innovation is 'inside-out'. Closed Innovation is characterised by the following rules:

- Hire the best and brightest people, so that the smartest people in the industry work for us.
- In order to bring new products and services to the market, we must discover and develop them ourselves.
- The company that gets an innovation to the market first will usually win.
- We should control our IPR so that our competitors do not profit from our ideas.

In the fifth regime, research is an integral part of the innovation process. Open Innovation is:

- Connect to the wealth of external knowledge to fill in the missing pieces of knowledge not being internally developed.

- Integrate internal and external knowledge to form more complex combinations of knowledge for creating new systems and architectures.
- Generate additional revenues from selling research outputs created from discontinued innovation projects to other firms for use in their own systems. IBM earned $1.9 billion on royalty payments in 2001; it spent $600 million on basic research that year.[96] It filed 3248 patents in the US in 2004.[97]

The open, collaborative approach to innovation fits very well in the drive for sustainable development. Sustainable innovation may mean different things to different people, but one essential aspect of sustainable innovation is communication with all stakeholders. The new approach to innovation also fits the new entrepreneurial spirit very well; entrepreneurship as a basic social value has been rediscovered. Carl Schramm, the president of the Kauffman Foundation, argues that it is not technology that lies at the core of the competitiveness of the US, as technology is available everywhere; nor education, in which the US is not leading anyway; nor the availability of financial resources, that move over the globe at the click of a mouse; but the entrepreneurial culture. The inevitable conclusion of Schramm is that entrepreneurship is to be nourished if the US is to stay at the competitive edge in the global economy.[98]

4.5 SUMMARY

This chapter can be summarised as follows:

- It has explored the evolution of industrial research and the opportunities for collaboration between universities and enterprises. After an early phase of Trial and Error, R&D became very much technology-driven with industrial laboratories having almost academic freedom in pursuing the developments they considered of interest. This stage of industrial R&D was highly successful, to such an extent that questions about the efficiency and effectiveness of R&D were hardly asked.
- Assessment of the output–input ratios of R&D led to the conclusion that R&D was too far from marketing, and a new stage set in – Market-Pull research in which the marketing function decided to a great extent what R&D was going to do. The search for a model to integrate the advantages of Technology-Push and Market-Pull led to strategy-driven R&D management in which R&D efforts were

subordinated to the strategic plan of the firm. This restored the balance between the long-term and the short-term view.

- The Tech-Business regime came as the result of three factors that reinforced each other: the switch from a cost centre to a profit centre for R&D; integration of research into value chains such as innovation and sales of technical service; and open-sourcing of research because no company could afford to master all required technologies.
- The evolution of the successive research management models came in response to changes in the markets, such as the development from emerging to mature markets. Each shift represented an increase in the complexity in the market and each time the research management techniques responded with a more complex, but also intrinsically more efficient system. The triggers to develop the new management systems came from the need to control expanding cost.
- The prerogative of profit-responsible management led to a loss of interest in 'free' fundamental research for supporting knowledge positions. Fundamental research is only carried out in support of specific R&D projects if a core technology needs deeper understanding, and preferably this research is outsourced to universities. The collaboration between industry and academia exploits the area of overlap between industrial R&D projects and publicly funded fundamental research.
- Smaller enterprises also use universities as places to which they can farm out R&D activities. In this case, the university functions not unlike an engineering contractor and projects in this area can be attractive for thesis projects of PhD students. In other words, large technology-driven enterprises seek other forms of collaboration with universities than smaller enterprises. This is an important conclusion for universities that will have to cater for both forms.
- Open-sourced research is the operational mode for R&D in Open Innovation. Open Innovation also includes the sale of spin-offs that the firm chooses not to commercialise itself, and the purchase of high-tech enterprises as an alternative to developing proprietary know-how.

5. Technostarters

5.1 MEET TECHNOSTARTERS

Having discussed the way in which universities can collaborate with technology-based enterprises for generating know-how and creating innovations, in this chapter we will focus on the other way of bringing know-how to the market: through the establishment of new firms. Depending on who takes the initiative, the university itself or an entrepreneurial student or academic, we distinguish university spinouts and technostarters.

Technostarters are students or academics who establish their own science- or technology-based firm. Technostarters are people who take the initiative and who are willing to take responsibility and risk. Together with the *cum laude* graduates and PhDs, they are the princes and princesses of the university and they should be treated as such. Successful technostarters persevere and are creative in finding solutions for the diversity of problems that occur on the road to a new enterprise.[99] They are optimistic, subscribing to the phrase attributed to Walt Disney: 'This goes to prove that nothing is impossible if you just put your mind to it.'

They are walking learning organisations, networkers who learn from others and from introspection, analysing their own progress: what went right and what went wrong and why. They have the instinct to spot combinations between technical possibilities and (latent) market needs. They have organisational talents and they are good recruiters; they can be charismatic as well as critical leaders and they have the skills to form a team.[100] The dream of many technostarters is to lead their own life rather than being employed. Technostarters are passionate people; they are dreamers who do.[101]

Technostarters often originate from universities: universities of technology, science and medical faculties of general universities, and agricultural universities. Corporate research and development (R&D) departments and independent research organisations also act as cradles for technostarters.

Like all entrepreneurs, technostarters perform a balancing act between supply and demand, technology and market. A beautiful technical idea is useless unless it matches some market need. Turning technology into business therefore involves not only the development of the technology, but in equal measure, the analysis and development of the market. Finally, to get

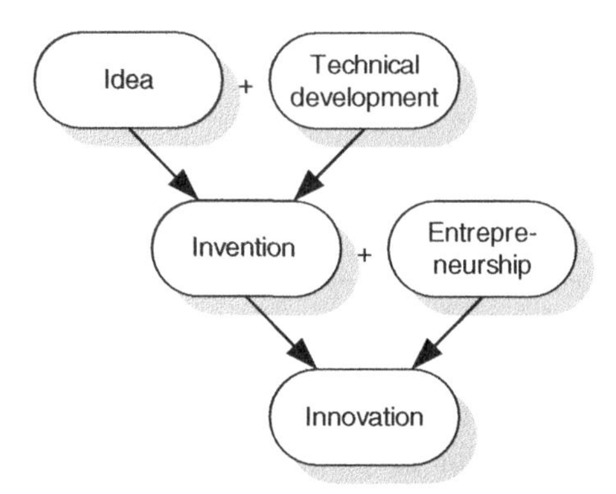

Figure 5.1 The value chain between idea and innovation

the new activity off the ground, capital is required and this creates the third market which the budding entrepreneur has to consider.[102]

Lots of people have creative ideas on which a new business activity could be based. They consider their idea as very valuable, but an idea as such is worth very little; its value comes from its application in the market. An idea can lead to an invention: a new product, process or service. The value of an invention is in most cases also limited; most patents are never used. Innovation is bringing a new concept successfully to the market. This requires market development and entrepreneurship. In the words of Jan Verloop,[103] former Shell Global Solutions innovation manager: Innovation = invention + entrepreneurship.

Many great technological innovators of the past – Edison, Bell, Eastman, Dell – were inventors as well as entrepreneurs. But they are the exception rather than the rule, and we will see later that in many, if not most cases the inventor and the innovator are different persons, raising the question of how matches between them can be made.[104] The point here is: an idea, however good, is worth nothing, an invention may be worth something and an innovation may be worth its weight in gold (Figure 5.1).

Starting a company requires a totally dedicated effort and this can put a strain on the starter as well as on his or her partner. The *Financial Times* columnist Lucy Kellaway was warned by a friend when her husband wanted to start a new journal in his own firm:[105] 'All I can really say is that you should be prepared for life to become complete hell. The amount of work involved is horrendous – as is the anxiety. Your life will be an unending crisis, putting out one fire after another.'

She admits this was all too true: 'You get to work harder than a junior hospital doctor and you earn next to nothing. Worse, you probably invest some of your own money which you are likely to lose. Any return comes in the distant future and only if the business takes off (which most small businesses never do).'

But her final word is: 'He is happy as a sandboy. He does something he is really good at, that he has control of and which he loves.'

5.2 WHAT MAKES A TECHNOSTARTER?

Not everyone is suitable for entrepreneurship. According to Adrian Atkinson, managing director of Human Factors International, a UK-based consultancy:

> Entrepreneurs are individualistic. They will start businesses up on their own, and work extremely hard at it, putting all their energies and focus into it. They do not recognise failure. They are intuitive, do not act rationally, and commit themselves without any regard to resources or financial constraints.

One might say they regard failure as the mother of success.[106] Atkinson's company published a very interesting overview of the characteristics of entrepreneurs versus enterprisers (people more suitable for employment in an existing firm) as shown in Box 5.1.

The GEM reports (see next section) distinguish between 'necessity entrepreneurs' and 'opportunity entrepreneurs'. We may assume that the vast majority of technostarters fall into the category of opportunity entrepreneurs. This speculation is supported by an investigation concerning the reasons why people want to be self-employed (which of course is not the same as being a technostarter). The outcome is shown in Box 5.2.

The reported outcome fits with the general observation that people in general, and students in particular, are more individualistic and more willing to take risks than they were in the past. Forty per cent of the alumni of Insead, a Paris-based business school, sooner or later start their own enterprise. Twenty per cent of Massachusetts Institute of Technology (MIT) graduates start their own business. Only 6 per cent of Harvard Business School graduates end up in large enterprises, a fact that made the school trade their general management course, which it had given for 80 years, for an entrepreneurship course in 2000. The entrepreneurship electives are the most visited at the University of Cambridge. Making money is no longer considered a negative attribute. For a long time, self-enrichment was looked down upon in Europe and Asia, and entrepreneurs were social outcasts. In the American culture of 'unlimited opportunities', people however would look proudly at successful entrepreneurs, with the idea that, 'If he can do it, so can I'. It seems that this attitude is spreading

BOX 5.1 ENTREPRENEUR OR ENTERPRISER? TAKE THE TEST!

You know you are an entrepreneur if:

- You are prepared to risk everything – personal assets and reputation – to succeed
- You will work all hours at the expense of your personal life
- You prefer to take decisions quickly and based on gut feel
- You like to dominate proceedings
- You work on the basis of trust rather than contracts

Examples: Sir Richard Branson, Charles Schwab

You know you are an enterpriser if:

- You prefer to work in a corporate setting
- You are rational and require evidence before taking a decision
- You focus overwhelmingly on wealth creation
- You draw regularly on highly competent team members
- You make big bets but with limited personal risk

Examples: Sir Christopher Gent, Jack Welch

Source: Human Factors International. Quoted in the *Financial Times*, 9 November 2004, p. 8.

over the world. The more liberal attitude towards entrepreneurship is not limited to Western cultures or affluent countries. In an interview Mr Sunil Mittal, the founder and chairman of the Bharti Group in India and the uncrowned 'India's king of telecoms', notes that:[107] 'In India, businessmen were always looked down on. The view was that these guys cheat on taxes and make profits by sucking money from the poor. We were never given credit.'

The change, he believes, has been gathering pace since the early 1990s, when a reformist economic team embarked on a policy of liberalisation in India: 'Wealth creation is being celebrated. People are coming out of colleges saying "I don't want to be a bureaucrat, I want to be an entrepreneur" and people like me are giving them hope that it can be done.'

Yet, there are strong barriers to overcome. Students are taught how to

BOX 5.2 REASONS WHY PEOPLE WANT TO BE SELF-EMPLOYED

Being self-employed: why do people do it?

53% • I want to take responsibility for my own future
52% • I relish the challenge of going it alone
48% • I want to be my own boss
43% • I have a unique idea
28% • I want to make more money
19% • I am unhappy in my job
8% • I want flexible working hours
6% • I am unemployed

Source: Shell LiveWIRE Young Entrepreneurs of the Year Awards, *Finalists Report 2004*, quoted in the *Financial Times*, 9 November 2004, p. 8.

play it safe: go to the right school, get good results, go to a good university and join a good company. Join the right societies, build the right networks. The message is: the more risk-averse you are, the more successful you will be. 'The pathological ability to avoid (difficult) things is, alas, very normal', according to Lucy Kellaway.[108] In France, on 28 March 2006, some 2 million students took to the streets to demonstrate against the abolition of the *contract première embauche*, the 'fixed first job', as proposed by the French government.[109] This is not exactly a movement to encourage entrepreneurship. Yet it may be more risky to work for a blue chip company than for yourself, as companies regularly lay off people without relation to performance. As an entrepreneur, you create your own life and your own risks.

However, for the majority of countries, entrepreneurship is in, not only in the US, but also in Europe, Asia and Latin America. We believe this attitude is stimulated by many large corporations that offer programmes to help technostarters create their own company. Royal Dutch Shell has the successful LiveWire programme for external technostarters and its GameChanger programme for internal entrepreneurs. DSM offers a wide range of facilities on its Research Campus in Geleen, the Netherlands and Philips Electronics has created an incubator on its High Tech Campus in Eindhoven, the Netherlands, where technostarters can share the extensive facilities this campus offers. This list can be extended with a multitude of other examples. As we saw in Chapter 4, the trend is for large corporations to open up their R&D facilities with the aim of sharing knowledge with other companies (even competitors), selling know-how and supporting starters. Universities follow this trend, albeit hesitatingly in most countries. MBA courses have been blamed for failing to educate top managers for the modern world,[110] even for causing the Enron fiasco and other scandals. A better route to the top of a corporation would seem to be to start your own enterprise, sell it after a number of years and then join a corporation. Entrepreneurship then is not so much a life fulfilment as a short-cut to top positions in existing corporations. For the corporation, it is much more attractive to hire former entrepreneurs who have proven themselves in the market and who know the ins and outs of entrepreneurship, rather than studious MBAs who may be good analysts but not necessarily good business leaders.

In a student population, typically there is a small number of die-hard entrepreneurs who will set up their company no matter what. On the other side of the spectrum, there is a large group with little or no affinity to entrepreneurship. In between are the latent entrepreneurs, people who might become an entrepreneur if the conditions were favourable and if they were confronted with the opportunity. The latent entrepreneurs might become entrepreneurs in a different capacity, for instance by taking over the family enterprise they work for if the owner has no successors in his family. Alternatively, they may find jobs in connection with entrepreneurship, for instance within a consultancy or venture capital fund. The gist of this argument is that efforts to stimulate entrepreneurship should start with creating awareness. This is the basis of our approach to education in entrepreneurship that we will describe in Appendix 2. Awareness programmes can also be successful outside universities. The Polish Agency for Enterprise Development, for instance, encountered an unexpected and overwhelming 6000 applications for entrepreneurial support when they opened a desk for this purpose.

5.3 THE IMPACT OF TECHNOSTARTERS

Since 1997, an international group of researchers, led by scholars from Babson College in Massachusetts and the London Business School in the UK, has tried to map entrepreneurial activities in 34 countries.[111] In addition to providing statistical data, the Global Entrepreneurship Monitoring (GEM) reports try to understand the relationships between entrepreneurial activity and national economic growth. To this end, the GEM reports define the Total Entrepreneurial Activity (TEA) as the percentage of adults (18–64 years of age) who are active as starting entrepreneurs or managing a young business of which they are also an owner, divided by the total workforce. The outcome of the 2004 survey is that in the workforce of the countries investigated (566 million) there are 73 million entrepreneurs (total population between 18 and 64 years of age in these countries was 784 million). The average TEA level in these countries comes to 9.3 per cent, with variations between countries from 1.5 per cent (Japan) to 40 per cent (Peru). The TEA percentage was 11.3 per cent for the US, 6.3 per cent for the UK and 4.5 per cent for Germany. The GEM report 2004 concludes that in the sample researched, 65 per cent of the entrepreneurs are 'opportunity entrepreneurs' (that is, driven to exploit a perceived business opportunity) while 35 per cent are 'necessity entrepreneurs' (driven by the absence of other satisfactory employment opportunities). According to the report, men are twice as likely to start a new enterprise as women. Most entrepreneurial activity is carried out by 25- to 34-year-olds, regardless of the level of income in the countries. It will be no surprise that these percentages vary widely between countries.

The TEA index is an aggregated compound that does not say anything about the number of starters, let alone technostarters. The GEM report 2004 notes that only 3 per cent of all start-ups qualify as 'business with high potential', defined as: 'those that expect to have few competitors, intend to bring innovations to the market, and use state-of-the-art technology'.

This comes as close to technostarters as can be measured statistically. However, it includes both 'nascent entrepreneurs' (people in the process of starting a new business in the year of consideration) and also 'young companies' (companies led by their owners that have paid salaries for more than 3, but less than 42, months). Unfortunately, the reports give no data that distinguish between these categories. Nevertheless, the number of technostarters and 'technostarted' entrepreneurs number roughly 2.2 million in the 34 countries investigated or – even more roughly – almost 3 per cent of the adult population. That means that technostarters are not a marginal phenomenon; there are simply a lot of them.

5.4 THE ROLE OF UNIVERSITIES

Technostarters are valuable for universities because of two reasons. The first reason is their role in the know-how carousel of which third generation universities (3GUs) are the centre. Technostarters interact with facilities of large enterprises and independent research institutes and in this way, they strengthen the hub and thereby the competitive position of the university. Technostarters are indispensable for the realisation of the third objective of 3GUs: commercialisation of know-how. Good facilities for technostarters will attract better students, an important argument at a time of competition between universities for the best and brightest.

The second reason is that technostarters render an indispensable contribution to the economy by creating new employment of a high level. This employment should offset the loss of mass-production-based employment. At a rough count, the world needs 1 million start-ups per year to offset the loss of jobs in mature companies. In addition, in the period 2003–08 2 million entrepreneurs will be needed to reduce unemployment.[112] And universities can deliver. The effect they can have was first brought to light by the now legendary 'BankBoston Report'.[113] This study found that if the companies founded by MIT graduates and faculty were to form an independent nation, the revenues produced by the companies would make that nation the 24th-largest economy in the world. The 4000 MIT-related companies (located worldwide) that existed in 1997 employed 1.1 million people and had annual world sales of $232 billion. That is roughly equal to a gross domestic product of $116 billion, which is comparable to the 1996 gross domestic product (GDP) of South Africa or Thailand. The study found that MIT 'imports' entrepreneurs as many companies were not spinouts of the university, but rather company founders who came to Massachusetts to benefit from the presence of MIT.

The MIT-related companies are not typical for the economy as a whole; they tend to be knowledge-based companies active in software, manufacturing (electronics, biotech, instruments, machinery) or consulting (architects, business consultants, engineers) businesses. Firms involved in software, electronics and biotechnology are at the cutting edge of technology. They are more likely to expand and export while they need a workforce of skilled professionals. About 150 new MIT-related companies are founded each year. There are only 106 companies with 1000 or more employees and these companies generate nearly 90 per cent of the jobs. There are 17 companies with 10 000 employees or more including Hewlett-Packard, Rockwell International, Raytheon Co, McDonnell Douglas, Digital Equipment Co, Texas Instruments, Campbell Soup, Gillette, Intel and National Semiconductor (some of these companies have merged with others; only six of the 17 companies had their headquarters in Massachusetts).

The BankBoston Report showed the vast economic benefits that a high-level university of technology can bring to a region and to the economy in general. It is no surprise that other regions have studied MIT and Stanford University and have tried to copy their success. The message is: strong universities can create impressive amounts of wealth, not only for the region, but also for the national and even global economy.

> Job creation is not an objective by itself. We have to understand that it is only with new products that we can participate in the international competition.

> Because of the open markets and globalisation, we will rarely produce mass-products in this country (Germany) . . . More economic growth can only be created by innovation, and growth will translate itself into more jobs . . . Many enterprises have gone bankrupt because of their single emphasis on mastering the cost spiral . . . We will always be an expensive country. Therefore we have to get back to the front line of technical progress.

These statements, made by Ludolf von Wartenberg, President of the Bundesverband der Deutschen Industrie[114] (Germany's main employers' association) characterise the dilemma of most Western countries. Mass production is shifting to Eastern Europe and Asia, creating a need for new, innovative and high-added-value production in the older industrial states. Mr von Wartenberg adds that this is a slow process. Although the major part of any new innovative business will have to come from established enterprises, many look to technostarters to fill the gap in economic activity and job creation.[115] All over the world, an impressive range of government or European Union (EU) supported programmes is being launched;[116] these are aimed at stimulating technostarters to create new companies, especially in areas where the loss of employment in mass production is hard-felt.[117]

Can technostarters live up to this expectation? Looking at the Intels, Dells, Apples, Suns, Amazons, eBays, Googles and many other technostarters that have become mature companies with revenue, profits and employment matching the largest traditional industries, one would be inclined to say: yes, they can. But economic analysis shows that the chances of a technostarter joining the ranks of the world's most powerful enterprises are as slim as those of a young amateur footballer becoming a Maradonna or Cruijff. Surprised by the absence of studies on the economic effects of entrepreneurial activities in mainstream economics, the investigators from the Global Entrepreneurship Monitor team tried to establish the link between entrepreneurial activity and economic growth at the country level.[118] By linking the GEM variable of Total Entrepreneurship Activity (TEA; the percentage of the adult population being 18–64 years old) that is either actively involved in starting a new venture or is the owner-manager of a business that is less than 42 months old) to economic growth, they conclude that the TEA rate correlates negatively for the relatively poor countries whilst it correlates positively for the relatively rich countries. The reason for this unexpected result may be that technostarters make only a small contribution to the TEA index and a high TEA index in poor countries indicates a lack of larger enterprises, with the small enterprises rarely having large growth potential.

Universities can be significant creators of wealth if they put their minds to it, and the benefits to the university itself can be considerable. They can do so by supporting technostarters or by creating new enterprises on their own initiative: spinouts initiated and managed by the university itself. The spinout option is used when the university wishes to keep the initiative, and when selling or licensing this know-how to an existing firm is the inferior option. The university will seek an entrepreneur to match the nature of the enterprise to be created. It is important to note that there are two quite distinct mechanisms for the creation of enterprises: 'bottom-up' based on the initiative of individuals, versus 'top-down' based on initiatives of a body of the university itself. The two mechanisms lead to different ownership structures and different distribution of property rights.

Either way, there will be direct income from licences, consulting, contract research and endowments. The indirect benefits lie in the attraction the university has for entrepreneurial students, academics and industry – either the industry that it helped create or the industry that it attracted. In this way, a strong regional network of knowledge-based enterprises and institutions can develop, from which the university, being at its centre, can benefit.

5.5 SUMMARY

This chapter has dealt with technostarters, students or academics who start their own, technology-based firm. We saw that:

- Technostarters are optimistic, perseverant and passionate people who are motivated by creating their own employment rather than being employed elsewhere. Entrepreneurship is very much in the air, and this is not confined to the developed world. Entrepreneurship has acquired a positive connotation and it is stimulated by many governments.
- Many technostarters originate from universities of technology, business schools and other academic education. However, an increasing number of technology-based enterprises and independent research institutes also support technostarters. Technostarters in these organisations are no longer seen as defectors.
- Technostarters are innovators; they create value by bringing an idea or an invention to the market. The role of the idea or indeed an invention in the value-creating process is limited.
- Technostarters create great economic value. The companies created in connection with the Massachusetts Institute of Technology in the USA would constitute an economy the size of Thailand or South Africa if they formed a separate nation.
- Although the number of technostarters in the world is unknown, a rough indication is that they form 3 per cent of the adult population.

- Universities stimulate technostarters because of their contribution to the economy and the challenge that entrepreneurship poses to an increasing number of students. In addition, they do so in order to enhance their own competitive position, as technostarters are an invaluable part of the know-how carousel of which leading universities are the centre.
- In addition to supporting technostarters, universities also take the initiative to create new enterprises themselves, using know-how generated by their research. Universities can receive substantial income from licenses, consulting, contract research and eventually endowments from the companies they create or help to create.

6. Financing technostarters and spinouts

6.1 FINANCING A START-UP

Financiers of new ventures, the third category of partners of the third generation university, are perhaps the partners the least known to university staff and technostarters. Most technostarters start with thinking about the product they want to create and commercialise. This is what they are good at, and marketing is something they have to learn. We tell them that an aeroplane needs two wings to fly: technology and market. It then needs a pilot – the entrepreneur himself. But the plane will still be grounded unless there is fuel in the tank – finance. The financial world is quite remote from university life and many new enterprises fail to make it because they underestimate or do not understand the role of financiers.

Financing in the early stages often has the form of equity participation. External financiers can help speed up the growth of the firm, by supplying extra capital and by bringing in experience. It is often better to participate in a rapidly growing enterprise than to muddle through on your own. The crunch is that financiers will often claim the right to change the management, thus being able to oust the founders from their management positions. This is very hard on the technopreneurs, but again the question is what do they want: a participation in a healthy enterprise or a nice way of passing the time? Many technostarters develop into good leaders for the more mature stages of the enterprise but there are also many that are good at initiating an enterprise but not at managing it in the later stages. In that case, they are wise to step back and let someone else do the job.

A new enterprise needs relatively little money in the early stages and increasingly more when it grows. Not only the quantities of the required funds are linked to the growth phases of the enterprise: so too are the forms in which finance is procured. Let us therefore take a look at the development phases of an enterprise and the amount of capital and the ways of financing required at each phase.

There are many ways of characterising the development phases of a firm and, compromising between literature and practical experience, we use one with five phases[119] (see Figure 6.1):

1. Design or pre-seed phase. For technostarters as well as spinouts, this phase includes the design of the product or service and checking its feasibility by addressing the market. It is a creative and playful phase with much soul-searching: 'Shall we go for entrepreneurship or not?' The technostarters need little money at this stage. They have their income as a student, their technical design is part of a university project, and all they need is money for testing the product and for market and intellectual property (IP) research. During the design phase it is still uncertain whether the firm can go ahead. It ends with the writing of a business plan, followed by a firm decision to go ahead – or not.
2. Development or seed phase. During this phase, a commercial prototype is developed, patent requirements are completed, marketing surveys and promotional activities such as presenting the product at an exhibition are carried out, promotional materials are prepared, and time is taken for talking to launching customers. The team is recruited and office and/or production facilities are prepared. Significant starting capital may be needed, and this money is at high risk because there are no revenues yet. The phase ends when regular production and sales have begun.[120]
3. Start-up phase. After the entrepreneurs have launched their product or service, money is needed for marketing activities, de-bottlenecking and expanding production, setting up customer services, and hiring more people. The risk is medium or still high. Profits are rare at this stage and if the company is in the black, the amount of profit will still be insignificant. This phase ends when there are clear signals that the company is breaking through, that 'it will make it' because sales are increasing, there are no longer liquidity problems and the profit margins increase.
4. Growth phase. At this stage the company is an early 'going concern' that is heading for growth. The company needs to reorganise itself, moving from an ad hoc, improvising management style to a more professional organisation with clearly delineated responsibilities, professional planning, professional attention to quality, procurement and logistics, plant expansion and expansion of the sales organisation. The excitement of getting the company off the ground is replaced by increasing professionalism and the implementation of sound business processes. If all goes well the company makes a good profit, but as the required working capital expands and more investments are required, the resulting cash flow will still be negative for a good deal of the growth phase. The phase ends when the company becomes well established, loans are being paid back and the profits provide an acceptable return on capital. The risks at this stage are significantly less

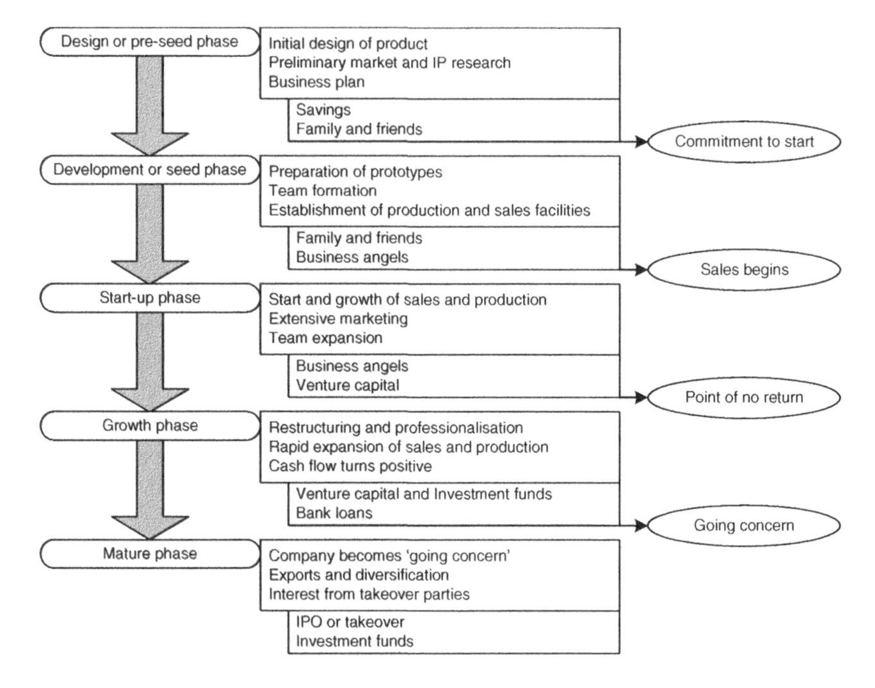

Figure 6.1 Phases in the development of a new enterprise

than in the previous phases and begin to approach the normal business risks of established firms.

5. Mature phase. In the mature phase the company may still be growing. The company now has a good financial track record, especially a track record for payments from debtors; it can finance itself and pay off loans. Activities concerning export, diversification and innovation of subsequent products are initiated. The mature phase can last forever, but often start-ups are bought out by large enterprises.[121] Many start-ups may never reach the mature stage before being bought out.

Figure 6.1 indicates the various ways of financing each phase. One has to realise that every company is different and there are no fixed rules as to how to finance a firm. The money for the design phase is usually collected from family and friends and the founders' own savings or their (part-time) jobs. If the new enterprise concerns a university spinout, the design costs are usually covered by a research project.

Although the financing of the design phase can be difficult for the starters, the real problems start when they go into development and the start-up phases. Financiers are reluctant to invest in these phases. Venture

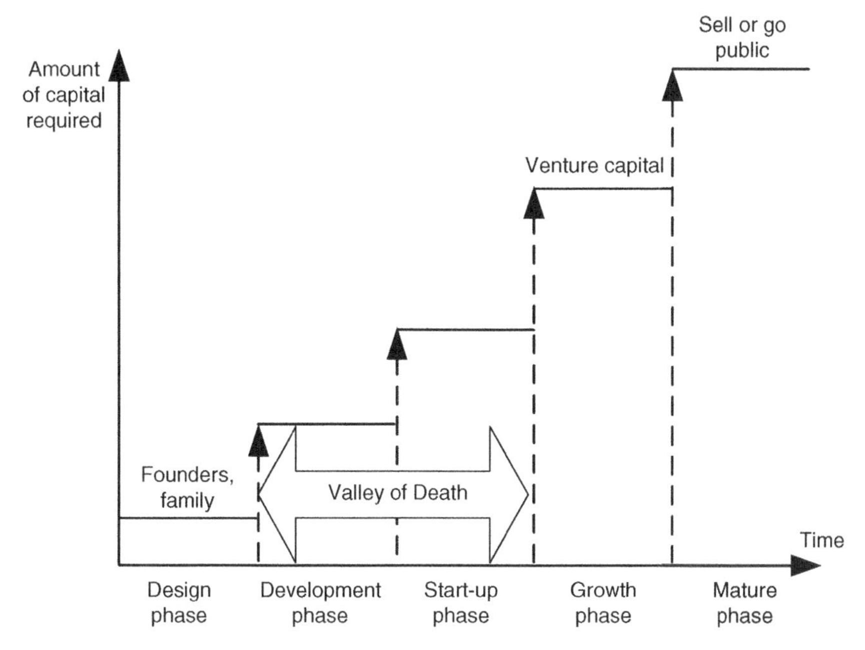

Figure 6.2 Financing the development phases of a start-up company

capital firms usually require a track record of several years of sound financial performance (especially debtors' performance) and they usually deal with larger budgets than are required in the development and start-up phases. Banks require collateral and do not in general consider an interesting concept as such. Only when the start-up phase has turned into the growth phase are venture capital firms or regular investment funds more likely to enter the game. Banks will then – at last! – be willing to provide loans on good debtors and fixed assets. Share participation from an existing firm in the same field is an option that is often used; this also brings in branch and technical know-how. When the company has matured, it can go public or be sold to an existing company that offers better opportunities for continued growth. Alternatively, the venture capital firm can sell out to investment funds, but this does not happen often.

The gist of this overview is that financing in the design phase, the growth phase and the mature phase does not present insurmountable problems. The problem lies in the middle: the development phase and, to a lesser extent, the start-up phase. These phases are often called the 'Valley of Death'[122] (Figure 6.2) as many potentially successful enterprises do not make it because of lack of money (water).

The Valley of Death is characterised as follows:

- More capital is needed than founders, family and friends can provide.
- The performance is too uncertain and too small to attract venture capital firms or investment funds.
- Banks cannot be used, as there is no collateral.

The Valley of Death can be overcome by experienced entrepreneurs and investors who have a more than average knowledge of the branch the start-up is working in, as well as of enterprise. For them the risks are lower than for other investors as they are in a better position to judge the risks and merits of the new enterprise. If they bring in capital, branch know-how and entrepreneurial experience, and if they are willing to open their commercial, technical and financial networks to the start-up, we call them business angels or informal investors. Business angels are often seasoned entrepreneurs who have sold their own company or drawn capital from it. Rather than go fishing, they enjoy putting their skills and experiences to use by financing and guiding start-ups. In this way, they can maintain their own network, enjoy the satisfaction that comes with guiding beginners, and make good money. For the start-up, a good business angel is a blessing: the starter can work with people who have been there before.

A typical example of the way this works is an angel investor who lives in San Rafael in Silicon Valley and started an information technology (IT) company in the 1970s; he sold it 25 years later. He spends about 20 per cent of his capital on high-risk ventures; the rest is for his pension and eventually his widow, as he says. He only invests in IT companies because he knows that business and the people that matter. He says he can only manage about six investments at a time, and he has the management team of a new investment visit him at home every Sunday morning to discuss business and progress. He will join the founders and managers in important meetings with customers or other concerned parties, evaluating the team's performance afterwards. 'With the phone calls and meetings I share with them during the rest of the week, I spend about a day a week working for them', he states. He will only invest in a company if he is reasonably sure his investment will be paid back ten times over in a few years. When the company has reached safe waters, he loses interest and he considers it is time for harvesting. In cordial agreement with the shareholding founders, he will then sell to a venture capital fund, another company or bring the firm to the stock exchange – doing an IPO, an initial public offering.

6.2 PRIVATE EQUITY, VENTURE CAPITAL AND BUSINESS ANGELS

Venture capital (that is, funds that finance the growth of young firms[123]) and angel capital are forms of private equity (PE).[124] Another form is buyout capital, funds that buy existing firms with the aim of breaking them up, turning them around and forging mergers, thus creating shareholder value. Private equity concerns equity investments in non-listed firms – companies whose shares are not traded on stock exchanges:

> Private equity is a broad term that commonly refers to any type of equity investment in an asset in which the equity is not freely tradable on a public stock market. More accurately, private equity refers to the manner in which the funds have been raised, namely on the private markets, as opposed to the public markets. Categories of private equity investment include leveraged buy-out, venture capital, growth capital, angel investing, mezzanine capital and others. Private equity funds typically control management of the companies in which they invest, and often bring in new management teams that focus on making the company more valuable.[125]

According to the European Private Equity & Venture Capital Association, EVCA, private equity investing 'can be broadly defined as investing in securities through a negotiated process'.[126] Small and medium-sized enterprises (SMEs) are financed almost exclusively by private equity as either they are not financed by share capital or the shares are not listed in a stock exchange. The shares are then with a closed group of investors as defined in the statutes, usually the founders and relatives. Shares can only be brought into the public domain by registering the firm with a stock exchange. The disadvantage of such a public listing is that the power of ownership is no longer exclusively with the founders and original shareholders, while the company has to give an extensive amount of information about its present and projected financial performance. If a company is growing fast, going public is a means to facilitate the attraction of share capital while the founders may wish to sell part of their shares.

There is no clear distinction between venture capital and angel capital. Both forms invest in share capital of the start-up or young enterprise although this investment may be accompanied by loans or deferred loans.[127] The term venture capital (VC) is usually associated with a fund:

- that is a legal entity that is operated by full-time management; the management typically receives a salary and a bonus that is related to the increase in value between the investment and the exit;

- that acquires money from a number of investors; the collective money is then invested and the investors do not participate directly in the firm that is the subject of the investment;
- that invests in enterprises that are already in the growth phase with a typical minimum of a few million dollars; it provides for a third round of financing, the first round being the financing by the founders and their friends and family and the second round provided by business angels.

Although the VC fund closely monitors the enterprise and has the right to take important decisions such as changing the management team, it does not have a day-to-day involvement in the management of the firm. By contrast, angel investors:

- Invest their own money directly or from a personal holding in the start-up.
- Often organise themselves in loose networks or groups with the objective to share research and scouting opportunities and to participate with more angels. If angels collaborate in the investment they will each participate directly, that is, without creating a common intermediary.
- Closely coach the managers of the firm they invest in, often making it the equivalent of a full-time job.
- Invest in the early stages of the start-up, including the design phase and certainly the development phase and start-up phase. This way, angel capital fills the gap in start-up financing between the 'three Fs' (friends, family and fools) of seed capital and venture capital; it provides for the second round of financing. A typical investment starts at $50 000 going up to several hundred thousands of dollars, but rarely exceeding say $1 million.
- Require a high return on investment, typically ten times the original investment within five years.[128] Good business angels realise an internal rate of return of 50 to 100 per cent of their portfolio.
- Often have an explicit exit strategy right from the start.

Angel investors are often retired business owners or executives, who may be interested in angel investing for other reasons in addition to pure monetary return. These include wanting to keep abreast of current developments in a particular business arena, mentoring another generation of entrepreneurs, and making use of their experience and networks on a less-than-full-time basis. Thus, in addition to funds, angel investors can often provide valuable management advice and important contacts.[129]

Jeffrey Sohl, director of the Centre for Venture Research at the University of New Hampshire, estimates that there are some 350 000 business angels in the US (2006) who invest $30 billion a year in 50 000 ventures, making an average investment of $600 000. Angel investors together invest more money than all venture capital funds combined ($24 billion vs $22 billion in the US in 2004).[130] There are some 40 000 business angels in the UK; European angels invest something between €10 and 20 billion per year. Venture capital funds invest on average $6 million in each venture. A typical VC fund has a capital base of over $100 million.[131] Beginning in the late 1980s, angels started to form informal groups with the goal of sharing deal flow and due diligence work, and pooling their funds to make larger investments. Angel groups are generally local organisations made up of 10–150 accredited investors interested in early-stage investing. In 1996 there were about ten angel groups in the US; as of 2005 there were more than 200. In 2004, according to the Centre for Venture Research, 18.5 per cent of deals that got through the early screens of angel groups and were presented to investors attracted funding, up significantly from 10 per cent in 2003, which is about the historical average.[132]

Angel investing is an old trade. Working at a workshop of the University of Glasgow, James Watt discovered significant improvements to the university's Newcomen steam engine. In 1765 he needed funds for the development, patent application and commercialisation of his version of the steam engine. He found a financier in Matthew Boulton, owner of a Birmingham foundry. In 1775, they formed a partnership, Boulton & Watt, making numerous further improvements. By 1824 they had sold over 1000 engines and eventually both became rich. The firm lasted for 120 years and still made steam engines in 1895 in Smethwick near Birmingham.[133] The first formal PE fund, American Research and Development (ARD), was established in 1946 by MIT president Karl Compton, Harvard Business School professor Georges F. Doriot and Boston businessmen. ARD made high-risk investments in emerging companies that were based on technology developed during the Second World War; its investment of $70 000 in Digital Equipment Company grew in value to $355 million.[134]

Many angels like to do business over a good dinner with a good wine, at which selected and well-prepared founders give a presentation of their start-up, followed by a 'shooting session' in which the investors ask relevant questions and see how the founders react. The Bay Angels gather round a table in a restaurant in Sausalito, the Cambridge Angels in Immanuel College. Angels will not only look at the value of the idea of the start-up and the data about future growth and income, they also closely evaluate the entrepreneurial qualities of the founders. If there is to be an investment, there has to be some kind of 'chemistry'. The deals however are strictly business. In some cases, banks offer sessions in which selected start-ups can present themselves to a forum of investors that are associated with the bank. Schretlen & Co., a Dutch private bank belonging to Rabo Bank, organises such sessions at five locations in the Netherlands, with a frequency of about six sessions annually at each location. The start-ups are screened beforehand by a consultancy that also helps the founders prepare their presentation. At TU Delft, the Foundation for Young Entrepreneurship organises workshops on how to write a business plan in which the workshops are led by volunteer-experts from professional service firms and a bank; these firms also sponsor the foundation. The technostarters are students from the university; they get academic credits for following the course. The credits are awarded by assessing a final and public presentation for a jury in which angels participate, after having signed a non-closure agreement. The jury evaluates as if they had to decide whether to invest themselves, answering three questions:

1. Is the business concept viable? This concerns products and cost, markets and price, the business model with sourcing, partners, servicing.
2. Is the team going to make it? (individual characteristics, operating as a team, support from angels or coaches).
3. Are the financial plan and the financing plan realistic?

In addition, the jury gives bonus points to those business plans that have an explicit and realistic exit plan (which most participants do not have).

6.3 INVESTMENT FUNDS

Before we embark on a discussion about financing strategies of start-ups with respect to IPR strategies of universities, we need to introduce the term 'carry' and the way it is used. The carry is roughly the value added between the start of an investment and the exit. The best way to introduce this quantity is to discuss the way investment funds operate.

The standard way of setting up an Investment Fund for Starters (IFS; Figure 6.3) is to create two bodies, the Fund as such and a (Fund) Management Company. The Fund provides money and does not employ staff; the Management Company manages the investments. The initiative to create a Fund often lies with a group of individuals who create a Management Company which then attracts investors to create the Fund. The opposite is also possible when a group of investors brings money together and then selects staff for the Fund Management Company.

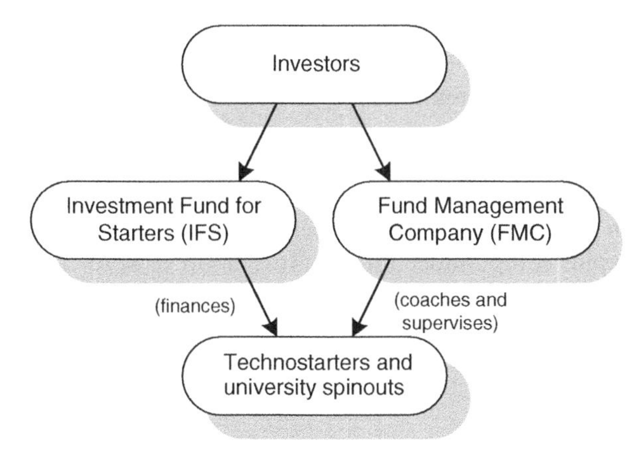

Figure 6.3 Structure of investment fund

The Management Company is the active partner; it selects the investment proposals, coaches and monitors progress and proposes an exit. In certain cases, the Management Company has full authority to invest and divest; in other cases, the investors have the final say in such matters, normally via an investment advisory committee. After the investment decision, the Management Company provides coaching and supervision of the start-up, both in the business and in the technical sense. Together with the enterprise, it will eventually propose an exit strategy to the investors. One might say that the Fund and Management Company together substitute the business angel; individual investors sometimes participate in the coaching of the new ventures by contributing their expertise in technology, entrepreneurship and the branch of industry. Sometimes a Fund is created or subsidised by the university (for example from endowment funds). Such a Fund may invest in spinouts and even have a monopoly to do so or at least a right of first refusal. In addition, it may or may not invest in technostarter companies. Governments may subsidise starter funds with an eye on the economic benefits they bring to the country. The Dutch government, for instance, gives a 100 per cent deferred loan to selected investment funds; up to €4 million, it matches the investment put in by the investors. The government then leaves the (dis)investment decisions entirely to the Management Company; there is no red tape. Payback conditions are very favourable and the scheme is one of the most effective and efficient around.

An Investment Fund always has a limited time frame; when its capital has been spent, the Management Company can start another Fund, possibly with the same financiers, possibly with others. The financial relationship between Fund and Management Company consists of two elements:

1. The Fund pays an annual fee to the Management Company's management; this fee is usually a percentage of the committed capital, that is, the capital that is committed at the start of the IFS, whether it is actually paid up or not.
2. The Fund pays a bonus based on the value creation, usually a percentage of the so-called carried value or carry, that is, the difference between the amount of money received at exit and the original investment(s) plus compounded interest. It is, in other words, the difference between the value created and the value that would have been obtained if the original sums would have been left to mature risk-free and at a fixed interest rate. This interest rate is called the hurdle rate or just the hurdle.

The carry is the reward for all who contributed to the success of the enterprise. It has to be divided, according to prior agreement, between the investors (founders and Fund), the Management Company and possibly others who have added value to the start-up. Although not common, university staff that adopt an active advisory role to the founders can participate in the carry. From the company's point of view, this is attractive as no fees need to be paid during the development of the firm, while a win–win situation is created nevertheless. The university can also claim part of the carry (or part of the shares) if it has intellectual property rights on the know-how the company is based on.

In a university, the tasks of the Management Company can be assigned to the office that supports all commercialisation activities. Such an office (later, we will call it the Support Team) can advise on whether certain know-how is better sold to existing firms, or whether it is more advantageous to start a new enterprise for it. The University of Leuven operates this way.

A private Investment Fund can play a larger role than just financing technostarters. In many cases, it is better suited to act as the manager of the technostart activities than the university itself. In this case, the Fund becomes the driving force in all activities concerning technostarters. This is depicted in Figure 6.4.

In this case, the Fund, with the blessing of the university, organises awareness programmes and lectures. The Fund then selects the enterprises that are ready for financing and tries to make matches between entrepreneurs and the technology of the university; it scouts such technology and makes an assessment of its potential in a start-up. The Fund can even run an incubator. The university can claim a percentage of the carried value and/or shares in exchange of intellectual property and its cooperation. In cases where such a private initiative is available, for instance from alumni, while the university feels it is not ready to pursue commercial activities

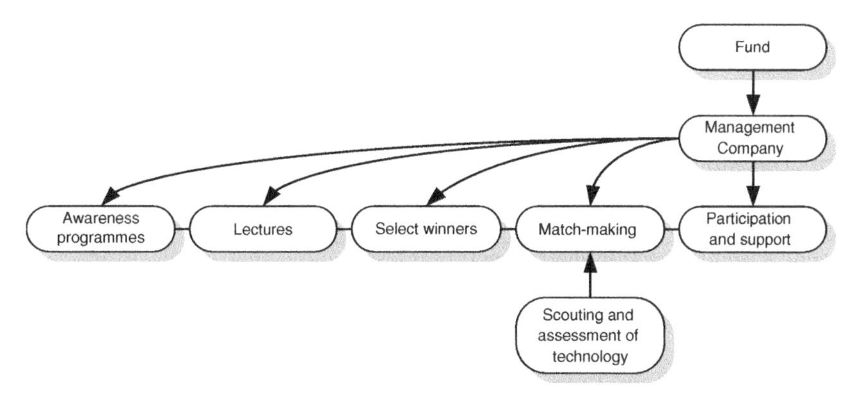

Figure 6.4 Fund-driven entrepreneurship activities

itself, a leading role for the private Fund is an attractive option as long as the university gets a reasonable share in the proceeds.

6.4 FINANCING AND IPR STRATEGIES

The expression 'concluding a deal' or 'deal-making' is used to describe the agreements between parties when an enterprise receives an investment, possibly in combination with a loan and with an agreement about the distribution of the carry. The deal-making is the crucial decision in the life of a technostarter, and unfortunately most first-time technostarters are not well prepared for it. This is because it is difficult for them to envisage the exit strategy, whereas the exit strategy is of utmost importance in the deal-making. Designing an exit strategy, when the enterprise has just been initiated is often counter-intuitive for the founders. They have to realise however that most technology-based companies will eventually be bought by large, existing enterprises or brought to the stock exchange; only a few last for a longer period of time as an independent company. Technostarters and university spinouts should always have their eye on the exit; the exit is the moment of truth. This raises several questions.

Firstly, should a start-up seek a participation of an existing firm that is active in the same field? The advantages are obvious: in addition to entrepreneurial experience, such an investor brings in much branch-specific and technical and commercial experience which will give the new enterprise considerable lift. The downside is that it may be difficult to sell the firm to a competitor of the investor. Another danger is that the investor may get familiar with the technologies and markets of the start-up and use them itself. An agreement to prevent this will have to be closed and this may incorporate complicated legal details. These risks are considerably less in the case of angel investments but then the clout of such investors might be smaller than that of an established firm.

Secondly, a share-participation by the university, whether in return of input in kind – intellectual property rights (IPR), support – or financial input, also has its pros and cons. The alternative is to conclude a licence agreement if the university owns the IPR. The advantage of a licence agreement is that the shareholder structure is less complicated and decisions can be reached more easily; this is especially relevant if the university is not experienced. The disadvantage of a licence agreement is obviously that liquidity is leaving the enterprise when it dearly needs it itself.

Thirdly, there is the form of the investment. The investors may like to give part of the funds required as a loan or deferred loan. In contrast to an investment in share capital, which can only be recouped at the exit, loans usually have to be paid back earlier, and in this way the investor reduces his risk. But for the young enterprise, paying interest can be a heavy burden in the early years when the revenue streams are small.

Tax reasons also can play a role. An investor may also seek a participation in the form of priority shares (preferred shares) – shares that give the shareholder privileges in case of bankruptcy. All these forms of investment are to the disadvantage of the normal shareholders (that is, the founders) and it is a matter of negotiation which form will be chosen.

Looking at it from the point of view of the university, a university has several options for its IPR policy:[135]

- exchange know-how for shares;
- exchange know-how for a share of the carry;
- licensing the know-how and receiving a fee, say for every product that leaves the company.

The IPR policy is often furiously debated in universities[136] and there are broadly speaking two views on this. One view, which one could label the short-term view, is that the university should make sure it has arrangements – for instance in the labour contracts with its employees and contracts with students – that will ensure that the university holds the IPR of all the knowledge created. Next, the university should exploit the IPR as much as possible in order to maximise its income from the knowledge it generates. Such a policy however may backfire in the sense that it puts potential founders off, resulting in fewer spinouts and technostarters than would have been possible. Other universities therefore follow what could be called the long-term view and which consists of a liberal IPR policy in which the university is not trying to maximise its immediate income, but focuses on the creation of a knowledge carousel, an atmosphere in which entrepreneurship flourishes thus creating an attractive environment for entrepreneurial students and academics. As we have argued before, such a policy enhances the competitive position of the university. In addition, the attitude of entrepreneurs towards the university will be more open, meaning that entrepreneurs can be approached easier when it comes to asking favours – student placements, guest lectures and eventually endowments.

Some pioneering third generation universities (3GUs) universities in the US and the UK originally adopted the long-term view, while they now tend to move towards the short term.[137] It makes a difference whether a technostarter uses mainly know-how he has created himself or whether knowledge that is not created by him is concerned. In the latter case, it is reasonable that the university receives returns on its investments in know-how creation. The argument against this is that it is often the better scientists who acquire the research grants or contracts, and they should be given a good share of the income if they are to be motivated to create the spinout; without them, it will simply not happen. In the case of students carrying out a thesis or PhD project, it is not always possible for the university to acquire the IPR; the knowledge created is in the public domain and the university then cannot stop a student using it for his or her own benefit.

The best solution is usually a compromise in which the university adopts a liberal policy while keeping a close eye on the possibilities of creating income from knowledge itself, maximising the entrepreneurial output of the know-how carousel rather than the immediate returns.[138] Much depends on the question of who acquired the research contracts or grants and who took the initiative to generate the know-how. In professional service firms, the power is with those who do the acquisition of assignments; in universities it is no different.

PART III

Organising the Third Generation University

Having given the outlines of a third generation university (3GU) in Part I and having discussed its main partners in Part II, we will now focus on the organisational aspects of the 3GU and the ways in which a university can migrate from the second generation university (2GU) to the 3GU model. In Chapter 7, we will discuss its general organisational, management and financial structure and its management practices. Chapter 8 focuses in on the organisation and facilities for know-how commercialisation. Finally, Chapter 9 addresses the question of how to migrate from the second generation university to the third generation university model.

7. Organisational structure and management style

7.1 ORGANISATIONAL STRUCTURE

Let us start our discussion on the management of the third generation university (3GU) by looking at its organisational structure. Traditionally, the activities of a university are carried out by faculties that address a certain scientific discipline, according to Aristotelian logic and its expansions. We saw however that most research nowadays is multidisciplinary or even transdisciplinary, whereby the research and development (R&D) activities are focused on subjects that involve scientists, engineers and designers of several disciplines. The teams that carry out transdisciplinary research organise themselves in cross-faculty teams, that is, teams consisting of members from different faculties and often from different universities and increasingly including non-university members too. This creates a matrix structure: the team members belong to the faculty, but work in the team that is an entity on its own with its own source of income (Figure 7.1).

Matrix structures in general signal a transitional phase as the new structure has not yet created enough confidence to replace the old, while the old structure, or rather its leaders, still fight for their survival. A matrix structure is unstable because it is based on conflicting principles, in this case discipline-based versus subject-based research and education. This often results in conflicts that take a disproportionate amount of time to resolve and that take energy away from the job to be done.

There is a trend now for cross-faculty teams to acquire a status of their own and this may show the way to a new and more effective structure. The teams become organised as transdisciplinary, faculty-independent institutions reporting directly to the board and renamed as a university institute with the name of the university before and the name of the object of research and education after it. These institutes are often responsible for the Master's courses and post-experience education[139] that correspond to their subject and the award of PhDs in their area of expertise. The university institutes attract their own second and third flows of finance (see section 7.3) and cooperate with industry and start-ups. They show a good deal of entrepreneurial behaviour, in the scientific as well as the financial

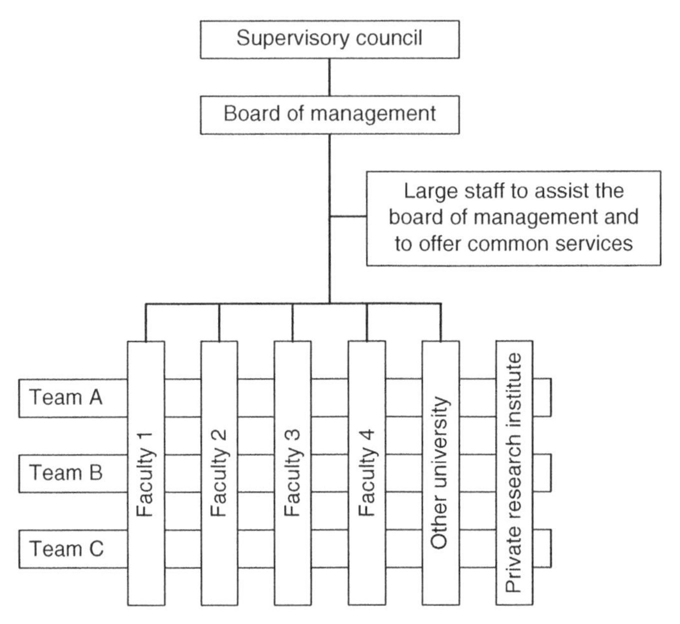

Figure 7.1 Traditional university organisation with faculties and cross-faculty transdisciplinary teams

sense; they are responsible for their financial well-being. They can be supported by a library and a small back office for finance and administration and information technology. University institutes form networks all over the world; they often cooperate in international projects. Words like 'coopetition' and other amalgamations of the words 'cooperation' and 'competition' describe their behaviour very well. As university institutes gain power at the expense of the faculties, there is a tilting of the organisation (Figure 7.2).

Where have we seen such tilting before? Since the Second World War, companies have become organised according to the functional organisational model. If the faculties of Figure 7.1 are replaced by functional departments such as marketing and sales, manufacturing, R&D and finance, the result is a diagram of the functional organisation of companies. The advantages of functional organisations are obvious: good quality and supervision of the functional activities, increased efficiency, and many possibilities for young people to develop themselves in the functional area. The weak point of functional organisations is the communication and decision-making across the functions, as the only cross-functional organ is the board of management. To meet specific demands, cross-functional teams, focusing on specific customer groups, products or regions, were introduced

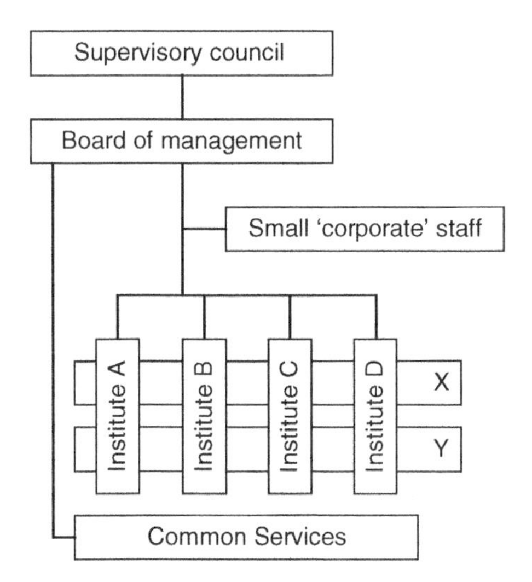

Note: X and Y are monodisciplinary professional societies replacing the faculties.

Figure 7.2 The organisational structure of the third generation university

with coordinating powers for planning and decision-making. Their creation resulted in a diffuse power structure and it became clear that a more radical solution was required if the company concerned was to cope with the turbulence in markets and technology. The solution came in the 1980s and was called 'business unit management'.[140] It consisted of three elements:

1. Tilting of the organisation: turning it 90 degrees, in such a way that the cross-functional teams – now called business units – became the dominant element of the organisation while the corporate functional structures either disappeared or became coordinating elements.
2. Empowerment: first of all by making the management of the business units profit-responsible for 'their' customer group or product group; next, at the lower levels of management, by empowering every manager and worker to carry out their tasks according to their own best practices and insights.
3. Change of culture: from introvert, company-oriented cultures towards extrovert, customer-oriented cultures. From 'inside-out' to 'outside-in'. From 'I work for my boss' to: 'I work for my customer'.

The business unit structure is now widely applied in industry; it fosters flexible behaviour, innovation and customer orientation.

Coming back to our universities, we can see many parallels. Faculties consist of scientists who work mainly in multidisciplinary teams. Balancing the work of these teams with the requirements of the faculties takes a heavy toll on the time of academics. Changes within the system do not help much. The tilting of the organisation, as depicted in Figure 7.2, with its true empowerment of the institutes and a change of culture, is very much like the change from functional structures to business unit structures in enterprises. It equally results in transparent lines of responsibility, innovative and entrepreneurial behaviour, and greater flexibility.

While the university institutes are responsible for the Master's courses and most of the PhD research, the Bachelor's courses are still the domain of the faculties. Alternatively, all academics can be transferred to university institutes and the faculties can be turned into a kind of informal 'professional societies' where people of the same discipline can exchange ideas and experiences on an informal basis. The Bachelor's courses are then organised by programme directors who are profit-responsible for the courses they manage (including their marketing) and who hire teaching staff from the university institutes.

In the structure of Figure 7.2, the central departments are split into a small Corporate Office, designed to support the board of management, and 'Common Services' or shared service centres, that are responsible for those services that demand central organisation because of economies of scale. These Common Services close service-level agreements with the university institutes. Sometimes common services can be outsourced; in any case, they have to compete with external service providers.

The conclusion of this section is that in a 3GU the university institutes become the main organisational element of the university. Contract relations between the board, the institutes and the Common Services make the organisation more transparent. Undergraduate teaching will remain the domain of the faculties. In addition, faculties may organise general Master's courses; if the university institutes organise the specific Master's classes, the two-track university has become reality.

7.2 THE MANAGEMENT STRUCTURE

The board of management is responsible for:

1. Setting the objectives of the university as a whole. This includes the definition of the university's portfolio of activities: which areas of research, education and commercialisation are going to be addressed?

2. The supervision of faculties, university institutes and Common Services in order to ensure that the objectives are realised.
3. The management of the external relationships that concern the entire university.

Concerning the objectives, the issue of the portfolio of activities exists as long as universities exist. In Chapter 1, we saw that only a few medieval universities included all faculties or all subjects of the Artes Faculty. Likewise, few universities would claim they cover all fields of arts and science. Choices become tougher as the costs of carrying out research increase; many universities have to narrow their scope. In addition, the issue of transdisciplinary research requires a new definition of the university portfolio as the university nowadays is not so much the sum of its disciplines but rather the sum of the subjects that are addressed in a transdisciplinary way.

The supervision concerns the faculties (if any are left), the university institutes, the Common Services and the Corporate Office.

External relations with companies that are cooperating with several research groups are the responsibility of the board of management as far as general agreements are concerned. The board can for instance close a framework contract with a large enterprise, from which several institutes will subsequently benefit. In addition, the board may have general relations with a National Science Foundation (NSF) type of institute while research groups may have contacts with the institute's departments that sponsor their specific research.

Our favourite model for the composition of a university's board of management is a five-person board, consisting of:

1. The president, responsible for the coordination of the activities, campus development, endowments, and representation to common external parties and the public.
2. The rector, responsible for the coordination and the quality of research, including PhD research.
3. A member responsible for the coordination and the quality of education and the application of modern teaching methods.
4. A member responsible for the collaboration with industry and commercialisation of know-how. This includes coordination of the marketing activities, running the marketing support department and the instruments of know-how commercialisation and cooperation, including the instruments to support technostarters and the technopark (if the university has one, including shared accommodation facilities for young enterprises). We will discuss the facilities that assist this board member in Chapter 8.

5. A chief financial officer, responsible for finance and administration, human resource management and facility management.

The faculties and/or the university institutes report directly to the president while they have functional supervisory lines to the other board members. The Common Services report to the chief financial officer. The Corporate Office, headed by the university's secretary, reports to the president, the specialists of this office working for all board members.

The organisational structure still leaves options open for the way in which the management is going to be carried out. Most universities have adopted the practice of strategic management to negotiate objectives and exercise control. The board then prepares a strategic plan for the university that includes targets for the university as a whole and its components. The objectives and strategies of faculties, university institutes and Common Services must fit the overall strategic plan. After the plans have been negotiated with the managers of the faculties, institutes and services, they become a management contract between the board and the responsible manager. The Corporate Office may assist the board but it is not part of the contract, meaning it has no involvement with the management of either university institutes or Common Services. The board of management will exercise its control in the three ways that are now mainstream in enterprises:

- Strategic control. The board has meetings with the management of each university institute and Common Services to check the progress on their strategic plan. There are several such meetings per year.
- Financial control. The board or its representative has regular meetings concerning the financial development of the unit.
- Professional control. The board has regular checks on the quality of the research, education and commercialisation of the university institutes.

This system implies that the board keeps an operational distance from the faculties or institutes; in terms of 'dos' and 'don'ts', the board's most important 'do' is: 'Don't do too much'. University institutes need to be entrepreneurial units, entrepreneurial in the scientific as well as the financial way. They should be empowered to hire their own staff, acquire their own research and educational projects, and make their own alliances, all within the framework of their strategies as agreed with the board.

Who will be the managers of the university? In a not too distant past, this question would have sounded superfluous. Hospitals were run by physicians, engineering consultants by engineers, law offices by lawyers, and universities by professors, the reason being that only professional leaders can have a vision on their subject, can motivate the professional or academic staff, supervise their work and make professional contacts. When organisations started to grow in size and complexity, managers were hired from outside the professional environment, partly because of the management experience they brought with them, partly because not enough professionals could be found who would be able and willing to take management positions. For the leadership of the university institutes we are very much in favour of restoring the practice of professional leadership. Naturally, such leaders would have to be willing to learn a good deal about management. They will have to accept that they should give up part (but only part) of their professional work in order to make time for leadership.

At the same time, we prefer the board of management to be composed of functional managers. The president should have a background in the management of complex professional organisations. The other members should be specialists in their fields. The managers of the Common Services should be experienced managers with a background in the subject of their service while the Corporate Office is comprised of a small number of specialists in fields that a university cannot do without. Such a composition of:

- functional leaders at the top,
- academic leaders of the university institutes,
- a team of experts supporting the board of management,
- professional managers to run the Common Services,

would in our opinion provide for a balanced way of management and leadership that would inspire the professional workers on the one hand, while securing the demands of efficiency and quality on the other.

A system with semi-autonomous university institutes will only work if the bill for failure would not be passed to the board of management. It would have to become common practice to dissolve a failing university institute and dismiss its personnel. That will sound devilish to the ears of university workers who have often been endowed with lifelong employment guarantees. But in enterprises, it is the most natural thing in the world. Likewise, failure or obsolescence cannot be tolerated in universities. Out of the ruins of failed enterprises, new business activities emerge. Likewise, dissolving an obsolete or failing university institute will allow its academics to enter new and challenging avenues.

7.3 FINANCING THE 3GU

The medieval university was financed by fees from students and donations from Church and state, which saw it as a status symbol as well as a source

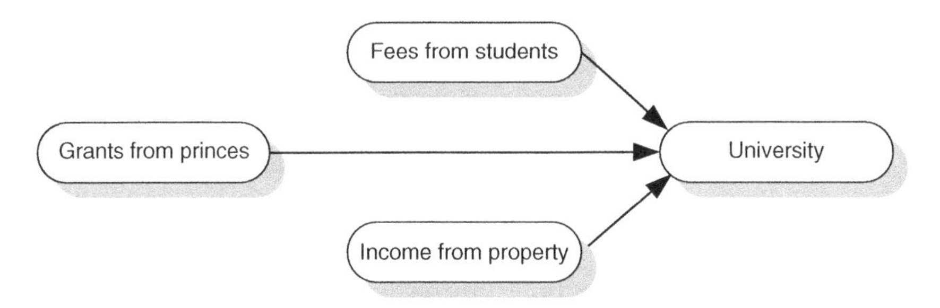

Figure 7.3 Schematic flow of finance to the medieval university

of income for their diocese, city or princedom. Like the monasteries, universities were permitted to acquire possessions (especially land, the currency of the time) that would grant them extra income and security in times of financial scarcity (Figure 7.3). This system made universities in part financially independent from the Church and state authorities.

The second generation university drew its income largely from the state; income from property became negligible although quite a few universities still own large domains of land and buildings. Initially, government grants were given as lump sums for education and 'free research'. This support is a form of input financing: the state pays for the availability of universities and delegates authority on how to spend the income to the universities. In Europe, this income is often called the 'first flow of finance'. Gradually, governments started to route funds for research through foundations such as the National Science Foundation in the US. Europe has similar national foundations as well as the newly established European Research Council.[141] This system of indirect financing introduces an element of competition as universities or academics have to compete for research projects. It constitutes a form of output financing (the state pays for deliveries), sometimes called the 'second flow of finance' (Figure 7.4).

In today's second period of transition, universities increasingly receive income from two additional sources:

1. Third parties, such as 'customers' concluding contracts for applied research or the use of know-how and income from post-experience courses. This is called the 'third flow of finance'.
2. Some universities are blessed with endowments (sometimes called the 'fourth flow of finance').

This is depicted in Figure 7.5.

The experiences with funding foundations have been positive and their operation has led to significant improvements in the focus and quality of

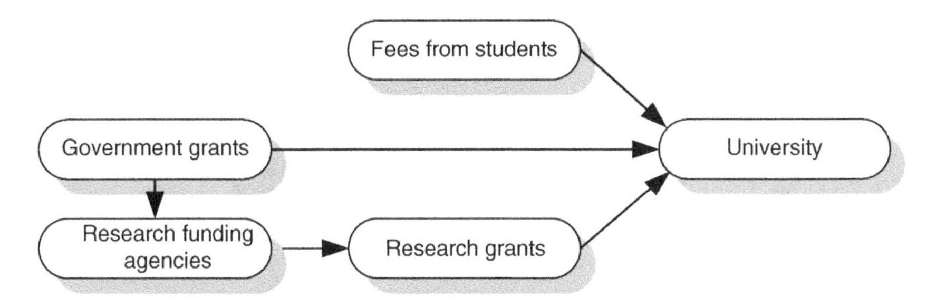

Figure 7.4 Schematic flow of finance to the 2GU

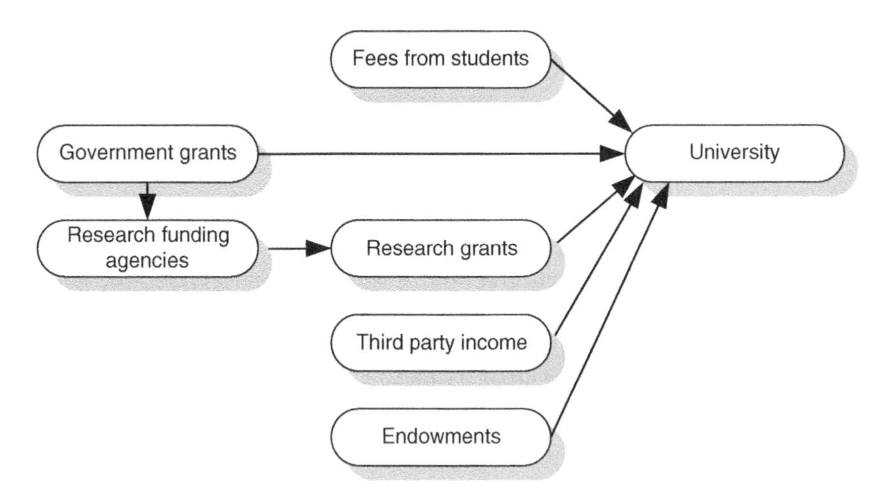

Figure 7.5 Schematic flow of finance to present universities

research. In many countries, however, the first flow of finance is still by far the largest source of income for universities. This way of financing results from the nineteenth-century view that governments are responsible for good educational practices, with schools and universities being their instruments. This made universities 'executive departments' of the Ministry of Education. *The Economist* has called it a 'Bargain with the state . . . a pact with the devil'.[142] This traditional view is now being challenged by the view that the responsibilities of state and universities must be disentangled. The government, representing the people and responsible for spending their money, has to decide how much of the national budget will be devoted to research and education and on which subjects it shall be spent. The research part of the budget is then offered for competitive bids through foundations – the second flow of finance. The education part of the budget goes

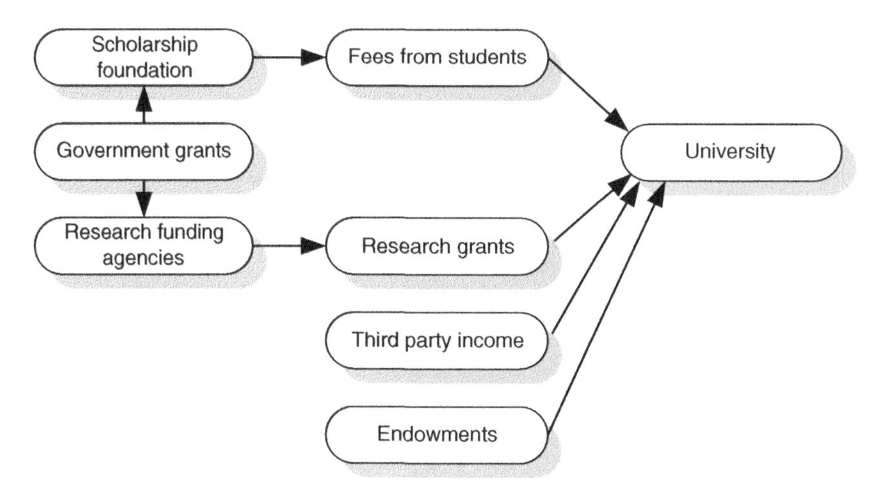

Figure 7.6 Schematic flow of finance to the 3GU

likewise to scholarship foundations that enable students to pay a fee corresponding to the actual cost of education (Figure 7.6).

With the end of the direct, first flow of finance to universities, the government involvement with the universities also ends and universities become independent organisations that set their own labour conditions and standards for exams. Rather than trying to ensure quality by government controls, the government relies on the market system of competition. The experiences with the independent universities in the USA show that the latter is more effective.

Many universities today are in a process of change, which we have called the second period of transition. Plotting the global versus national orientation against the amount of financing from fixed budgets versus programme financing (Figure 7.7), we can plot the 2GU in the lower left quadrant and the 3GU in the upper right. Universities in transition often receive a substantial first flow of finance to cover their Bachelor's courses and monodisciplinary research; these activities have a national orientation. For the financing of Master's courses and PhD research they depend increasingly on second or third flows of finance while these activities have an international orientation as such activities are part of a global competitive environment.

7.4 GOOD UNIVERSITY MANAGEMENT

There are some 30 000 universities in the world and many of them have management problems. Yet there are hardly any management courses for

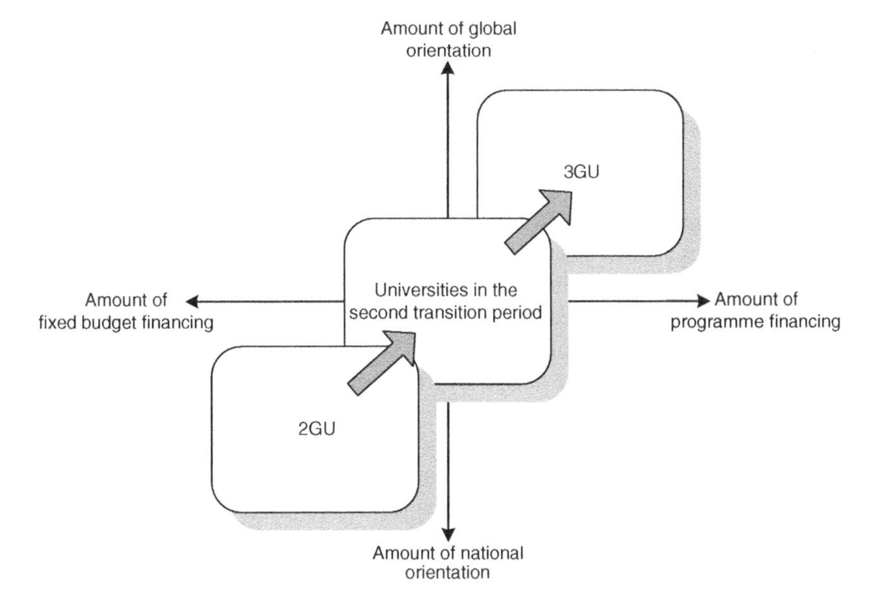

Figure 7.7 Universities moving from 2GU to 3GU

university leaders and there is a surprisingly small body of literature on the subject.[143]

Ask an academic in such a place how the work is going and the answer will be twofold. Answer 1a is that he or she is working on an exciting subject and they are making interesting progress. Answer 1b is that they are working with some challenging partners (the names of some international industries and other universities follow). Answer 1c is that they have such nice talented young people in the group who are really promising. So everything looks well. Then you ask: 'How is it going with the faculty?' and the faces start sagging. The complaints concern the bureaucracy, the lack of resources, lack of a strategy or even the slightest consistency in the management of their department or faculty, the difficulties in getting rid of underperforming subordinates, the anger over unfair appointments or promotions. Apparently, the work is challenging but the organisational setting is not. The question of why some universities have such a gap between professional motivation and organisational demotivation is intriguing, and despite a host of literature on the subject of managing professional service firms, of which universities are a subcategory, the answer is evasive.[144]

A possible clue is that much of what we know about management is what we learned in industrial enterprises – we have been doing that for some 250 years – and that this body of experience is at odds with universities and professional service firms in general. Traditional industrial enterprises[145] are characterised by:[146]

- specialisation (breaking up the work process into small uniform segments);
- standardisation (of work-elements, jobs, components, output);
- synchronisation (between elements of the production and logistic processes and with society in general);
- concentration (all the work is done in one enterprise: car manufacturers also make the rear lights);
- maximisation (of output);
- centralisation (of the design of the production and logistic processes, planning and organisation).

One only needs to envisage a car production line to get the idea. Industrial organisations are centrally designed and require strict control – also of details – if they are to operate well. As the price of the product is a major item of the marketing mix, they have a need for strict cost control as well.

Professional service firms are characterised by exactly the opposites of the above elements:

- Professionals create all or most elements of their service themselves, alone or with a small collegial team.
- Each service they render is made to measure and different from the previous one.
- The synchronisation with society is very limited. Professional service firms for instance train their own personnel to a large extent (learning on the job). Working hours are flexible and professionals are encouraged to work at home. Their professional and private lives are very much mixed up.
- Support is hired, from the lunches ordered outside or offered by a contractor, to the leasing of cars, printing facilities and so on.
- The quality rather than the quantity of output is maximised as workers are motivated by the recognition that comes from solving interesting problems.
- Professionals have to find their own solutions; there is no central top-down instruction on how to do the work.

This implies that professionals need a different management approach than industrial firms; they should be given freedom and encouragement, with control limited to the quantity and quality of output. If they generate enough income, there is no need for detailed cost control because, if universities are lavish with goodies (information technology equipment especially) and fair with the distribution of status (the corner room) they give their employees double motivation: through their work and through management. As a result, the employees work harder (they feel responsible for their output) and they make more money than the costs of the goodies that are only a small percentage of the budget anyway.

There seem to be three reasons why this heaven is not universal:

1. The values underlying the management techniques from the industrial era are deeply ingrained: a 'good' manager is never satisfied and always critical, he is constantly looking for savings, however small, and he works his head off controlling every detail. In a university, such an attitude is disastrous.
2. Professional competition, which is healthy, can turn into jealousy – which is not. A good father likes his children to perform better than himself. Likewise, a good senior academic takes pride in the achievements of his team members, even if they outwit him. However, when jealousy or fear for status or position prevails, the juniors become humiliated by overly critical comments – which they do not know what to do with as professional work can always be improved and it is difficult to distinguish justified criticism from nagging, especially when one is young.
3. Organisationally, universities and professional service firms are jungles. Mintzberg has called them 'ad-hocaries'.[147] In order to strengthen their positions in a world in which formal power has little value, university leaders tend to seek allies. In return for loyalty, cronies ask favours and objectively unjustified favours create disproportionate unrest in the faculty. In addition to that, the leader and the group of cronies often form an informal, inaccessible ring that blocks information. It makes them feel invincible; like Shakespeare's *Henry V*: 'We few, we happy few, we band of brothers'.

In an industrial firm, if one cog fails, the entire system comes to a halt and this is immediately noticed. Corrective action is taken and if it is not, it will soon show up in the financial results or in a high illness rate, turnover rate of personnel or a high rate of complaints from customers. If indicators such as these show good figures, the supervisory board or the non-executive directors may assume that all is well. Not so in a university or professional services firm. A university is comprised of a conglomerate of small teams. If one team performs financially badly, the results can be counterbalanced by those of high-achieving groups, resulting in a satisfactory overall result (never mind that the good performers are punished and the bad ones rewarded). In other words, the financial results are not a good indicator of the performance of a university. There is no immediate necessity for the university leaders to solve the problems of a malfunctioning group, and many prefer to keep a peaceful and collegial atmosphere rather than be hard on poor performers. Social indicators such as sickness leave, personnel turnover and social unrest or industrial action are equally inadequate to measure the performance of a university. If such figures are low in an industrial organisation, they indicate that things are going well. In a professional service firm, good signals can hide a lack of motivation and mismanagement. When there is tension in a professional service firm, the professionals will continue doing their job, partly because of professional pride and partly because of their sense of responsibility vis-à-vis the customers. They will stay on the job as long as the work is interesting, focus on the work and their teams, and put up with the nasty aspects of the organisation. Quality indicators are just as ineffective as the financial and social indicators. Many universities organise visitations – visits by a team of external experts who assess the educational and research performance. The visitations committees focus on output (courses, articles, theses), and while the organisation is malfunctioning, the quality of output may be perfectly thrilling, courtesy again of the professional pride and sense of responsibility of the professionals. All this goes to say that the methodologies of management and supervision that worked well in the old traditional industrial enterprises are grossly inadequate in universities.

Yet it is important for university management to know whether the academics are properly motivated. Professional workers can only perform and develop themselves well if they put their heart and soul into their work. When they are confronted with what they perceive as unjust management practices the quality of the work will suffer, but only in the long term as, rather than fighting the system, they will look for another job. The essential question in managing universities and other professional service organisations is how to keep the professionals motivated while maintaining direction and performance. The typical academic is a sensitive person with a large ego and limited social skills. Although they will never admit it, many top scientists are lonely people. The art is to provide a secure environment in which talents can flourish, while keeping people on track to achieve the desired results. Given these general observations, some suggestions can be given concerning the management of universities, without any presumption of completeness.

First, there is the management aspect. Good deans realise that their appointment marks a turning point in their life which requires them to acquire a whole new set of skills while they have to leave part of their previous life behind. One dean told us:

> When I was asked to take up the dean's position in the Medical Faculty, I hesitated. I realised that I had to run a highly sophisticated professional group, including 'difficult' persons and a substantial budget. I had neither the training nor the experience to do the job. It would take much of my time and I would have to cut down on my dealings with patients, lecturing and research. At the same time, it was a challenge and I also felt I could not refuse. When I took up the job I realised I needed help. First, I sought a personal coach to help me manoeuvre in the yet uncharted territories. Second, I appointed a management assistant of a good professional level to take care of the planning and accounting of activities. Third, I registered for a two-week course in hospital management. It took me a year to get the job under control and to create a vision of what I wanted to achieve with the faculty. Then I started attracting top candidates for three new chairs in order to strengthen our performance. Their appointments and other changes in personnel took me another year. Gradually, I started delegating certain responsibilities to the department heads, which not only reduced my workload but also gave them a better understanding and appreciation of the managerial tasks. With about half my time still working professionally, these were 'tropical years'. Several times, I considered giving up my work as a physician but each time I decided not to do so, as I felt I would weaken my professional vision and authority. You need to stay at the edge. Although the combination of physician/researcher/lecturer and manager is still very demanding, it gives me great satisfaction to create a world-class team that is recognised internationally. As a professor, you like to see your name printed. As a manager, you enjoy even more seeing the names of your people printed.

Attention should be given to all academics (and others) in management and leadership positions. Tacit management talent is to be monitored and courses are to be given before or at the time of appointment to a leadership position: short seminars for section leaders, more extensive courses for board members, deans and heads of department. The selection process for leaders must be based on leadership qualities on the one hand and the ambition to lead the faculty or institute on the other, rather than the usual: 'It's Jack's turn'. It is advisable to offer executive coaching services for the newly appointed. It is important to have women as managers in universities and to work explicitly towards a goal of about 50/50 men and women in management positions. This not only serves the natural objective of equal opportunities but also results in a healthier management culture.

Second, there is the financing and reward system. Academics and professionals serve two masters: the development of their own talents and professionalism as well as the realisation of the required output. Workers in industrial organisations focus on output; workers in universities tend to focus on their own development and the development of opportunities, with outputs just being a means, not an end in itself. A culture and an administrative system should be created that makes academics responsible for the scientific as well as budgetary results. This can be achieved by making teams (sections) responsible for the result and creating proper boundary rules. A good rule is that a team receives 85 per cent of the net revenue resulting from its activities, with the remainder going into a faculty's or institute's innovation fund, created for supporting new academic activities. There should be clear rates for the revenues for the services a team renders: lectures, theses projects, fundamental research and so on. Likewise, the costs charged to the team should be equally transparent. The team then works as a mini-enterprise and this creates a good spirit and a sense of responsibility that also benefits the scientific results. Much research is sponsored or contract research. Although the professionals themselves are the main marketing persons, negotiating contracts, let alone the legal details, are not every researcher's cup of tea. Support from a specialised marketing team is therefore to be recommended, while such a team should realise it only has a supporting and stimulating role. Concerning remuneration, most universities reward their employees according to input characteristics (level of education, annuity). In contrast, industrial firms reward their personnel by output characteristics: the better and more you perform, the more you get paid. Universities can also adopt output remuneration; it prevents financial losses, for instance, if a young academic gets his doctorate and therefore a higher salary, even if his output remains the same. The message should be: 'Nice that you got your PhD but in order to get a higher salary, you will have to show how your output increases.' Finally, there should be transparent procedures for accepting newcomers and promotions and for investments.

Three, the work itself. Working for a customer who is waiting for the result is motivating. If there are no such customers, it is useful to create deadlines as this will give a sense of purpose. Teams that supervise or just assist research establish interactive patterns with the researcher which can help him overcome hurdles and maintain a sense of direction. Most academics find a mixture of teamwork and individual work rewarding. There is too much emphasis on teamwork nowadays, which does not mean that it is not important, but major breakthroughs in thinking are often an individual act. It is the interaction between teamwork and individual work that produces the best results.

Finally, it is important to create feedback on the motivational health of the community, as we saw that other reporting systems do not provide for this. One way is to conduct periodical anonymous trust-surveys, asking all employees how they evaluate their job and working environment. If answers are given in quantitative figures, the results can be compared between teams and as a function of time. When there are reasons for concerns, corrective actions can be taken. Another tool is exit interviews with staff leaving the university, identifying the reasons for leaving. Still another is the creation of the function of ombudsman, an independent professional, possibly a retired academic with management experience, to whom complaints can be addressed, anonymously if so desired. Many universities lack such feedback loops that are indispensable for keeping the system on track.

8. The know-how commercialisation function

8.1 THE MARKET OF KNOW-HOW COMMERCIALISATION

Before we can design the structure of the marketing department of the third generation university (3GU), we need to know which customer categories are being served. A university basically has three kinds of customers who can at the same time be its partners:

1. Large technology-based enterprises. In Chapter 4, we saw that many such enterprises, whether in traditional branches of industry or in information technology (IT) or life sciences, discontinued their pure scientific research while they still needed these activities to support their exploratory research. They are therefore interested in sharing pure scientific research with universities or farming them out altogether.[148] Large enterprises are much less interested in cooperation concerning product and process development as they can carry out these activities themselves better and faster.
2. Production firms. Companies that are not involved in fundamental change have no need for basic research and exploratory research or pure science. Their innovation efforts focus on product and process development while they may need applied research occasionally.
3. Young knowledge-based firms, either technostarters or young enterprises. Research is their *raison d'être*. They often stem from a pure science project and they need applied research as well as development activities. If they are successful and if they stay independent, they become large technology-based enterprises.

The needs of the university's clients and/or partners are depicted in Figure 8.1 (adapted from Figure 4.1).

Let us now look at the market from the perspective of the university. There are basically two ways of promulgating know-how (Figure 8.2):

- through existing enterprises;
- through the creation of new enterprises.

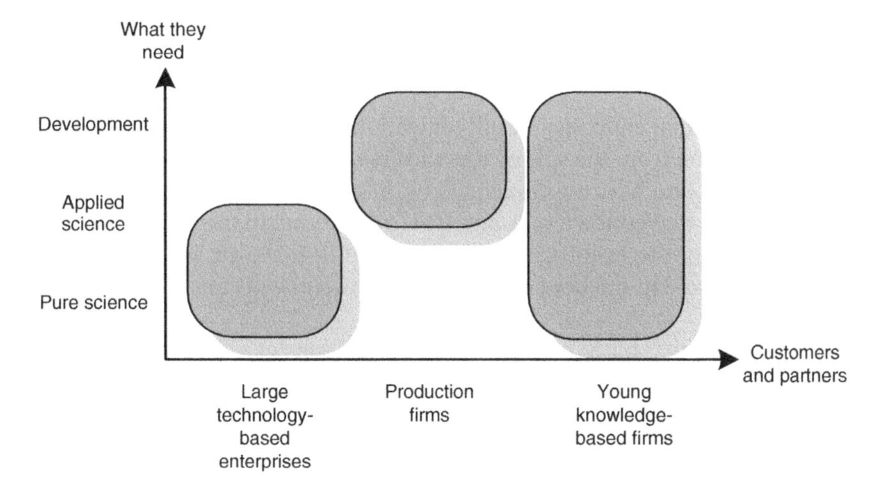

Figure 8.1 *The market: the university's customers or partners and their needs*

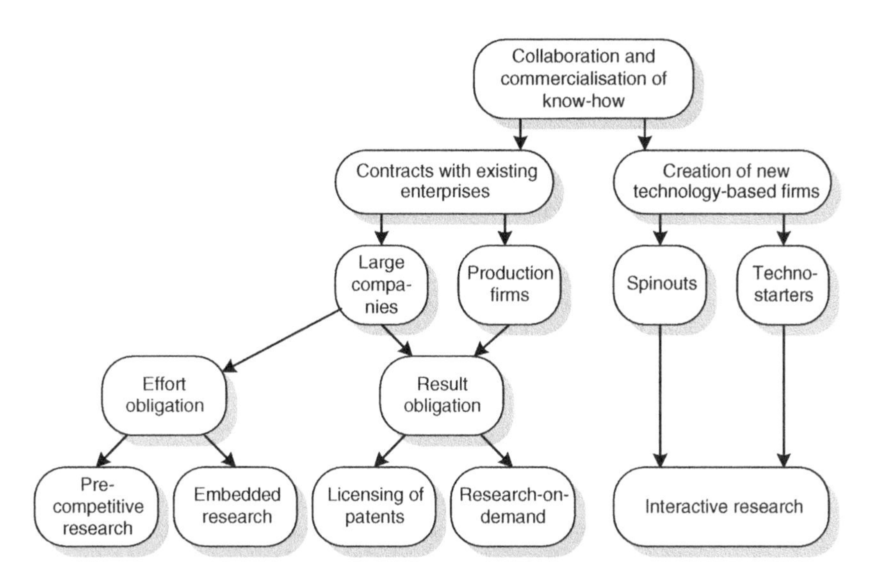

Figure 8.2 *Patterns of collaboration and sale from the university's point of view*

The collaboration or commercialisation with existing firms can take two basic forms:

- Projects that concern a 'result obligation', meaning there is a concrete obligation from the side of the university. The contracts are straightforward and have a well-defined output.
- Projects that concern only an 'effort obligation'. In this case, the exact nature of the result cannot be specified in advance; parties simply collaborate in the hope that something useful will emerge.

In each of the two basic forms, two concrete forms can be distinguished. The two forms in the category of result obligation are:

1. Research-on-demand. The objectives and terms of reference of the research are well defined. The client pays for the research, in full or in part, and concludes a contract with the university similar to a contract with an engineering consultant. The contract defines future ownership of the resulting know-how. Research-on-demand can be contracted by corporations, small and medium-sized enterprises (SMEs), consortia of companies, governments or government agencies, branch organisations, other research organisations and perhaps other clients. The university will usually only accept projects that serve a scientific interest. Research-on-demand usually has a development or applied nature and Master's students can give valuable inputs. The initiative for the cooperation can come from the client as well as from a university staff member.
2. Sale or licensing of patents. In this case, the research at the university has already been completed and a patent may have been awarded or applied for. With this know-how available, the university can try to find a buyer or user of the know-how. In most cases, it is advisable to grant a licence, meaning that the university is still the owner of the know-how and that it can licence the know-how to another party in case the licensee defaults on using it. The licence can have the form of a royalty to be paid every time the know-how is applied in a product or it can be a lump sum or annual fee. Large enterprises often wish to own the know-how, especially in cases in which a basic technology is concerned, as it gives them full control and the right to use it in as many applications it wishes, without having to renegotiate the contract each time with the university.

The two forms in the category of effort obligation are:

1. Pre-competitive research. This form of research is meant to develop basic technologies that will be turned into applications by the

sponsor(s) themselves. The client can be a single sponsor but more often the client is a group of companies and possibly other institutions, sometimes organised in a foundation. If there are several participating enterprises, they can still compete with the applications that are derived from the basic research and for this reason this collaboration is permitted by anti-trust law. A good example is the development of production technology for the manufacture of chips; companies can share this know-how and still compete in the design of the chips they bring to the market. The idea of pre-competitive research allows competitors to benefit from the savings in time and cost from the cooperation in the shared basic research. The subject of the research is decided by the sponsors and the university together. It can be carried out by PhD students and/or staff members. For the university it can be a rich source of publications – paid for externally. The initiative for this type of research often comes from a senior academic well known in the field of the particular science.

2. Embedded research as carried out at the University of Cambridge (section 2.1). In this case, researchers from the university and an enterprise are working together at the same location. This type of collaboration is usually between one sponsor and one university. The reason for enterprises to engage themselves in this kind of research is that they can stay in touch with cutting-edge technology. For universities it can again be a rich source of publications.

Collaboration in pure science and licensing of know-how are reserved for the happy few universities that comprise the Type 4 and Type 5 universities (see Figure 3.1) while research-on-demand can also be carried out by Types 2 and 3.

For the establishment of new enterprises there are, as we saw before, again two options:

1. Spinouts of scientific projects. In this case, the university or its subsidiary owns (part of) the know-how. Universities can adopt a systematic approach to identifying possible spinouts to avoid know-how that could have been commercialised being left to rot on the shelves. More effective than stocktaking is to stimulate researchers to create spinouts by giving them a fair share of the benefits. Spinouts can be the result of predefined initiative or they can be an unintended spin-off of research that was only meant to advance science. The university or its subsidiary is usually a shareholder, in full or in part. The researcher will often not be the chief executive officer (CEO) of the new enterprise although there are plenty of examples where they are and where they

are very successful. Some academics still argue that it is unethical to let commerce benefit from government-sponsored research. However, know-how that can be used should be used, and the best way to exploit it is using the market mechanism.
2. Technostarters who use their thesis project (or another project that may not even be linked to their university education) as the base of their enterprise and who own the know-how or who license it from the university. If the university does not own the intellectual property rights (IPR), there is no immediate financial benefit for the university from the value created by the technostarter. However, technostarters can engage later in contract research with the university or hire technical or other consulting services. In addition, technostarters who have become successful entrepreneurs may lavishly endow their alma mater at a later stage in life.

The cooperation between spinouts or technostarters (in their early stages) and the university concern neither a result obligation nor an effort obligation. It is often an informal, non-structured cooperation with Master's students having a placement in the firm and academics offering unpaid advice. For this cooperation, we have adopted the term 'interactive research'.

Naturally, Figure 8.2 is quite schematic and there are many mixed versions of research while small companies can also sponsor activities listed under large enterprises.

Contract research is catching on in European universities. In the UK, Imperial College made €65 million in 2003–04, just ahead of Birmingham University and Leeds University. Imperial College had 53 spinouts in that period, putting it ahead of Manchester University (48) and Oxford University (45). Newcastle University has the highest number of staff employed to engage with commercial partners (134), followed by Staffordshire University (110) and Oxford (96). These data from the Higher Education Funding Council for England can be compared with US data from the Licensing Survey of the Association of University Technology Managers. These data show that US institutions created one spin-off for every €90 million of research expenditure with about €35 million per spin-off in the UK. However, US institutions generated a licence income of 3 per cent of their research expenditure against UK institutions' 1.1 per cent. Apparently, US institutions are better in exploiting intellectual property while UK institutions are better at creating start-ups.[149]

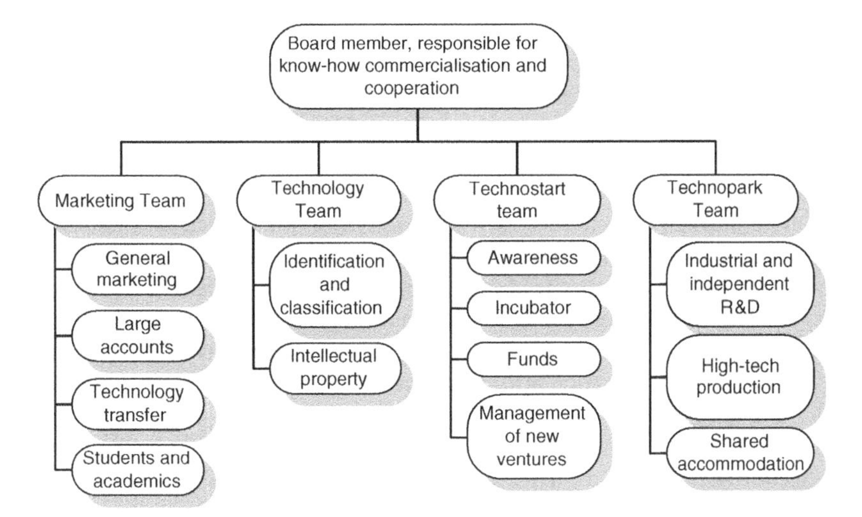

Figure 8.3 Organisation of the commercialisation of and cooperation in research

8.2 ORGANISING COOPERATION AND COMMERCIALISATION OF KNOW-HOW

In section 7.2, we introduced the board member responsible for cooperation and know-how commercialisation. This board member has four tasks, for each of which he or she can be supported by a team (Figure 8.3).

Firstly, there is a Marketing Team with four activities:

1. General marketing activities such as the website, the distribution of brochures and journals, organisation of events where the university presents itself, hosting guests, and all other activities that will identify and inform possible partners and clients and/or strengthen contacts with them and put them in touch with the academics concerned.
2. Activities concerning large accounts. This means assisting university institutes and faculties with:
   a. identifying and targeting potentially large clients (industrial, governmental, other research institutions), and maintaining relationships with them;
   b. the drafting, closing and administration of framework contracts with large clients, either research-on-demand or pre-competitive research;
   c. attracting corporate and independent R&D organisations to use facilities in the university's technopark (see below).

3. Technology transfer activities for production companies, the place where smaller companies or other clients can contact the university with questions, requests for student assignments, requests for research and suggestions for other cooperation. The technology transfer team should have good and up-to-date knowledge of what the university has to offer and where it can be found.
4. The marketing activities of a university are not limited to customers and partners in creating and commercialisation of know-how and the university also competes for the best students and academics. Hence, the Marketing Team may assist university institutes in bringing their courses and vacancies to the attention of those concerned, by website, advertisement, participation in events where students meet universities and so on.

Secondly, there may be a Technology Team which assists university institutes and faculties with:

1. The identification of all know-how in the university and its classification into three categories:
   a. suitable for licensing or sale;
   b. suitable as a subject for a new venture;
   c. not suitable for commercialisation.
2. Matters regarding intellectual property. The team advises on how to protect know-how by patents or otherwise, and may apply for patents on behalf of the institute or faculty and administer them when granted.

Thirdly, the Technostart Team is responsible for activities related to new ventures. Together with the institutes or faculties, it will run awareness programmes and the incubator and, if there is no logical place in the institutes or faculties to coordinate education in entrepreneurship, it can also perform this task. The Technostart Team can act as the shareholder for spinouts. The Technostart Team will be discussed in section 8.3.

Finally, the Technopark Team will be responsible for the real estate management of:

1. land and/or housing on the grounds of the university that are leased to the partners of the know-how carousel;
2. shared accommodation facilities (housing and services) for young ventures that have outgrown the incubator.

Real estate management is comprised of the procurement, maintenance and administration of land and buildings. We use the term 'Technopark'

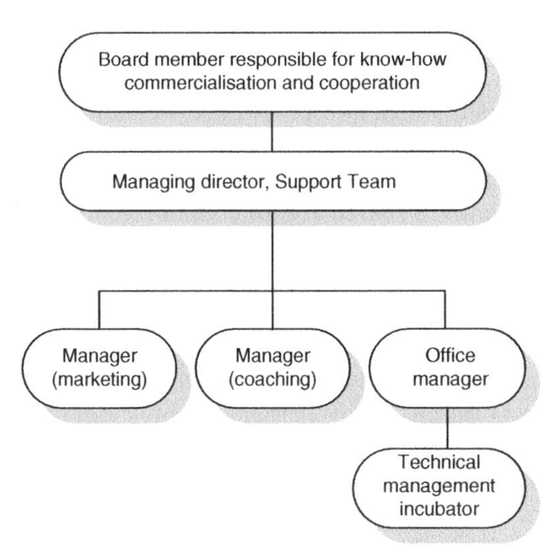

Figure 8.4 Support Team for technostarters

for the area, preferably on the university's land or otherwise close to it, where partners of the know-how carousel and young ventures can lease facilities or build their own premises.

For many universities a structure like the one shown in Figure 8.3 is too elaborate, especially when activities concerning technostarters are just beginning. Such universities can start with a simple structure as depicted in Figure 8.4. Here the team consists of only four staff members. When the tasks are expanding, a university may migrate its support from the structure of Figure 8.4 to that of Figure 8.3.

A good example of an effective organisation can be found at the Catholic University of Leuven (K.U.Leuven) in Belgium,[150] set up with ample funds from the regional government. In 1972, this university established K.U.Leuven Research and Development (KUL R&D), as an organisation responsible for the commercialisation of the university's know-how, either by licensing or by establishing new ventures. It owns and manages the property rights. With KBC and Fortis, two commercial banks, it has set up the two Gemma Frisius investment funds of €12.5 million each (the banks hold 40 per cent each in these funds and the university 20 per cent) as the business angel; the venture capital structure was far less developed in Leuven than it was in Cambridge. The position of KUL R&D is stronger than that of Cambridge Enterprise as Leuven always and fully owns the university's IPR.[151] KUL R&D supports itself by retaining 8.5 per cent of revenues. The university gets another 8.5 per cent and the rest is shared by the department and individual researchers who can receive up to 50 per cent of revenues.

K.U.Leuven has incorporated 'service to the community' as its third objective. It has set up various science parks such as the Haasrode Science Park, a 120-hectare site which houses several dozen university spin-offs and international high-tech firms that together employ some 5000 people. Haasrode includes a business incubator with office space for 70 companies and the Business Centre, a shared accommodation centre which houses not only IT companies, but also multimedia, communication and industrial coating firms, human resource bureaus, import–export firms, a print shop and a translation bureau. The Arenberg Science Park offers 90 000 m^2 of working space and the Termunck Science Park 120 000 m^2 and 35 hectares of land. Two more centres are being prepared in former company offices, the Ubicenter and Campus Remy. Perhaps the most impressive creation of K.U.Leuven is IMEC (Interuniversity MicroElectronics Centre) which claims to be Europe's leading independent research centre in the field of microelectronics, nanotechnology, enabling design methods and technologies for information and communication technology (ICT) systems. Founded in 1984 by the legendary professor R. van Overstraeten, it carries out pre-competitive research with virtually all the world's major ICT corporations that can also use the facilities for their own research. IMEC's research budget was €230 million in 2006 with €35 million coming from government grants and the remainder from industries such as Intel, Samsung, Philips, ASML and ASMI. These companies expect the research component of the cost price of electronic devices to go up to 40 per cent of revenue in 2020. In addition, the semiconductor industry is going through a transition phase, incorporating nanotechnology and transdisciplinary research. These factors make collaboration more a necessity than a desirability and this explains the interest of these enterprises. IMEC offers many services. In addition to the facilities mentioned it gives many courses and seminars; its population is highly international. Finally, K.U.Leuven operates a number of high-tech networks, including DSP Valley (DSP stands for digital signal processing), the Leuven Security Excellence Consortium and others. For ambitious students it is paradise.

Agriculture and food processing are rapidly becoming high-tech industries, and agricultural universities are organising themselves to bring knowledge to market.[152] The Netherlands is the world's third-largest exporter of agricultural produce (€20 billion annually) with 10 per cent of the country's gross national product (GNP) being generated by the agri-food industry and with 4.5 per cent of the country's population active in this area. This achievement in a small and highly industrialised country with inclement weather owes an awful lot to systematic technological developments, with the Agricultural University as the driving force together with a number of specialised institutes of applied agricultural and food processing research. These centres have been merged with the university to create Wageningen University and Research Centre (WURC). WURC has become the powerful centre of what is popularly known as Wageningen Food Valley. It includes corporate and independent research centres (Unilever, DSM, Keygene, Heinz, Nestlé, Givaudan, Campina, Seminis Vegetable Seeds, Noldus IT, TNO Process Innovation and many others), educational institutes, institutes for industrial genomics such as Nutrigenomics, institutes such as the Institute for Food Safety and the Dutch Plant Protection Agency, incubators (biotech start-ups include Genetwister, Catchmabs, Checkpoints, Plant Dynamics, Porifarma and many others), science parks, innovation clusters, a conference centre and all kinds of networking activities, geared towards life sciences, food, health, nutrition and agriculture. It has the Food Valley Innovation Link, the transfer bureau for SMEs, a link with China, Food Valley Society (a club of 45 enterprises in the area), and many other facilities. In short, one can see the know-how carousel in operation outside the traditional high-tech fields of electronics and information technology.

An alternative to the activities carried out or stimulated by the university itself is to rely on private initiatives that work closely with the university. Alumni and/or university spinouts can take initiatives to start an investment fund or organise business plan competitions as an educational as well as a selection tool. The advantage of a private initiative is that it is faster and more flexible than university efforts as enterprise is quite unfamiliar to most universities. In the absence of private initiatives, the university has to take its own future in hand. The most successful cases (for example Massachusetts Institute of Technology – MIT, Stanford, Cambridge) are a combination of private and university initiatives. In each case, government support is needed and governments should not be reluctant to be lavish with financial support since a know-how carousel that creates new enterprises is the best possible investment in high-quality employment. This applies to highly industrialised countries that see traditional industrial manufacturing moving out to low-wage countries as well as to developing countries that want to make a balanced entry into the world's markets.

A final note on the marketing of research. Like other professional services, research can only be sold by the professionals and researchers themselves, although they can be assisted by professional marketers and legal and other specialists. Herein lies the bottleneck of the commercialisation of know-how: the professionals often have neither the interest nor the qualities to pursue commercial opportunities; they prefer to do their professional work. Since they usually have no experience with know-how contracts – and since they are mostly not interested in the details – the support of marketing experts is essential.[153] It is strange therefore that few universities can claim to have a marketing support team, although some European universities have a common bureau in Brussels to lobby for EU research projects.

8.3 THE TECHNOSTART TEAM IN DETAIL

We will now discuss the tasks of the Technostart Team of Figure 8.3 and postulate that a good supply of four kinds of 'raw materials' (Figure 8.5) is required in order to create a successful 'factory' for new technology-based firms (NTBFs), whether student-initiated (technostarters) or university-initiated (spinout).[154]

In order to succeed, all flows need to be present. If any of the four flows is lacking, the 'factory' will not work, however well the other flows have been organised. The winners are the ones who have it all.

We will now discuss the four flows in more detail.

The Flow of Technology

To get the flow of technology going, universities can adopt four instruments:

- A financial incentive structure for the individual researcher who is the source of a spinout. If there is no financial or status reward, then there is no incentive to compensate for the hassle inevitably involved in transferring know-how to a spinout.
- Awareness programmes for academics and students, aimed at developing an instinct for spotting commercialisation options for their research.

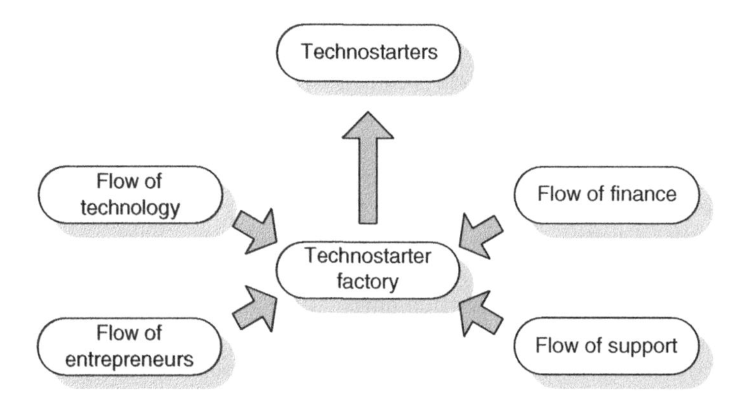

Figure 8.5 The four flows of 'raw materials'

- Support to faculties and institutes.
- Stocktaking and acting on know-how that can be commercialised.

The Flow of Entrepreneurs

Only a few students enter a university with the explicit aim of finding a subject to study with which they can start their own enterprise. The same applies to academics. Awareness programmes followed by educational activities should get the flow of entrepreneurs going. We will discuss details in Appendix 2.

The Flow of Finance

As we saw in Chapter 6, informal investors are crucial to university start-ups and technostarters. But the problem is that, at least outside the US and the UK, the concept of informal investing is only just beginning to develop, and the market between informal investors and starters is still emerging. Universities cannot wait for an informal investment culture to develop. Therefore, they have to develop other means of financing start-ups – for the benefit of university spinouts as well as for technostarters. The three most common financial support schemes are:

1. A university investment fund, like the Gemma Frisius Fund at K.U.Leuven. Such a fund will come with a management company as described in Chapter 6.
2. Matchmaking sessions where start-ups can present their business plans to an audience of investors who will 'roast' them with critical questions. Such sessions can be attractive for informal investors. The university should carefully select the serious and professional informal investors, who are really going to put in some effort and not just money. Such investors can be registered by what can be called the Platform, a body that organises matchmaking sessions and that also carries out a pre-selection of start-ups that are permitted to present their business plans.
3. A fund that provides deferred loans with favourable conditions for start-ups. The capital for such funds is provided by state grants or grants from endowments or other university resources.

The Flow of Support

Last but not least, the flow of support. This is delivered in five ways:

1. working space, offices or development places, usually referred to as incubator facilities;

2. professional support;
3. coaching;
4. technical support;
5. publicity.

Incubator Facilities

There are as many definitions of incubators as there are incubators.[155] Expressions like 'incubator-plus' and 'accelerator' are used for basic incubators with enhanced services. We would like to define a basic incubator as a work space with facilities such as broadband that can be rented by start-ups and technostarters on favourable terms. The residence time for start-ups can be limited and sometimes rents increase annually to create an up-or-out system. An important side-effect of incubators is that the tenants can exchange experiences and benefit from each other's advice; this is often as valuable as the advice given by professionals.

Professional Support

University start-ups and technostarters, like all entrepreneurs, need specialised advice on topics such as marketing and market research, intellectual property rights, finance, administration and reporting, quality management, logistics, procurement and so on. During the early phases of the enterprise, the founders will have problems in paying for these services and they should have the opportunity to get them free of charge, at least during the initial stages. In Delft, a group of alumni created the Foundation Network Young Entrepreneurs Delft, in which professional auditing, marketing, management consultancy and intellectual property rights (IPR) bureaus and a bank participate. The foundation gives the course 'Writing a Business Plan' (Appendix 2, section A2.3, pp. 201–3) and offers free advice during the early stages of an enterprise. The interest of its partners in doing this is a mixture of positive publicity, access to potential new clients, training for their young experts, keeping in touch with high technology, and just plain fun. The foundation has helped to create about 30 enterprises in the period 1981–2006.

Coaching

In addition to the specialist support discussed above, start-ups can greatly benefit from coaching by experienced entrepreneurs. As Luke Johnson writes in a recent column: 'Entrepreneurs often have low boredom thresholds and are weak in day-to-day micromanagement that every business needs . . . The wise founder hires a detail person, someone who enjoys process and paper work'.[156]

We would add that those entrepreneurs who do hire such persons often make their lives difficult. This is just an example of how entrepreneurs can benefit from good coaching, especially from those who have been there before. Coaching however is one of those activities that most people think they can do without any training, but good coaching is a profession in itself. We therefore suggest that coaches are selected, even if they are not paid. Coaches should be willing to invest time in their development as coach.

Technical Support

Technostarters often use their thesis (MSc or PhD) as the technical foundation for their enterprise. As this is part of their course, the technical support and supervision are included and free of charge. Many academics like to continue supporting technostarters on a personal basis after they have left the university.

Publicity

Positive publicity stimulates all of the four flows of the technostart 'factory', as nothing breeds success as much as success itself. Publicity about successful technostarters can help create role models. It can also stimulate endowments.

9. Implementation and assessment of 3GU

9.1 CHANGE MANAGEMENT

Universities that want to migrate from a second generation university (2GU) to a third generation university (3GU) face an uphill battle. The 3GU comprises a number of characteristics that are contrary to the very idea of a 2GU, and members of the academic community will have to be convinced that the values held for so many generations have to be modulated and supplemented. Unless the university's leadership adopts a carefully balanced plan for the migration, efforts to bring about change might lead only to frustration and confusion, making things worse rather than better. Change management is a profession by itself. Before moving to the specific 2GU–3GU migration, we will therefore first offer some general experiences.

Few things are as difficult as good change management, a critical attribute for the successful implementation of the 3GU. Mark Twain is quoted as saying: 'I am all for progress but it is change I don't like', and Lord Palmerston supposedly answered Queen Victoria when she suggested some change: 'Change, madam, change? But aren't things bad enough already?' With their long histories and deeply embedded traditions, these attitudes characterise many academics.

Or do they? The common misconception is that the 'lower down' one looks into an organisation, the more rigid people's attitudes are. In earlier research in a number of companies, we tried to discover the extent to which this notion corresponds to reality (this section is based on two corresponding publications).[157] The conclusion is that change is an emotional issue: 'People are willing to change; they just don't want to be changed'. The extent to which people are willing to change depends very much on the management of change. The research showed that three types of employees can be distinguished, those who have:

- Inclination to change, meaning an active, anticipatory and self-adjusting attitude. Inclination to change can be defined as the perceptible endeavour to be constantly examining one's own perfor-

mance and that of one's department and adapting it to meet the demands emanating from the dynamics of the company's 'environment' or from changed ambitions of the organisation. People in this category do not need to be motivated to change; they are motivated already and the management challenge is to prevent their energies from being diverted and to align them with the objectives of the change process. The group of people with an inclination to change is usually small, say 10–20 per cent in a population.
- Willingness to change, meaning a perceivable willingness to go along with the changes that arise from the demands made on the organisation by the dynamics of the 'environment' or by changed ambitions. This term is related to passive willingness; not objecting but being prepared to do something if someone else takes the initiative. People who are willing to change form the majority in a population, say 60–80 per cent. Their attitude can be summed up as: 'I did not invent this change idea, but I am a reasonable person and if you have reasonable arguments I will listen and eventually go along with it, even if I have to make sacrifices.'
- Incapability to change, a fundamental attitude against any changes or even a desire to return to the times of the 'fathers'. No matter how many good reasons for change are given or how many guarantees against personal setbacks, the worker or manager will resist or sabotage the changes. This group is again a minority, say 10–20 per cent of the population.

If a change process is badly managed, people that are incapable of change can influence the 'willingness to change' group, meaning that a majority will be against the changes that are then most likely to fail. On the other hand, if the process is well managed, the influence of the group with an incapability to change will have little influence.

Organisations incorporate an enormous amount of inclination to change and willingness to change. Employees' willingness to change is as great as the extent to which they are motivated. A common management omission is that the reservoir of inclination to change is not exploited as much as it could be. Good ideas are not voiced because there are no facilities for hearing them and because no one asks for them. People with ideas are regarded as troublesome, as 'a kind of background noise disturbing the normal course of business'.

Successful change management depends on three factors:

- the extent to which there is a high so-called potential for change in the initial situation;

Table 9.1 Potential for change at the initial situation

The potential for change is:	
Low	High
• no confidence in management	• there is a great deal of confidence in management
• poor internal communications	• good internal communications
• no clear, or badly communicated, objectives and strategies	• clear, well-communicated objectives and strategies
• defensive strategy	• offensive strategies
• weak corporate culture, non-homogeneous culture or various cultures	• strong unified corporate culture, people are proud of their company
• company has a weak or poor image	• company has a good image
• nebulous or complicated organisational structure	• comprehensible organisational structure
• the organisation is part of a larger entity and dependent on others for its decision-making	• organisation is independent or decentralised
• the organisation has a successful past	• young and dynamic organisation
• operating results are average	• operating results are excellent or very poor

- the extent to which the characteristics of 'good' change management are applied;
- the selection of a change strategy that is fit for the specific situation.

The potential for change is a characteristic of the initial situation. Its elements are summarised in Table 9.1. If the potential for change is low, it might be wise to spend time to increase it by removing bottlenecks and solving issues that have probably been in the background for some time, resulting in negative attitudes though not harming the operational activities to a serious extent. Such an apparent peace rapidly vanishes when a change process starts and the elements of a low potential for change start to bite. As management may not be aware of the unresolved issues and therefore of a low potential for change, it is recommended to carry out a measurement that can give an indication of the potential for change and improve it if necessary.

The characteristics of good change management (Box 9.1) have much to do with motivation. Motivation in turn stems from objectives and communication. If people believe in the purposes of the change, they are willing to go to great lengths to make the change work, even to sacrifice some of their personal interests.

BOX 9.1 CHARACTERISTICS OF A 'GOOD' CHANGE MANAGEMENT APPROACH

- things are 'put out to air' in advance, so a decision does not arrive like a bolt from the blue
- the purpose of the change is completely clear, meaning not vague, inadequately explained or 'overpacked'
- there are provisions for participation and adjustment, especially where individual matters are concerned
- there is a genuine intent to communicate and excellent tools for communication
- changes are implemented in their entirety with 100% feedback to all concerned
- people are given enough leeway to give the changes some measure of personal interpretation. Management must then indicate some kind of framework

Features of poor change management are roughly the opposite.

Ambitious targets, such as the realisation of a competitive know-how hub or 3GU, release much positive energy. Such ideas are easily carried by those with an inclination to change and they will be supported by those with a willingness to change, provided there is good communication. This communication should take place before as well as during the change process. The ideal communication process prior to a major change is to prepare a strategic plan in which large numbers of employees participate. Managers can look down on such procedures ('We know the outcome already') but, as Mao said: 'The plan is nothing, the planning is everything.' A well-led strategic planning process often results in involvement and commitment of the participants to act towards the realisation of targets and the change process then is much easier than in situations in which such a common understanding is lacking.

For the choice of change strategy, one should first analyse the objectives of the change process. These objectives can be defensive or offensive. A defensive objective occurs when the organisation is out of balance with its environment; there is a strategic gap to be closed. If the need to close this gap is ignored, the situation will move from bad to worse. Closing the gap is a defensive change strategy because, when completed, the organisation has merely caught up with the competition; it has not obtained a competitive advantage. When management – often new management – comes to the conclusion that although things are going well, they could be going much better, ambitious targets can be set and for the realisation of this strategic stretch an offensive change strategy is to be selected. The organisation seeks to obtain a competitive advantage in terms of a new business model, new technology, new marketing methods, better organisation, and better motivation of personnel and so on.[158]

A typical example of an offensive change strategy is the step-by-step approach (Box 9.2). The change process is split up into a number of steps or working phases, going from the general to the specific. Each working phase is followed by a communication phase with a predetermined and unalterable time horizon. After the communication phase, the management takes a non-reversible decision concerning only the contents of that phase. This decision kicks off the next working phase, and so on. There are usually three phases: the first to define the strategy, objectives and business model, as well as the main lines of the organisational structure and the desired culture. The second phase concerns the detailed organisational structure, designed by project teams of employees for each organisational unit. The third phase is the design of support structures and the assignment of the jobs in the new organisation to the employees.

BOX 9.2 CHARACTERISTICS OF THE STEP-BY-STEP CHANGE STRATEGY

- thorough preparation of the process, with a clear timetable with fixed dates for the completion of the respective phases
- the change process is split up in phases
- after each work phase, intervals are planned to accommodate for communication, decision making and preparation for the next phase. This way, the next step is taken when the previous one has been completed and 'digested'
- the work/design during each phase is carried out by managers who will be responsible for the situation after the change
- these managers are appointed at the start of the next phase, the higher managers after phase 1, the others at later phases
- the detailed preparation for the next phase starts when the previous one is finished
- the actual change takes place when the last phase is completed, i.e. during the change process the old situation is still prevalent

Universities that move from the 2GU to the 3GU model need to apply an offensive change strategy. Since there is no immediate threat to the survival of the university, the need for change may be difficult to communicate, especially in a conservative environment. The step-by-step approach involves many managers and academics in the phase of analysis and major decisions, while they get much freedom in designing the detailed structure and working parameters as far as their own faculty or department is concerned. The use of the step-by-step approach will take time, often one year or more. This apparently slow progress has a high score of success. Time is needed if many people are to be involved and committed. The strategy has the advantage that the community can get used to the new situation while on the go. When the process is finished and the university changes to the new model, there is no need to train people to work in their new functions as they have participated in the design of these functions themselves. All this makes the step-by-step method a powerful tool for changing universities into the 3GU model. We will therefore elaborate on it in terms that are more specific for the university transfer towards the 3GU model.

9.2 INTERVENTION MODEL

If we are to use the step-by-step approach, we first have to identify the actors in order to build an intervention model. The university actors in the transition process towards a 3GU can be listed as follows:

- Board of management and the university as a whole, including the faculties as suppliers of know-how and the university community as a whole as carriers of the transition process.
- Educational centres for education in entrepreneurship, for instance in the Faculty of Management.
- The teams of Figure 8.3 that support the commercialisation activities of the university, including the Technostart Team.

This leads to three levels of intervention (Figure 9.1) that we will call board, education and support.

Step 0

First of all, the board and other major leaders of the university such as the deans and the secretary have to be committed to the necessity to change and the direction it should take. To this end, the change process starts with a general presentation of 3GU concepts and their background for this group.

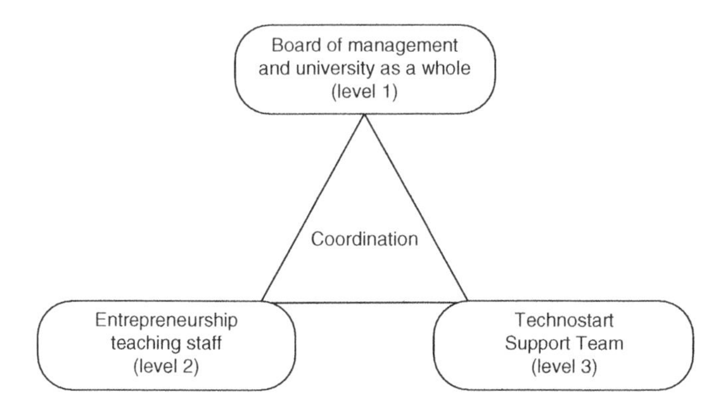

Figure 9.1 Intervention model

Once the leaders are committed to the realisation of the 3GU concept and the road the university should follow, the real work can begin. We call this preliminary phase of 'decision-making on principle issues' Step 0. It is essential that all major players in the university subscribe to the two basic notions – 1) 3GU as the end result and 2) the choice of an organic change process – as differences in opinion will be exploited by those opposed to the change once the process is under way. The board and the major leaders must stick together; to this end and for supervising the process, they create the Steering Group of the change process. During Step 0, the Steering Group produces a short document ('Basic Report') outlining:

1. the reasons that make change inevitable or desirable;
2. the basic concepts of the 3GU, 'translated' to the university's own situation;
3. the stages and timing of the change process.

Step 1

In this step, there is groundbreaking work to do for the board of management and the Steering Group; as there are not yet functionaries for the change process on the levels of education and support, there is no work yet at these intervention levels. First, the Basic Report is presented to all members of the university – staff and students, academic and non-academic – and to other major stakeholders. The report is to be presented by the president or rector as the population has to hear it from 'the horse's mouth' in order to consider it trustworthy. The Steering Group can then set up working teams (members from across the faculties and departments, and including students) to design solutions to various issues covered in the Basic Report. These teams can organise 'hearings' in which anyone can participate. After a pre-set and unalterable point in time, the teams report back to the Steering Group which then decides upon the final text of the 'Phase 1 Report'. After this, the board appoints:

- the professor of entrepreneurship;
- the board member responsible for the commercialisation of know-how and collaboration with industry (hereafter C&C; see Section 7.2);
- the four managers to assist this board member, that is (Figure 8.3) the managers of:
  - the Marketing Team;
  - the Technology Team;
  - the Technostart Team;
  - the Technopark Team.

Step 1 ends with a festive presentation of the final Phase 1 Report and the installation of the working groups of Step 2 which start the next cycle of work–communication–decision-making.

Step 2

To start off, the Steering Group installs six working groups, headed by the board member for C&C (intervention level 1), the professor of entrepreneurship (intervention level 2) and the four managers (intervention level 3). Their tasks are as follows:

1. The group of the board member for C&C will include the other board members. They will prepare a strategic plan, resulting among others in the establishment of an innovation fund from which the necessary changes will be financed. Following the completion of the plan, the board can adopt the commercialisation of know-how and collaboration with industry as the third university objective. The board at this stage can initiate the creation of the first university institutes, or promote cross-faculty teams to this status. The role of the institutes in giving Master's Courses and in awarding doctoral degrees should be formalised.
2. The working group of the professor of entrepreneurship can design the university-wide programme of education in entrepreneurship, followed by the detailed design of essential courses. At the same time, this team, together with the Technostart Team, can start organising awareness programmes in entrepreneurship for students.

3. The working group of the marketing manager can start modernising and adapting the website, and start other marketing activities, while they can start approaching large accounts in order to identify their interest in collaboration. The group should check addresses of alumni and prepare a good database.
4. The working group of the technology manager can prepare a proposal for the intellectual property rights (IPR) policy of the university that specifies which parties will receive which remuneration in the event of successful sales of know-how or the creation of new firms. In addition, the group can identify the chairs or sections of the university that are most likely to create possibilities for know-how commercialisation, whether through licensing or new start-ups.
5. The working group of the technostart manager can start creating incubator facilities. It is attractive to have an 'entrepreneurship building' including an incubator as the 'face' of the 3GU. Preferably, the entrepreneurship building has a lecture room where lectures in entrepreneurship and awareness sessions can be given, and where office space for network partners is available. Eventually, this building should comprise displays of successful alumni-entrepreneurs who can act as role models for students. At the same time, the group can start approaching financiers and ask selected financiers to participate in lectures.
6. The working group of the technopark manager can start preparing or acquiring land and buildings for the technopark and the shared accommodation. Although the users for these facilities are yet to be attracted, procedures to acquire land and buildings are often laborious and they should start at this stage in order to be ready in time.

Step 2 can end in a market-type presentation to the university's community of the results and the further plans of the working groups in order to inform and invite reactions. During Step 2 it is advisable to keep the community informed, for instance by publishing special editions of the university's periodicals devoted to the change process, and by organising events. After the board has studied all reactions, it decides on the final results of Step 2.

Step 3

In this step, the six functionaries appointed at Step 1 can assume their regular tasks as described in section 8.2, while the board can move towards the final stages of the 3GU:

- converting all lectures into English;
- creating funds for foreign students;

- creating special facilities for the top stream of students (the two-track university);
- creating a Design Faculty;
- increasing the number of university institutes until most or all research activities take place in these institutes, as well as most or all Master's courses and PhD projects;
- with a group of other universities, a process of gaining political clout aimed at the loosening up of relations with government departments can be started.

During Step 3, all parties should extend and solidify the respective networks of the university (see next section).

In practice, a change process will differ from the process outlined above, if only because the initial situation is different. In any case, it is good to have a systematic plan[159] and to report regularly on progress made, as not all members of the university community or the know-how carousel will be aware of what is going on, and it is vital to keep their support.

9.3 ASSESSING PROGRESS: THE TRIPLE SIX MODEL

In this section we will propose the so-called Triple Six Model as a tool for evaluating the university's progress on its way to becoming a 3GU. The model is based on the observation that there are three categories of factors that characterise a university's progress on the way to becoming a 3GU (Figure 9.2). These factors strongly influence each other.

The first category comprises the intrinsic quality factors: the values, attitudes and assets that are essential to a 3GU. Such factors cannot be changed overnight. The second category includes specific instruments for know-how commercialisation and technostarters as discussed in Chapter 8. Such instruments can be procured at a much faster rate than the intrinsic

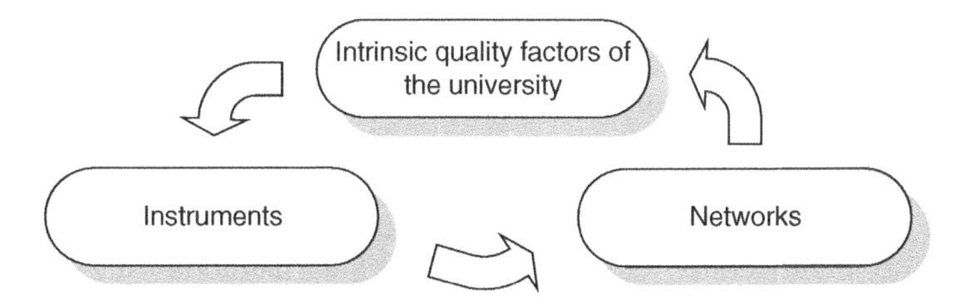

Figure 9.2 Categories of factors comprising the 3GU

factors can change. Finally, a 3GU is a network university, and the quality of its internal communication and its contacts with external parties to a large extent define its effectiveness. Networks take time to build, the time constant lying somewhere between those of the intrinsic factors and the instruments. Each of the three categories is made up of six factors, hence the name Triple Six Model. We will now proceed to discuss them in some detail.

Intrinsic Quality Factors

A university is made up of staff (academic, management and support staff) and students, led by vision and strategy, held together by organisational structure and culture, and endowed with land, buildings and funds. Tradition directs these factors to the Humboldt university model, with its emphasis on research and scientific education. Such factors cannot be changed easily, even if the will is there. For this reason, we call them intrinsic quality factors.

The first intrinsic quality factor concerns the intrinsic values of the university: its vision, mission and philosophy. For a 3GU, the vision should clearly outline the ambition of the university to become a (global) know-how carousel and state that cooperation with external partners (corporations, start-ups, other research and development institutions, professional service firms and others) is seen as essential to the excellence of the university's standing. The mission should state that the three objectives – research, education and commercialisation of know-how – are of equal significance. By the 'philosophy' of the university we mean the business model, especially the question of how the university sees itself in relation to external partners. This is where the concept of the know-how carousel comes in as well as a statement of how the university plans to commercialise its know-how: new ventures, licensing or sale of know-how. It is easy to put these thoughts on paper; it is much more difficult to bring them alive and have them accepted by the university's community and stakeholders. When evaluating the extent to which the university satisfies the 3GU vision, mission and philosophy, one should not only take the text into account, but most of all the degree to which the ethos is alive and seen as a guiding line for the entire university community.

The second intrinsic quality factor is the extent to which there is an innovative and entrepreneurial structure and culture. A statement that the university strives for innovation is meaningless if the financial structure favours existing lectures and traditional teaching methods. New courses and teaching methods require considerable time investments; unless there is a compensation for the efforts required, faculty will naturally focus on improving existing courses. The organisational structure scores low when faculties are the main organisational element. The score is higher when university institutes report directly to the board (and have their own personnel and profit and loss accounts) and when the services are transferred to a common service unit or shared service centre. If there is a free market in which such centres have to compete with external suppliers, the score is even higher. An element of this intrinsic factor is the composition of the board of management, especially whether there is a board member solely responsible for cooperation and commercialisation of know-how (see section 7.2). The organisation and staffing of the functions of this board member (Figure 8.3) is an equally essential element. The extent to which the culture (values and attitudes of staff and students) is innovative and entrepreneurial is more difficult to measure. Ideally, the university should regularly conduct enquiries into the attitudes of all its personnel. If there are no means to conduct such enquiries, one can measure by taking samples. Organisational culture is very much driven by organisational and financial structure. The idea that culture is a rather fixed element that can only be changed by great efforts and over long periods of time is to a large extent untrue. If the financial award system is changed, culture change will follow rapidly.

The third intrinsic quality factor concerns the attitudes of the student population. Which students does the university want to attract? The marketing of the university as exemplified by its website, printed materials, advertisements and other means should address the type of students the university prefers. If the university has entrance exams, these exams should not only measure intellectual capabilities but they should also include questions concerning the attitudes, values and goals of the candidates. Many business schools assess incoming students by individual tests, group discussions, sports events and referee assessment (by alumni), the idea being that the quality of student output is determined as much by the quality of their input as by the quality of their education.

Factor four concerns the quality of staff and the way staff are selected and promoted. All too often, only intellectual characteristics and previous research results are challenged, vide the advertisements in journals for vacancies. Teaching abilities are notoriously absent in such advertisements (and in the subsequent selection procedures) and we have not yet come across an advertisement in which innovative, entrepreneurial or commercial qualities are demanded. Yet staff members of a 3GU should have such qualities in similar amounts to their intellectual qualities and their ability to successfully carry out research. In short, the fourth factor should measure the integral qualities of the academic staff (or at least, all qualities should be present in the total workforce; it is neither necessary nor possible

BOX 9.3 INTRINSIC QUALITY FACTORS

1. Vision, mission and philosophy
2. Organisational and financial structure and culture
3. Attitudes, quality of student population and selection tools
4. Same for academic staff and promotion systems
5. Availability of land and buildings
6. Availability of innovation fund

that every staff member possesses all qualities) as well as the marketing, selection and promotion systems.

If a university has the advantage of owning large areas of land and a large number of buildings, it can more easily set up incubator, shared accommodation and technopark facilities than if these facilities are scarce. In this context, campus universities have a distinct advantage over city universities which are often spread out in different buildings over sometimes large distances.

Finally, and in line with the statements above, the presence of a fund for new activities, say, the university's innovation fund, is a valuable asset. Such a fund can finance new courses, innovation in education, new areas of research and technopark facilities. As it will take considerable time to collect the means for such a fund – for instance from contributions from industry or endowments – we have listed it as an intrinsic factor.

Box 9.3 summarises the intrinsic quality factors discussed above.

Specific Instruments

The second category of key success factors for entrepreneurship and technostart are instruments specifically designed to foster entrepreneurial activities, whether top-down (university start-ups) or bottom-up (student and academic technostarters). The range of instruments follows the four-flow model as outlined in section 8.3 with research into entrepreneurship to be added. The instruments are summarised in Box 9.4.

Networks

We stated earlier that the 3GU is typically a network university. This means that the collaboration with outside partners is far more penetrating than the cooperation and communication with other universities and industry in the second generation model. The kinds of partners – and hence networks – are summarised in Box 9.5.

BOX 9.4 SPECIFIC INSTRUMENTS FOR ENTREPRENEURSHIP

1. Awareness programmes and publicity
2. Educational programme on entrepreneurship
3. Incubator facilities
4. Shared accommodation facilities and technopark
5. Financial infrastructure
6. Research on technostart and entrepreneurship

BOX 9.5 NETWORKS

1. Coaches
2. Informal investors and other financiers
3. Professional service firms
4. Corporations and independent R&D organisations
5. Intra-university networks (networks within the university)
6. Inter-university networks (networks with other universities)

The roles of coaches and informal investors and other financiers have been highlighted in Chapters 6 and 8. Professional service firms such as auditors, management, marketing and IPR consultants are the lubricating oils that enable the machinery work (section 8.3).

Making the university part of an international know-how carousel increases its competitive position. Institutes of applied science and technology are an important partner in the know-how carousel as the example of Wageningen University has illustrated.

Interuniversity networks play an important role already, either as formal agreements between universities or as informal and personal contacts between academics who meet at conferences, correspond about publications or act as external examiner in exams. Interuniversity networks strengthen the 3GU. They facilitate cooperation in research and education, and the exchange of experience with cooperation and commercialisation of know-how. Temporary exchange of students and staff is an option that can be very effective.

9.4 CONCLUSION

This completes the book. This chapter has tried to sketch the road that universities can take in order to benefit from developments such as international competition, the possibilities to commercialise the know-how generated, the possibilities offered by enterprises to join in collaborative research, governmental deregulation, the emergence of transdisciplinary research, the renewed interest in special education for the best and brightest, and other trends that change the role of universities in a fundamental way. The changes have been put into a historical context, showing it is not the first time that universities have changed in a fundamental way. Finally, and based on consulting activities with universities, some hands-on recommendations concerning the realisation of a 3GU have been given.

Universities are valuable institutions; they have a central position in our civilisation and they are a major source of our prosperity. They are carriers of our culture in general, and in the context of this book, the science and technology culture. Adapting our universities to the demands of the time is therefore a task that transcends the importance of their daily management.

Appendix 1: Understanding innovation

A1.1 INNOVATION AND ENTREPRENEURS

Why Companies Innovate

In this appendix, we will present a concise overview of some mechanisms of technological dynamics and innovation. Companies innovate because they compete. If they do not compete, for instance in centrally planned economies, they have no need for innovation. The Darwinian jungle of the free enterprise system requires companies to defend their products and services constantly. One way of doing so is by improving quality–cost ratios. If new technology is applied to upgrade existing products and services, we call it defensive innovation. Successful defensive innovation allows a firm to maintain its competitive power but not to improve it.[160] To realise growth, companies have to launch new products or services. Offensive innovation aims at a significant improvement of the competitive position of the firm, either by launching new technology-based products that will drive the old, inferior, products out of the market, or by creating completely new products that offer solutions to entirely new problems. Taken together, technological innovation helps enterprises realise new business and defend existing positions.

Technological innovations are often accompanied by organisational innovations. Quinn describes a number of what he calls 'organisational revolutions' that accompanied technical innovations in the information industry.[161] Innovations in services often have a technological as well as an organisational component,[162] another argument for transdisciplinary research including, in this case, technological as well as organisational research.

Innovation thus changes competitive power. New technology, and especially radically new technology, gives 'first-movers' the opportunity to obtain positions of leadership; Apple and Skype are good examples. First-movers are followed by 'follow-the-leader' enterprises, which develop their own technological or organisational edge with an eye to the leaders; Dell is a good example of this. Finally, there are the 'me-too' companies that do not develop technology of their own but buy licences or use freely available technology and adapt it to specific markets. Whatever the type of company or its position, in order to survive it is imperative to innovate.

The higher the technological and market dynamics, the more innovation one can expect and the more opportunities there are for entrepreneurship. For the coming decades we can expect a lot of technological dynamics: the complete revision of our energy systems, the maturing of life sciences now that we begin to understand the role of RNA, and still many innovations from the information and communication technology (ICT) cluster. At the same time, globalisation and high economic growth in a large part of the world change lifestyles and this will lead to market dynamics. El Dorado for entrepreneurs, except for the fact that there are more of them and the competition will be stiff.

Market economics, entrepreneurship and innovation are closely linked. The social market system is the best system of economic and social organisation for creating prosperity, security and sustainability. Entrepreneurship in a fair, competitive environment in which democratically elected governments map out the playing field is its instrument. Innovation, the successful development and application of something new, is realised through entrepreneurship.

Innovation and the Entrepreneur

Darwin and his followers taught us the mechanisms by which natural life is sustained on this planet.[163] The mechanisms are surprisingly simple: mutation and selection. Existing species mutate because of spontaneous modification of their genetic code. Some of these mutations are gradual like the increasing length of the giraffe's neck. Others, like the emergence of birds, are radical. There is evidence that in times of crisis, when the very existence of a species is threatened, mutation is more radical.[164] Mutation creates new versions of the species and some of these are better equipped to survive external circumstances than the originals. If so, new species substitute the older ones. In Herbert Spencer's inimitable language this is known as the 'survival of the fittest', a phrase he coined after reading Darwin's *Origin of Species*. If a new version is less successful than the original, it becomes extinct.

Adam Smith and his followers had a similar argument about economic life.[165] Under a free enterprise system, entrepreneurs establish new companies (mutation) and the market decides whether these start-ups become successful or not (selection). As with natural life, mutations can be incremental or radical. Either way, successful mutations create wealth for the customer (who benefits from a better quality–price ratio) as well as for the entrepreneur. With this incentive, entrepreneurs are tempted to engage in the risky venture of creating new products or services. The system of free enterprise makes the production sector ever more effective and adaptable to changes in demand.[166]

The entrepreneur spots a window of opportunity, an idea as to how a market and a technology can be combined to generate business. He has a vision of how his idea, when realised, will create value in the market. Entrepreneurs are: 'dreamers who do, who take hands-on responsibility for creating new business. The entrepreneur may be the creator or inventor but is always the dreamer who figures out how to turn an idea into a profitable reality.' [167] In other words, entrepreneurs first have a vision, and then they get things up and running.

Entrepreneurs are matchmakers between supply and demand. The entrepreneur may see many opportunities but he will only put his energy and resources into those opportunities that he expects to add value to new or existing customers. The opportunity can consist of a certain application of (new) technology, a new way of financing or organisation, a new standard (the International Organization for Standardization – ISO freight container) or the proverbial gap in the market, a hitherto unrecognised need, or a customer function that is not satiated with existing products or services.

Entrepreneurs who put new technology to use are the technological entrepreneurs. They use technology as the driving force, the competitive edge. The Austrian-American economist Schumpeter was foremost in pointing out the role of the entrepreneur as innovator or renewer. Schumpeter defines an entrepreneur as someone who creates radical innovations or true renewals, rather than gradual renewals. His definition of radical innovations, *Neue Kombinationen* (new combinations), became widely known and, indeed, entrepreneurship is about making new combinations between different technologies or between technology and markets. In Schumpeter's time, such new combinations were made mostly by new entrepreneurs who, when successful, would push traditional firms off the product lifecycle and substitute them to become established companies themselves. Schumpeter labelled this role of entrepreneurs as 'creative destruction'. Nowadays many 'new combinations' come from large enterprises.[168] Either way, technological entrepreneurs change the world by bringing new technological applications to the market: fire, the wheel, bronze, iron, the steam engine, electricity, telecommunications, polymers, solid state electronics, pharmaceuticals, various 'green revolutions' and so on. Hence, the technological entrepreneur is a mediator between technology and market. (Figure A1.1)

He will monitor technological development and develop technology himself, by looking at his market and assessing what he can sell. At the same

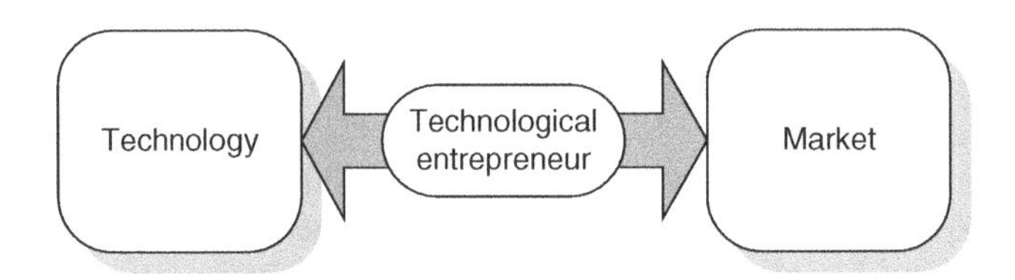

Figure A1.1 The technological entrepreneur as matching agent between technology and market

time, he will watch his (potential) customers, analyse their needs and wonder whether the technology he can develop might create value for them. Nelson and Winter extended the role of the entrepreneur as mediator between so-called technological trajectories (technological trends, like miniaturisation or digitisation) and selection environment (a wider concept than market, including societal demands).[169] They point out that new technology does not arise at random, but at a particular time; technologists will deploy certain technology, such as mechanisation in the nineteenth century, chemistry in the early twentieth century, and information technology in the later twentieth century. Such technological trajectories are more than just technical disciplines that are being advanced, they include notions such as: replacing manual labour by machines, substituting natural products by industrial products, and so on. A technological trajectory acts as a driving force, but also as a constraint since available talent is directed towards the implementation of the trajectory while other possible 'trends' have to wait. When a trajectory is exhausted, talent will shift to another technological paradigm, and sooner or later there will be a new trajectory. Similarly, the selection environment is an extension of the market as the factor that determines the fate of new technology. Non-market factors, such as the need for sustainability or safety, scarcity of resources and political considerations, may favour a particular technology while hampering the introduction of another. In addition, 'market' means not only the buyer of the product, but also the ultimate user. For instance, for a new aeroplane, not only the reaction of the airline matters, but also the reaction of the passengers, airports, legislators and many others.

Innovation is therefore a powerful tool (but not the only tool) in the struggle for life in a competitive environment. The driving force in innovation is the entrepreneur, who thinks and acts and who is the matchmaker between supply and demand. Technological entrepreneurs put new technology to use; together with philosophers, scientists, true political leaders and artists, they are the ultimate change agents of this world.

Now, if technology plays such a dominant role in the free enterprise system, let us explore what we are talking about.

A1.2 TECHNOLOGY, INVENTION, INNOVATION

The word 'technical' stems from Greek *tekhnikos*, 'skilled in a particular art or subject', and *tekhne*, 'art, skill, craft'. The sense narrowed to 'having to do with the mechanical arts' (first recorded in 1727). A technician is a person skilled in the technique of a particular art or craft. Technology comes from Greek *tekhnologia*, *tekhno* + *logia*, literally 'the science of craft', or the 'systematic treatment of an art, craft, or technique'. The meaning, 'science of the mechanical and industrial arts', is first recorded in 1859.[170] Technology nowadays is the science of the industrial arts, the science of technical skills and processes; some people use the expression 'technical sciences', which is the same as technology. A technologist is someone who has scientifically studied the phenomena that lead to the understanding and subsequently the design of technical processes. The word 'technology' is also used for the formal body of knowledge that the technical sciences have produced and is documented in patents, articles or otherwise. One can say: 'We will invest in a plant for product X and we bought the technology from company Y'. Know-how is also knowledge including formal knowledge (technology) and tacit knowledge; hence it has a wider meaning than technology. Technology in the sense of the 'science of technical processes' is also called applied science. It tries to understand phenomena and to design processes with the aim of doing something with this knowledge, that is, putting it to practical use. Pure science aims to investigate natural phenomena and their role in nature, to broaden our understanding, 'know-why', *la science pour la science* (Figure A1.2). Sometimes insights from pure science form the basis of technological development, but this is not a necessary connection: much technology is the result of technological research alone. The word 'research' means pure scientific as well as technological investigation. In industry, we use the expression 'research and development' (R&D) as one concept, meaning the efforts carried out with respect to applied science.

Technology can lead to an invention, a new (hitherto unknown) device, process or algorithm that has been shown to work. Not all inventions are based on scientific reasoning; many are ideas developed by trial and error. An invention may originate from a technical idea, an observation of a need or a problem for which a solution can be found, or combinations of these. If an inventor can prove that his invention is original, he can ask for a patent. The word patent comes from the French *lettre patent*, 'open letter',

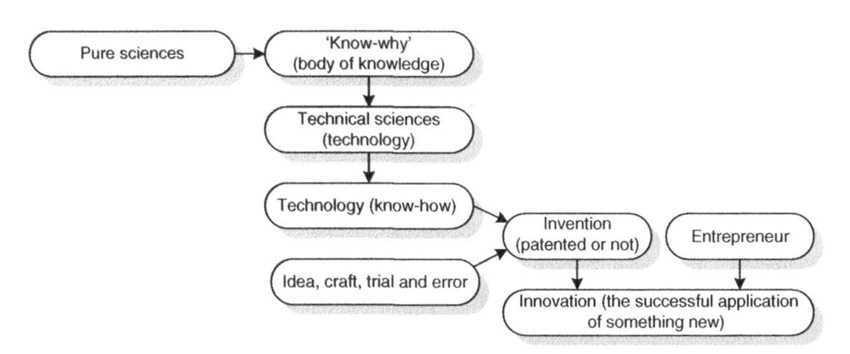

Figure A1.2 Summary and coherence of definitions

a letter given by an authority to give the addressee a monopoly of a certain issue; this could also be a toll road or mine, for instance.[171] Patent now means the 'copyright to an invention', 'exclusive right', monopoly – nowadays a temporary monopoly.

Most patents are never commercialised. An invention, patented or not, is nothing but a possible start to an innovation. It is only when an invention has been put to use that we speak of an innovation. Innovation is the successful introduction of something new; successful as shown by acceptance in the market or other use. This implies that the process that leads up to an innovation is only partly a technical process, scientific or not. It is also very much a commercial process – bringing the new product to market. Innovation requires technical as well as market development. The success of great innovators always stems from the combination of an appreciation of the possibilities of a technology with a vision as to what role it can play in society, how it will be absorbed in the market place. In other words: an idea is nothing, an invention is something and an innovation is the real thing. One can speak of marketing innovations, organisational innovations and technological innovations; the three often, but not necessarily, go together.

To conclude, technology is the sum of technical sciences and the body of formal knowledge these sciences have brought forward. Technology can lead to inventions and inventions can lead to innovations if the know-how is used, in the market or otherwise. Entrepreneurship, technology and innovation are different qualities but they are closely linked. However, not all entrepreneurs are innovators and not all innovations stem from technological development. Likewise, innovators are entrepreneurs; but not all entrepreneurs are innovators.

Now that we had a closer look at what technology means and what it can do, let us look at technological dynamics.

A1.3 TECHNOLOGICAL DYNAMICS

There are four ways in which a technological entrepreneur can use technology to drive an innovation. The four ways form a classification of technology according to their effect in the market.

Technological surprise is the creation of a totally new technology that is used to satisfy an as yet uncovered or unknown need. Fire and sleds were technological surprises and so were stone axes, spears, wool, cotton and torches. Photography and digital computing were technological surprises. Technological surprises create new companies or rejuvenate existing industries. Polymers (partly a technological surprise, partly substituting natural materials) were invented and brought to market by existing companies; software was developed mainly by new companies. The question why certain technological surprises are realised by existing companies and others by start-ups is an intriguing one. A technological surprise can be a new combination of existing technologies. Sony's Walkman is a good example: existing radio and audio cassette technologies were used to create a portable radio–cassette player. This met a hitherto unsatisfied and even unknown consumer need: listening to music while on the move.

Technological proliferation is the process by which existing technology is applied to completely different use. CD-ROMs and DVDs are proliferations of compact disc technology. Radar technology has proliferated with completely different applications such as the microwave oven and systems for speed control. Laser technology has proliferated into a wide range of uses, medical for instance (eye operations, dentistry, physiotherapy) or its use in readers of compact discs and many others.

There are not many examples of pure technological surprise as most new technology is used to drive the old inferior technology out of existing applications. We call this technological substitution. The steam engine was designed for driving pumps to drain coal mines, which was previously done by hand or horse-driven pumps. Later, steam engines were used to drive factories (substituting horsepower and watermills), trains (substituting horse-drawn carriages), ships (substituting sail) and, in Holland, pumping water from reclaimed land (substituting windmills). Steam engines, in turn, were eventually substituted by combustion engines and electrical motors. Combustion engines will probably be substituted by a combination of fuel cells and electrical motors. In all these cases, a new technology with a significantly better performance–cost ratio drives the existing technology out of the market. The market or use is the same, but the need is fulfilled in a significantly better way. When the new technology hits the market, there is a real discontinuity. Gaslight substituted candles, which in its turn was substituted by electrical light. Within electrical light, various technologies have substituted one another: the incandescent lamp, sodium lamp, mercury lamp, fluorescent light, LEDs. Open source software is a real game changer, as it will stimulate competition in markets that were hitherto dominated by monopolistic suppliers. Note that technological proliferation and technological succession overlap: a proliferating technology can substitute an existing technology.

The most common application of new technology is technological escalation, the incremental improvement of existing technology. Chips are getting more powerful as well as cheaper, thanks to technological progress. Luboil technology is continuously and significantly improved, thus improving the reliability of motoring. Naturally, for commercial reasons manufacturers wish to suggest that such innovations are actually breakthroughs by naming the improved version the umpteenth generation or the like. But, in the case of technological escalation, the basic technology is the same and so is the market use. This does not mean that this form of technological renewal is inferior. On the contrary, entire business sectors depend on technological escalation for their development. In the construction sector only a few technological surprises (prestressed concrete, mud shield tunnelling) and substitutions (power tools, electronic measuring equipment) supplement the annual series of relatively small improvements in existing technology; over the years, this results in impressive improvements in productivity. Since the arrival of powered weaving and knitting machines in the nineteenth century and polymer fibres in the twentieth, the textile industry has depended on technological escalation (non-wovens did not replace knitting and weaving; denim was a technological escalation with great impact). Even the spectacular development of solid-state electronics can be labelled as technological escalation since the birth of the chip in 1957. In other words, our increase in prosperity depends very much on modest, non-spectacular, systematic technological escalation. Technological escalation is almost exclusively carried out by existing companies; it can be relatively easily imitated and this would make a start-up too vulnerable. Because of its easy imitation, technological escalation has a defensive nature; one may increase one's market share but the gain is not likely to be permanent as the competition will strike back. Technological surprise, substitution and proliferation can give the innovator a defendable and significant improvement in his competitive position, even wiping out the competition (which uses old technology) completely. Therefore, such innovations have an offensive nature and they are indeed game changers[172] that change the market as well as the playing field.

The link between the four roles of new technology in the market is illustrated in Figure A1.3.

		Technology is:	
		New	Existing
Application is:	New	*Technological surprise*	*Technological proliferation*
	Existing	*Technological substitution*	*Technological escalation*

Figure A1.3 Technologies according to their effect in the market

Sometimes the distinction is made between 'outside-the-box' and 'inside-the-box' innovation. 'Outside-the-box' stands for radical innovation, game changing innovation, revolution, discontinuity, something quite new. 'Inside-the-box' refers to gradual innovation, evolution, more or better of the same. This distinction is made because the management tools to bring these kinds of innovation to fruition are completely different. Technological surprise and technological substitution comprise 'outside-the-box' innovations while technological escalation and technological proliferation lead to 'inside-the-box' innovations.

Technological Escalation

When the main quality over cost ratio of a developing technology is plotted against time, often an S-curve of some kind results (Figure A1.4).

The curve has its S-shape because the learning process during early development escalates; more opportunities for improvement arise as the development progresses, causing the curve to grow exponentially. This is reinforced by the scale effect: increased scale of production leads to lower cost per unit, hence to larger production volumes, hence to larger scale effects. After a point of inflexion, growth in the quality–cost indicator becomes slower and accelerating growth turns into decelerating growth. This is caused by the diminished scope for improvements while the impact of additional scale effects becomes smaller. Eventually the curve will approach an asymptote and then the technology has fully matured. After this, the quality–cost curve will increase slowly but often steadily, as improvements will continue to occur or as new sub-technology can be incorporated. Take for instance the combustion engine used in cars: the technology is over 100 years old but electronics, 16-valve and other techniques have greatly improved the efficiency of the engine while catalysts have reduced the amount of hazardous wastes. The steam engine has improved by an average of 2 per cent per year for over 150 years. Exponential growth however never lasts forever. The so-called Moore's

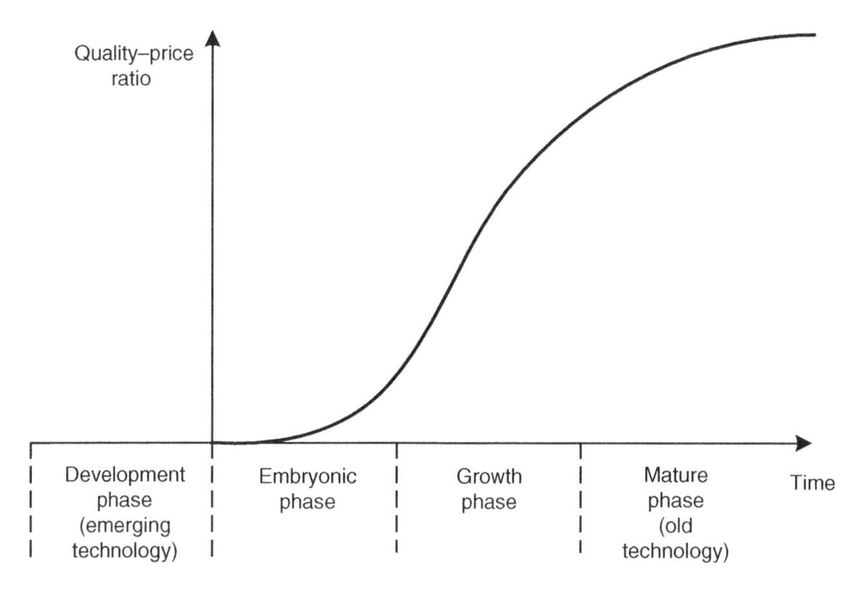

Figure A1.4 Technological escalation

Law (named after an Intel director and founder) states that the quality of chips (measured as the number of components on one chip) doubles every 18 months while the costs halve in the same period. Although this rule reasonably represents past development, but it is not a 'law' as all developments in nature will eventually slow down to reach some asymptote. Note that mature technologies may enter a second life in which development is speeded up after a prolonged mature phase of marginal improvements; high-speed trains are a good example.

Technological escalation is reinforced by market dynamics, resulting in the well-known product life cycle. The driving forces in adopting innovations change as the diffusion of the innovation in the market progresses.[173] In the product life cycle, turnover in dollars or euros is plotted against time and this results in another S-shaped curve with embryonic, growth and mature phases and possibly a decline phase. The market dynamics are best known as the process of diffusion or adoption as described in an influential book by Rogers.[174] Rogers noted that customers have different attitudes towards new products or new technology in general. Some people will buy the new technology immediately, no matter the cost, while others wait to follow first-movers. Rogers distinguishes five kinds of users (Figure A1.5), the number of adopters forming a Gaussian distribution.

Note that all together we have five interlinked S-curves: the effects of

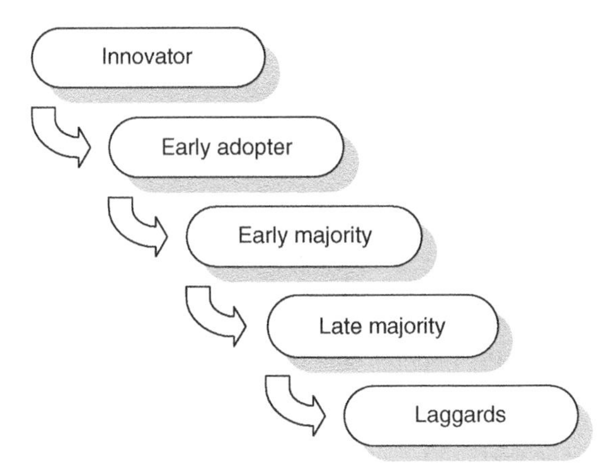

Figure A1.5 Adopter categories in technology diffusion as found by E.M. Rogers

learning and increasing scale together form the process of technological escalation. Escalation combined with market dynamics results in the product life cycle. This is illustrated in Figure A1.6.

Many formulae have been suggested to describe the S-curve. One of the early suggestions was made by Fisher and Pry in 1971 and this curve can still be used if one wants to keep things simple.[175] The formula is based on the observation that the rate of development is proportional to:[176]

- the number of remaining improvements and customers (those who have not yet bought the new technology);
- the probability that the improvement is implemented and that a remaining customer swings to the new technology.

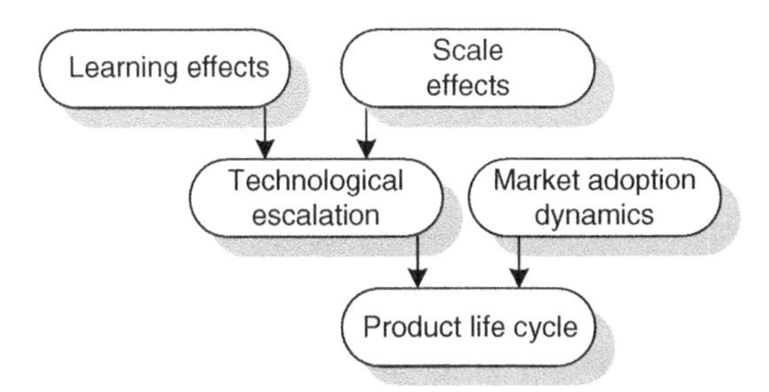

Figure A1.6 The five S-curves of the innovation process

The formula then is:

$$\frac{dF}{dt} = P_t \times (F_t - F)$$

in which:
F is the number of users
F_t is the ultimate number of users
P_t is the probability that a new person will adopt the technology

The probability P_t is assumed to be proportional to the number of users – those having already adopted the new technology – and some factor k. This means that the more people that have already adopted the technology, the more are likely to adopt it in the future. The factor k represents the effectiveness by which the new technology is advocated and the attractiveness as seen by the user.

This means:

$$P_t = k \times F$$

Substituting this in the formula above results in the Fisher–Pry formula:

$$\frac{dF}{dt} = k \times F \times (F_t - F)$$

If F is normalised, by defining $f = F/F_t$, going from zero to one and symbolised by f:

$$\frac{dF}{dt} = k \times f \times (1 - f)$$

which illustrates that the rate of development or adoption at any moment is proportional to the number of current users and the number of potential users remaining. All formulae for S-curves use this basic principle.[177]

The factor k determines the rate of adoption or development: the larger its value, the faster the new technology is adopted or developed. The factor k is the result of many factors governing the speed of diffusion. Innovation is enhanced if:

- The new technology has a large advantage over the old; the greater the relative advantage (quality over cost), the faster it will be adopted.
- The perception of the new technology as being advantageous is large, meaning that the advantages are well communicated and easily visible.
- The complexity of the new technology is low; one can understand its use immediately as well as how it is going to be used and operated.
- The new technology resembles the old technology. Edison used this effect when he called electricity 'electrical mains', referring to 'mains',

the term then used for gas distribution which was the technology to be substituted.

- The new technology is 'backwards integrated', meaning that one can still use other equipment or software when the new technology is adopted. This effect is used by Microsoft in its new versions of system and application software; for a long time the Windows software was even backwards compatible to the original MS-DOS software.
- The risks in adopting the new technology are isolated, meaning that if the new technology is a failure it will not affect the usability of linked equipment or software. If you buy a bad new LCD screen it will not cause your computer to break down. Another way of saying this is that the new technology is reversible: adopters do not enter a world from which there is no return.
- The new technology is sustainable and/or it has a positive image; it adds to a desired image of the user, and there are no technical or other negative side-effects.

Technological Substitution

In the case of technological substitution, a second S-curve, representing the development of the new technology, appears on the board. This second one does not necessarily start at a higher quality–cost ratio than the 'old' technology. Now imagine the situation of Figure A1.7.

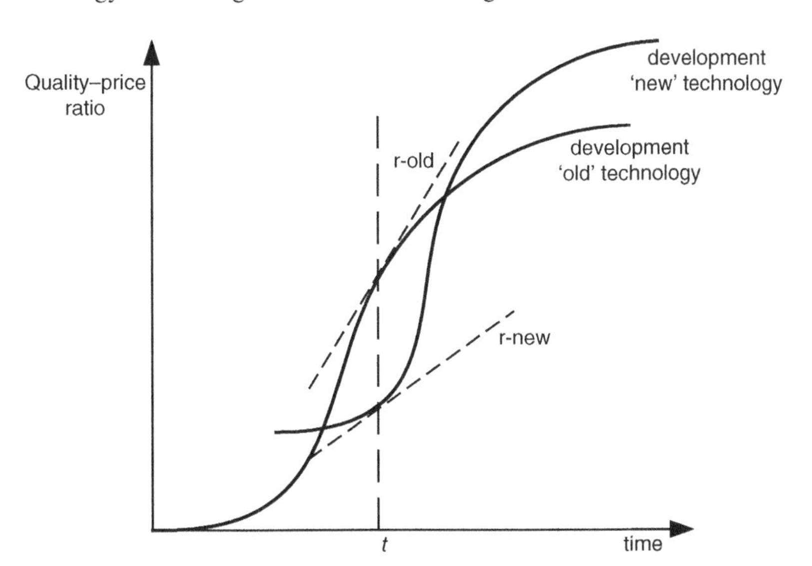

Figure A1.7 Technological substitution

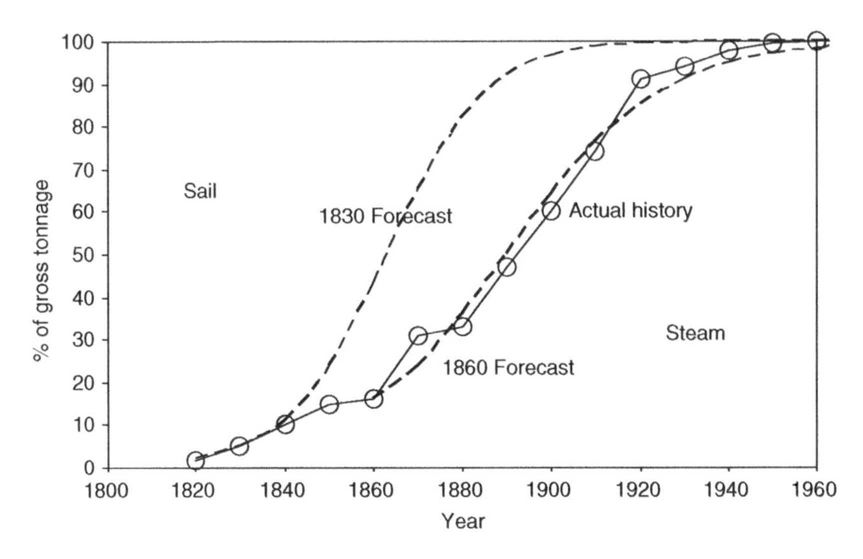

Figure A1.8 Substitution of sail by steam ships

Here we see the developments ('escalations') of the existing technology ('old' technology) together with that of a challenger. This challenger does not seem to be a serious threat at moment *t* in the figure. The quality–cost ratio is lower and even the speed of development, represented by the tangents r-old and r-new, is lower. One might wonder how this new technology can ever become a threat if the challenger starts with a backlog and develops even slower than the original technology. The answer is that the factor *k* of the new innovation is higher, that is, it has more advantages and acceptability and the resulting S-curve is steeper. This is a treacherous phenomenon that has caused many a company to underestimate the threat of technological substitution and go bankrupt.

Another treacherous phenomenon is the fact that 'old technologies fight back'. Consider Figure A1.8 which depicts the substitution of sail ships by steam ships in the nineteenth century.[178]

The first steam ships appeared around 1810 and substitution started slowly. Based on the data available in 1830, a first forecast was made using the Fisher–Pry or a similar formula. We can see though that the actual development runs behind the forecast of 1830. When in 1860 a new forecast was made, based on the data then available, a curve emerges that closely resembles actual history up to the Second World War when the last sailing ships were substituted.[179] One may conclude, the more data, the better the forecast, and that is undeniably true. But comparing these curves with similar ones, there seems to be a systematic error in that early predictions are always too optimistic. There is a simple explanation for this. In the case of the sailing ships the technology of the ships had not been fundamentally changed since the invention of the East India ships in the seventeenth century. When steam came onto the market, sailing ship technology was considerably stretched: the American clipper with its sharp bow was designed for speed (it did up to 20 knots, outperforming steam) and the schooner with gaff-rigged sails enabled it to sail closer to the wind and thus required relatively small crews; the schooner was used as early as 1630 but it was only fully developed in the second half of the nineteenth century.[180] The phenomenon that an old technology only fully develops after being challenged by a new one can be observed in many instances, and it is a source of miscalculations by analysts who make forecasts that are overly optimistic. In 2000, Jürgen Schrempp, the then president of DaimlerChrysler, announced that his company would put 100 000 fuel cell powered cars on the market in 2003. He did not deliver on this prediction, apparently because traditional engines could be stretched to meet the California emission standards (in addition, the performance–price ratio for the fuel cell cars developed more slowly than expected). Competition by suppliers of the same technology is apparently not strong enough to squeeze the last drops from the development bottle, whereas technological substitution is. The old technology is not only pushed to its limits of efficiency but, often, also to its limits of appeal. We still admire the windjammers and locomotives of the early twentieth century; we admire the mechanical calculators, cameras, balances and typewriters of the 1970s, and in Holland we adore the seventeenth-century windmills while protesting against the high-power windmills that are now being installed. Apparently, old technologies reach their summits of beauty and appeal just before becoming obsolete. The lesson is: when preparing a business plan for a new technology, take the stretch capabilities of the old one into account; know your enemy.

When a new technology challenges an old one, there are three possibilities:

1. There will be a 100 per cent substitution as in the cases of the substitution of steam power by combustion and of mechanical devices by electronic ones.
2. The substitution will be partial, resulting in a dynamic equilibrium between old and new technology. As late as the 1970s, the polymer industry expected that the substitution of natural fibres (wool and cotton especially) by man-made fibres (such as nylon, polyester and polyamide) would be a total substitution and they were drawing their S-curves in order to plan capacity and predict the moment of victory. But then the old technologies started to fight back with denim and

crease-free woollen clothes, and labels for pure wool and cotton that matched the natural life-trend, that emerged after the hippy-era. Since then, all kinds of mixtures of natural and man-made fibres have come into use, creating the dynamic equilibrium.

3. The new technology never comes to fruition as it is itself substituted before it reaches the age of maturity. The original rayon reinforced rubber tyre was, in rapid technological successions, challenged by the nylon, polyester and glass fibre reinforced tyres until the real winner, the steel belt tyre, took all. These substitution processes created havoc in the tyre industry, leading to international consolidation of the industry with Michelin, a hitherto relatively insignificant player, becoming the world market leader with plants in the US; this was previously unthinkable. So, insightful innovation pays, especially if you understand the key to the solution; in this case, the heat transfer dynamics in the tyre.

Long-term market dominance can be obtained by serial substitution, meaning launching a new innovation before the previous one has matured. Such serial self-killers become their own most serious competitors as they introduce the new technology when the competition has just mastered the previous one, and this gives an enterprise the best possible competitive position as companies that are able to realise serial substitution become unattainable for competitors and acquire 'permanent' leadership. IBM in the 1960s and 1970s came up with new generations of mainframe computers before the competition was fully aware of what was going on. Sony's mission today is 'to destroy its own products'; it fights its own LCD flat television screens with its plasma screens, and it devised affordable high-density digital cameras while the classic versus digital substitution was still in full swing. Philips has been in the forefront of applying new technology to lighting; the ends of each technological substitution have been depicted in Figure A1.9.[181] Note that here there is a physical limit to the development as the ratio of lumens–watts cannot exceed the 100 per cent efficiency point. We call a series of successive technological substitutions technological succession and new challengers should move up the curve if they are to make sense. The challenge to 'unattainable' positions based on in-house technological succession often comes from unexpected quarters. Anyone who had predicted in 1960 that Texas Instruments would become a competitor to the Swiss watch industry would not have been taken seriously. Yet electronic watches would have eradicated this industry from the market had it not been for a new trend that made watches a fashion item rather than an instrument to read the time. The first reaction of the Swiss industry was that 'customers would always prefer the real thing' (the 'real thing' always being

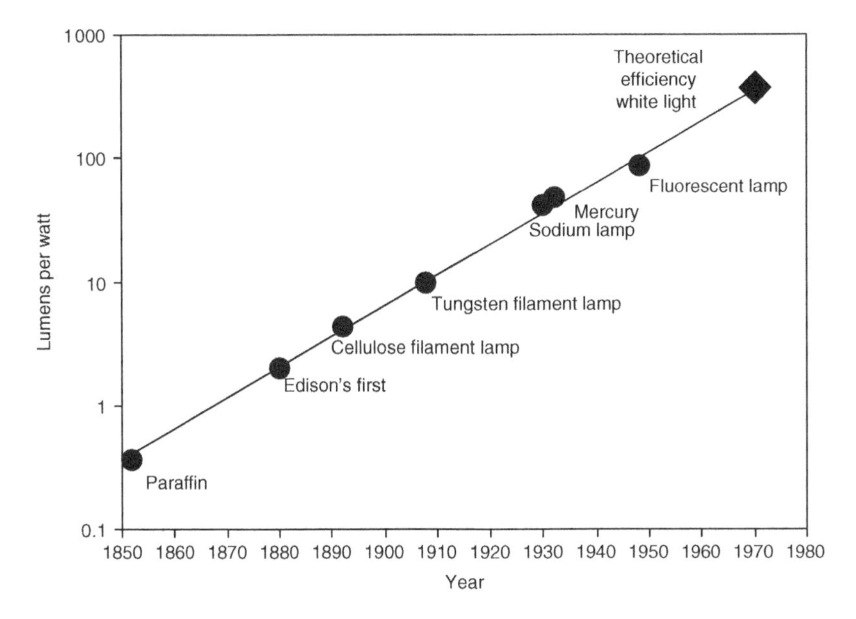

Figure A1.9 Technological succession

the old technology; it is an example of ostrich-like head-in-the-sand behaviour). Manufacturers of mechanical scales and cameras used the same argument and the lesson is that one should sell one's shares in companies using this argument. IBM at first completely underestimated the role of the personal computer, then the role of the systems software for it. Sony might find that television itself becomes obsolete when Internet technologies substitute it and plasma TV sets become museum pieces.

Technological Proliferation

The laptop used for writing this book and the chip inside it are both innovations. But they are of a different nature. A chip as such, however fast, is not worth a dime; it is only useful if and when it can be used in a personal computer (PC) or other appliance. Therefore, we call a chip (or rather, solid-state electronics) a basic innovation, defined as a building block to be utilised in applications. With this basic innovation, we can make various so-called applied innovations or applications: the dynamic random access memory (DRAM), the static random access memory (SRAM) and others. Again such applied innovations are useless unless they can be combined to yield a product innovation or product.[182] The innovativeness of a product innovation rests in the creative combination of applied innovations and the design and marketing of the result. We think of a PC as a dressed-up chip, but we might equally regard it as a dressed-up hard disc drive, screen, battery and other elements, not mentioning the software, mouse technology and other peripherals. Each type of innovation is in its own way the compromise between technology push and market pull. If a basic innovation can be used directly in a product innovation, such as liquid crystal technology, it coincides with an applied innovation.

The idea that product innovations are based on one basic innovation is as popular as it is misleading. The story goes that book printing was invented when the imprint of a wooden letter in the sand gave the inventor the idea. The reality is very different.[183] When the first book, the Gutenberg Bible, was produced by Johannes Gensfleisch zum Gutenberg in 1456, it was not as revolutionary as one tends to think. Since the eleventh century, written texts had begun to substitute oral agreements, especially in England. In the fifteenth century there was a well-developed branch of commercial writers' firms, we would now say publishers, with early professional quality management, production planning, budgeting, contracting, financial management, and so on. After the great pestilence of 1350–1450, there was a shortage of supply (writers) and abundance of demand of writing as trade picked up. So the market for printing was already there. Writers' firms started to innovate. Reading glasses were invented, thereby extending the working life of writers beyond the period when they became myopic. Block books were another invention; an entire page was cut in wood and used for repetitive printing; the technique was derived from coin minting and imprinting seals. Johannes Gutenberg viewed writing as the endless repetition of putting down the same letters and he sought to industrialise exactly that process. This vision was his innovative moment; the next major use of the industrialisation principle came only in the seventeenth century when Maurits of Orange developed the industrialisation of military technology[184] while the Industrial Revolution was even further away. Gutenberg was trained as a goldsmith and he invented the right alloys for the punch (the prototype to be copied), the relief in reverse (the negative) and casting metal for the letters, punctuation marks, and so on. His letters had to be equally tall in order to obtain levelled printing. This was difficult enough, but in addition to his moulds and alloys he needed to invent a press (he modified a screw wine press), ink (he used pigment and linseed oil as did the painters at this time) and paper. The product innovation 'book printing' was hence enabled by a number of basic innovations.[185] The message is: an innovative product is almost always the result of the combination of a number of basic innovations; one basic innovation alone is often pretty useless. Another lesson is that technologies as different as book printing and reading glasses were actually competing new technologies.

Rogers[186] uses the expression 'technological diffusion' for the adoption of a product innovation in the market. The expression is also used to describe the processes by which basic innovations proliferate into applied innovations and further into product innovations. This diffusion process involves many people in distinctive roles, as the example of agriculture in the US and the Netherlands illustrates. The agricultural sector is characterised by the presence of many small firms, each too small to develop basic, applied or even product innovations. Yet the sector's innovativeness is second to none. This high rate of innovation has been achieved by agricultural universities and common research centres, fundamental as well as applied, and a multitude of transfer agents ranging from extension services and model farms to schools, courses, printed and other media. These transfer agents act as two-way channels; in one direction the knowledge obtained at R&D centres is modified and individualised to reach the farmer; in the other direction, farmers' problems are communicated upstream via extension services to research centres. Just as important as these instruments is the innovative culture of cooperation and coordination shown by farmers' organisations and the Ministry of Agriculture. Much of the work in the innovation infrastructure is carried out by volunteers, senior farmers who spend considerable time sitting on boards of schools or institutions. The cooperative culture is enabled by the fact that farmers do not see each other as competitors. It is questionable whether the agricultural 'model' will survive modern developments. Industry (the food, machinery, pesticides and other industries) increasingly takes over the role of innovator and the farmers simply have to follow. More recently, there has been a merger between the classical agricultural 'model' and industry-driven innovation, as both models tend to cooperate in the technoparks that comprise university and common research and development facilities as well as the industrial R&D and facilities for technostarters. For food companies and agricultural institutes participation in successful technoparks becomes mandatory because of the high level of synergy between the participants and the quality and efficiency attained as a result. One may expect that only a small number of such parks will maintain a top position in the world while others will become less relevant followers.

The recognition of the agricultural 'model' has led to the concept of know-how infrastructures (the way in which technology and market needs diffuse in a network of various participants, with each participant playing a vital role, such that missing one player is to miss the entire effect) or innovation infrastructures. These models have been elaborated into the concept of a national (or regional) innovation system (NIS) by which the innovation capabilities of a nation or region can be analysed, monitored and subsequently improved.[187] NIS models are widely used nowadays, for instance for the EU accession of Central and Eastern European countries and for stimulating innovation in the Russian Federation.

A different lesson from the agricultural 'model' is that 'innovation requires networking': the network is the message. This fits with modern notions about the structuring of large firms by using networks.[188] Just as a food company cannot innovate without the cooperation of extension services, so large electronics firms need technostarters and small firms as partners in their innovation processes.

A1.4 PRODUCT AND PROCESS INNOVATIONS AND STANDARDS

Most of our examples so far relate to product (or service) innovations that are innovations directed towards the market. We have to distinguish these from process innovations – innovations leading to an improvement in the firm's production functions such as manufacturing, logistics, quality systems and others. Process innovations are often 'invisible' to the customer except that the product quality may have improved or the price is lower to reflect lower production cost. The management of process innovations has to deal with an 'internal customer' rather than an external customer. This makes it quite different from (and in general less risky than) the management of product innovations.

In Figure A1.10, product innovation is plotted against process innovation; this results in the innovation map for the firm. Product innovation requires process innovation if the new product cannot be manufactured using existing manufacturing technology. An example is the hand-in-hand

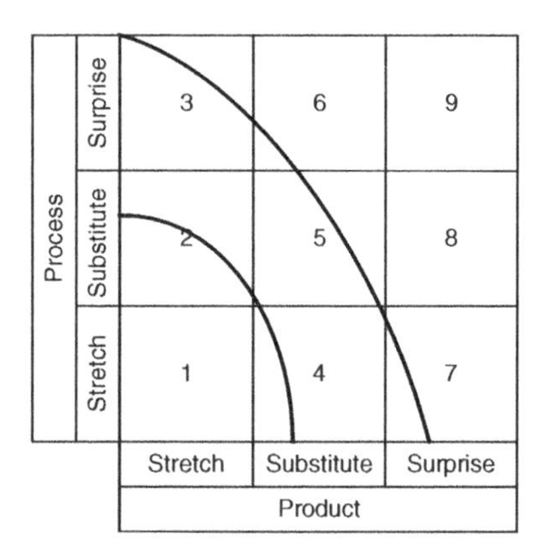

Figure A1.10 Innovation map of a firm

innovations in chips and wafer steppers, the machines to produce chips. Such 'twin-innovations' occur in cells 1, 5 and 9 of Figure A1.10. Innovations along the vertical axis of Figure A1.10 usually proceed much more smoothly – and are less risky – than the ones on the horizontal axis. Number 1 innovations concern improvements in product and/or process; these are simply a 'must' while adding little competitive power. Making an existing product with a substitute process or even a revolutionary process, that is, innovations 2 and 3, do indeed offer defendable competitive advantage. The time pressure here is often strong as competitors might be on the same track. A surprise product innovation will often require a corresponding process innovation and one can find but few examples of innovations in cells 7 and 8. Plotting the major innovations for a firm on the grid of Figure A1.10 not only gives the chief executive officer (CEO) a fair idea of their nature and risks, but it can also help to assign the management level responsible for the innovation process. The two hyperbolas divide the matrix into three parts. Innovations in the part to the left are the domain of 'operations'. The innovations in the middle layer will be the responsibility of business unit management. The innovations in the top and right section comprise 'outside-the-box' innovations that are not linked to existing business. These will be top management's responsibility until they become new business units.

There is a third possible result of innovation, standards, with yet again another way of innovation management. Formulating and executing standardisation policies are tricky as win–win situations can be close to win–lose situations, which are the normal strategy in competition between companies. We define standardisation as: the development, implementation and successful acceptance of common rules for performing specific tasks.[189] This definition is broad: it includes the rules for playing chess as well as the rules that enable you to call any telephone in the world from the phone on your desk. Standards only work if all who perform the specific task adopt the standard. This adoption can be enforced, de facto enforced or voluntary. If there are many users of a standard, it will be impossible to reach agreement and national governments will have to step in. This leads to public standards such as the metric system, the voltage of public networks and so on. Public standards are often international and there are international bodies that coordinate the national and private enterprise interests such as the International Organization for Standardization ISO in Geneva. Some, but not all, public standards are obligatory; this depends on national regulation policies. The standard of the ISO container for instance leaves every company free to define its own container standard. However, the ISO standard for containers has been widely adopted and it would be virtually impossible to ship a container of deviant dimensions. The ISO system has not been able to gain similar acceptance of household waste containers. In Europe alone there are over 120 different standards for such containers, presenting an interesting challenge to the manufacturers of refuse collection vehicles. The width of railway tracks, the size of nuts and bolts and the standards for telecommunication are all part of the public domain, enforced by law or not.

Original standards are often developed by business leaders, frequently the original innovators. The originator has three options:

1. He can keep the standard protected (secrecy lasts longer than patenting, vide the Microsoft software standards).
2. He can share the standard (for payment) with competitors, thus increasing the likelihood that the standard becomes widely accepted and that market development is fast.
3. He can put it in the open domain (as Philips did with the audio tape cassette) with the same but even stronger effect.

Eventually, the standard may migrate into the public domain and become an enforced standard (like the electricity voltage; the 110 volt originated from Edison and his company). Option 3 is a so-called open standard that can be used by anyone, usually free of charge. Closed or proprietary standards (options 1 and 2) are protected for use by the innovator himself and parties he licenses the standard to; the standard then becomes a marketing instrument. The initiator of a standard can develop the standard alone, or cooperate with competitors to arrive directly at option 2 above (for example the DVD standard of Philips, Sony, Matsushita). Sometimes a large group of individuals and enterprises develop the standards together, for instance the Linux standards for system and application software.

In defining his standardisation strategy, an innovator is subject to conflicting driving forces. Choosing the closed standard option can bring considerable benefits as the Microsoft example obviously shows. Microsoft managed to create a de facto monopoly. Sony, on the other hand, uses proprietary standards to encourage customers to buy its different products which together form a system. The conditions for the successful adoption of the closed standard strategy are:

- The firm has to be confident that it can enforce the standard throughout the entire industry (Microsoft) or that it can increase its market share by using the systems approach (Sony).
- The firm must be able to protect the standard, either by patents or by secrecy.

If the innovator fails to meet these requirements, several private standards will compete in the market, slowing the adoption of the innovation, as consumers buying a product with a losing standard will deem the product useless before its lifetime is up. The three standards for video cassette recording (VCR) of Philips, Sony and Matsushita (the last winning the game with its VHS standard) are responsible for the relatively slow market adoption of VCRs and the two competing standards for high-definition DVDs will no doubt slow the adoption of this technology. Choosing the open standard option reduces the innovator's competitive advantage but speeds up the adoption process and this results in faster returns on investment. The downside is that all the work on the standard benefits the competition as much as the innovator. It is therefore only beneficial if the innovator can realise first-mover advantages. Choosing the cooperation strategy (as with the CD and DVD standards) has similar advantages; it is particularly valuable in situations where the innovator is not powerful enough to enforce his standard in the industry or if he wants to speed up the adoption process, perhaps because a substituting technology is already in the making. However, if the innovator has a strong technological lead and he does not want to wait for consensus with competitors, he may successfully choose the go-it-alone standardisation strategy.

Functional standards should be distinguished from technical standards. In the construction sector, for instance, a wall can be specified in technical terms: so many bricks of a certain type and so much plaster and isolation. The functional standard would consist of a defined strength, permeability for sound, heat, moisture and appearance. Functional standards challenge the ingenuity of innovators: perhaps new materials should be developed to meet the standard and save costs. With technical standards the playing field of an innovator is limited to improved logistics and the like. It is obvious that functional standards foster innovation and that technical standards hamper technological development.

Standards can have long lives. The width of railways is generally considered too small but it will not be altered easily as the cost would be monumental. Once the first railway with its corresponding locomotives and carriages had been built, the standard for other railways was set. But the standard may be even older than the early railways as it is likely that the railway width was derived from the distance between the wheels of nineteenth-century carriages as the inventors most likely took an existing carriage, changed the carriage wheels for iron wheels and put the thing on rails. There is a speculation that the width of carriage wheels, in turn, is derived from the width of the wheels of Roman carts, as these carved tracks in the stone roads and later carriages had to have the same width to secure stability. True or not, this example shows the rigidity of standards. Many administrative systems are based on the COBOL software language of the 1960s, a standard that is considered by many as absolutely obsolete (ref. the year 2000 problems), but it is likely to stay for a very long time as the costs of rebuilding the software packages does not outweigh the efficiency disadvantages of the COBOL-based systems.

A1.5 THE INNOVATION PENTAGON

Many companies today wrestle with the question of how they can be more innovative. This concerns not only large technology-based enterprises, that use approaches outlined above, but also smaller companies. For them, we have developed a tool called the Innovation Pentagon that we will outline in this section.

The first step for an enterprise to become innovative is to get rid of some ideas that may have worked in the past but that are misconceptions today. Such misconceptions include:

1. Innovation is something creative, surrounded by a certain mystique.
2. Because it is a creative process, innovation cannot be steered. All the company can do is to establish a sound R&D department and effective ways in which potentially successful results can be transferred to the operating departments such as manufacturing and marketing and sales.
3. The development of new products, services or processes must be carried out in secrecy as they constitute future competitive power. This power is the source of wealth of the company and it cannot be jeopardised by letting competitors in on the secret.
4. R&D is a cost centre. The more applications emerge from R&D, the better the costs will be covered. Projects that do not make it to the market are regarded as failures.
5. The CTO – chief technology officer – should be a respected technological wizard who will solve the problems of the future.

These 'beliefs' have to be turned into their opposites:

1. Innovation is a normal business practice that certainly requires creativity but not more than say the marketing or manufacturing departments.
2. Innovation is based on strategic choices that stem from the strategic planning of the firm. Rather than bringing results of R&D to marketing and then to manufacturing, these functions are involved in

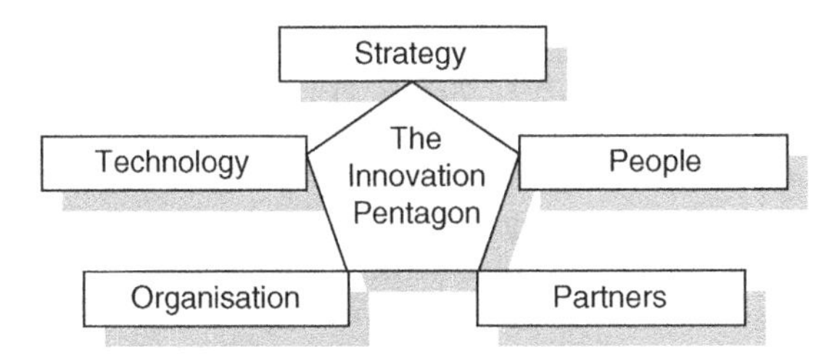

Figure A1.11 The Innovation Pentagon

innovation processes right from the start, using the strategic plan of the firm or a business unit.

3. Collaboration with clients and suppliers helps in finding good-value propositions for them. Such collaboration reduces the risks of innovation. The know-how available outside the enterprise is much larger than the know-how inside, and if this can be employed, the innovations come faster, cheaper and better.
4. R&D is a profit centre that has to earn its living by contracting activities from internal and if possible external parties. Spin-offs of innovation projects are inevitable. If they cannot be employed by the firm itself they should not be regarded as failures but rather as business opportunities for which alternative ways of commercialisation have to be found.
5. The CEO and the managers of business units are the drivers of innovation. There can be an innovation manager (not a technology manager) who coordinates the innovation activities. This manager is more a networker than a technical wizard although he or she should have a thorough understanding of technology and should be able to communicate with scientists, technicians and commercial staff in an effective way.

The approach then proposes that the extent to which an enterprise is innovative is determined by five factors that all need to be present in an enterprise if it is to be truly innovative[190] (Figure A1.11). We will now discuss these five factors.

Strategy

If you don't know where you want to get to . . . '*then it doesn't matter which way you go*',[191] said the Cheshire Cat to Alice in Lewis Carroll's famed *Alice's Adventures in Wonderland*. Many entrepreneurs rely on their gut feel or intuition when it comes to investment decisions and they distrust formal procedures such as strategic management, discarding them as theoretical exercises that have little to do with business practice. Modern strategic management processes blend intuition and rationality, arriving at decisions that bring the 'dreams' of the entrepreneur hither in a way that is rationally and financially sound.[192] Innovating within established enterprises requires a careful choice of what they want to achieve.[193] When the strategic plan has been prepared, innovation projects that will help to realise the plan's objectives will have to be selected. There are three criteria by which investment proposals – including innovation projects – are to be judged:[194]

1. Financial return, the extent to which the investment is profitable.
2. Strategic affinity, the 'match' with the strategic plan (a company is not investing in areas that may be profitable but that are outside its present and future scope).
3. Social and environmental acceptability. A company is not going to invest in a venture that is controversial vis-à-vis social and environmental aspects.

Organisation

When the innovation projects have been selected and due objectives have been set, a proper organisational structure will have to be built. As stated above, profit-responsible managers, whatever their level, are responsible for the innovation projects. They will employ one or more project managers to execute the innovation projects. These project managers need not be technological wizards but rather managers who understand the business processes as well as the technical headlines.[195] They should be good organisers as well as good networkers. A good organisation of innovation includes good evaluation techniques involving managers from all company functions such as finance, marketing and manufacturing, and a good procedure as to when and how the innovation project is to be evaluated.[196]

Partners

The investment proposal of an innovation project will include the partners with whom the development will be carried out. There are many different reasons why a company can collaborate with others; the main topics are:[197]

- Combining complementary capabilities. This can have different formats, such as company A has market access and company B has the technology or the partner has knowledge that is needed and it saves time and expenses compared with building up one's own

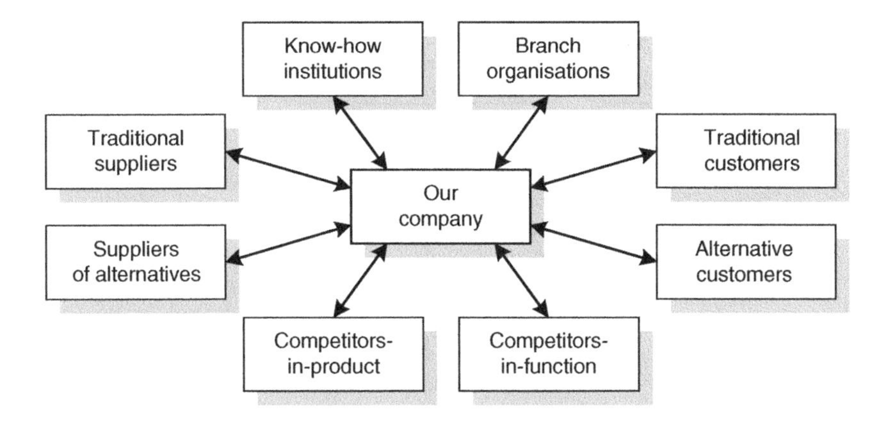

Figure A1.12 Potential partners in innovation

capabilities. Sharing capabilities is the most important reason for collaboration.

- Cost sharing. Saving expenses is an obvious reason, but is rarely the only one.
- Risk sharing. A joint approach to the market can reduce the chances that someone else enters the market earlier.
- Developing common standards. Controlling the standards can be a major element of competitive power. Existing standards can hamper or block new breakthrough innovation, but a new common standard can create a fertile platform for follow-up innovation.

Potential partners are depicted in Figure A1.12. Collaboration with suppliers and customers is a common phenomenon. It is sometimes more attractive to collaborate with suppliers of alternative materials or services or future customers rather than the traditional ones. Collaboration with competitors is tricky if it leads to similar products and competition can only be carried out on price. We distinguish competition-in-product from competition-in-function, referring to the situations in which competitors offer basically the same solutions versus solutions based on different technologies. Collaboration with competitors-in-function is more complex but often also more attractive. In the case of small and medium-sized enterprises (SMEs), branch organisations sometimes take the initiative to innovate and seek companies amongst their members to work together. Collaboration with know-how institutions, universities, professional service firms, engineering bureaus and so on should be distinguished from the role of such entities as pure suppliers. In any case, it is essential that a

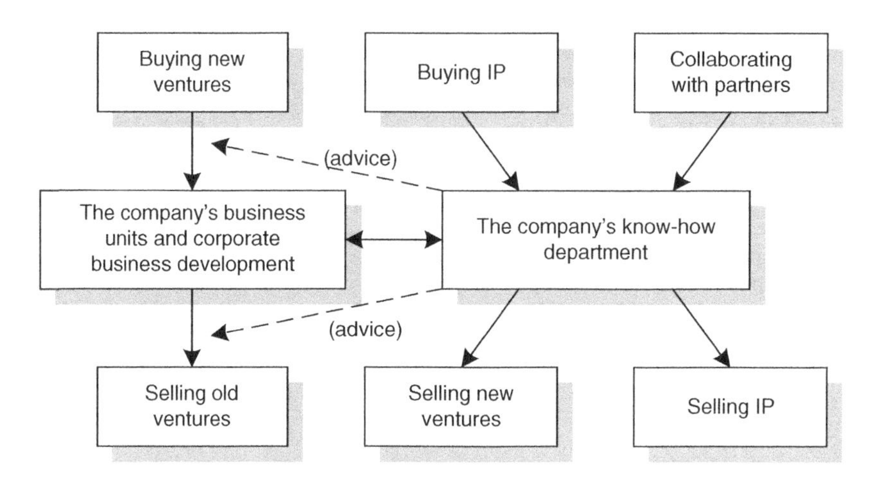

Figure A1.13 The technology department as innovation centre

company stays in touch with all potential partners in order to have up-to-date information about their possibilities and desires.[198]

Technology

Although technological expertise is no longer the one and only success factor for innovation, such expertise is a prerequisite for the development of new or improved products, processes and services. The technology manager in a small company is not only leading innovation projects, he is also buying and selling know-how just as large companies do. As such, this is the liaison with organisations such as universities. The role of the technology department of a large firm is depicted in Figure A1.13; small companies have similar activities.

People

Finally, we come to the people element of the Innovation Pentagon. Some call it an innovative culture. 'Corporate culture is the biggest deterrent to business creation', according to Harvard's David Garvin.[199] Corporate culture comprises the attitudes and informal aspects that govern the behaviour of those working in the firm. Norms and values guide behaviour and habits. The culture is often formed from the personal and business norms and values of the entrepreneur who started the firm. The culture is reinforced by the selection of personnel who should 'fit' the culture, and by 'stories' (the myths and sagas of the firm, the heroes and the pundits) that people tell each other. Through culture the people working in the firm distinguish themselves from those working in other firms. Culture is the non-formal element that supplements structure in creating attitudes of people in a firm. As norms and values are deeply rooted, culture is said to be difficult to change. We would like to challenge this conventional wisdom; changes in reward structures or organisational changes for instance have an almost immediate effect on a company's culture. Changing the culture by swapping an authoritarian management style for a learning style in which management can be challenged takes more time. A company that wants to become (more) innovative has to address the culture issue; it requires more than allocating a budget and installing proper structures. Culture is only one element of the human factor when it comes to innovation; personal knowledge, experience, attitudes and skills are other elements.

Together, the elements of the Innovation Pentagon can be regarded as the corporate innovation system. This term is derived from the concept of the national innovation system as coined by Christopher Freeman as a replacement of the earlier term of 'know-how infrastructure'.[200] The starting point of his theory is the observation that the national environment can have a considerable influence on stimulating, facilitating, hindering or preventing the innovative activities of firms. Initially, only elements such as the quantity and quality of national R&D and education were recognised as contributing to a nation's industrial innovation. R&D measures were taken as indicators of technical change, for instance in the Science Policy Reviews conducted by the Organisation for Economic Co-operation and Development (OECD). During the 1950s and 1960s the evidence grew that the rate of technical change and economic growth depended more on the efficient diffusion of technology than on R&D spending as such. The success of innovation depends very much on good communication between market and 'operations' with the technologists and it is often required, especially in branches comprised of many small enterprises such as agriculture, to build transfer or 'translation' institutes between users and suppliers of know-how.[201] The lesson learned from this discussion is that the same holds for large enterprises where design centres sometimes play the role of such an intermediary.

Appendix 2: Educating technostarters

A2.1 THE FUNNEL MODEL AND SYNCHRONISED EDUCATION

In the historical overview of Chapter 1, we saw that the medieval or first generation university aimed to create critical professionals (theologians, physicians, lawyers); it was not designed to create investigative scientists. This task was added in the Humboldt or second generation university, while education for professionals was maintained. The third generation university (3GU) adds entrepreneurs to the list of students to be educated (Table A2.1). The education of professionals, scientists and entrepreneurs can take place in undergraduate courses, graduate courses and post-experience courses or seminars.

Table A2.1 Education tasks of the three generations of universities

This type of university:		Educates:	
1st generation university	professionals		
2nd generation university	professionals	scientists	
3rd generation university	professionals	scientists	entrepreneurs

This appendix will discuss the funnel model for an educational programme in entrepreneurship, which is comprised of a number of stages in which the entrepreneurial intent increases after each stage, while the number of participating students decreases as students who are no longer interested in the subject drop out.[202] (Figure A2.1).

This cascade model has the following stages:

1. In the first stage, the interest of the student is awakened by an awareness programme or a mandatory course[203] such as 'Introduction to Entrepreneurship'. After such a course, the student may go to the next stage or call it the end of the road as far as entrepreneurship is concerned.
2. Students whose interest has been raised can follow an elementary elective, say a course such as 'Turning Technology into Business'. After this

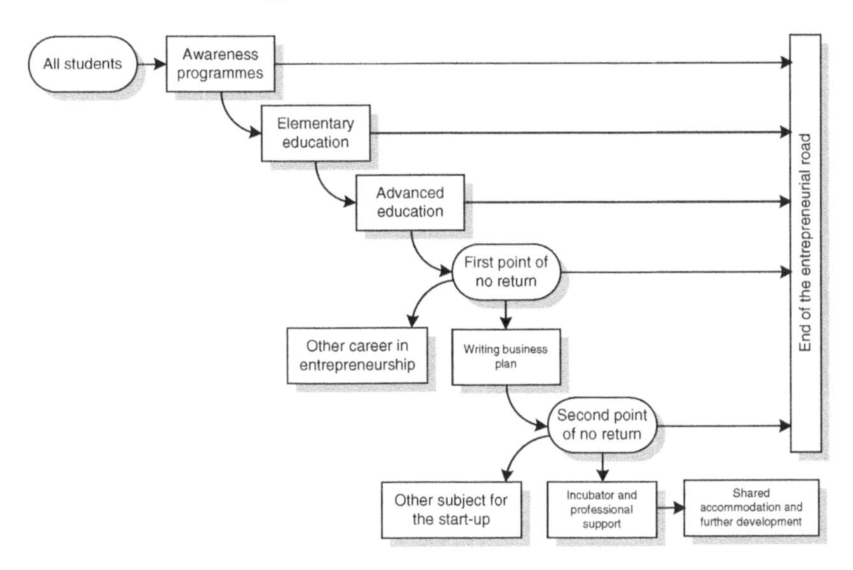

Figure A2.1 The way of the technostarter

course, the student can opt out of the entrepreneurship programme or go to the next stage.

3. At the next stage, the student can opt for an elective advanced course such as 'Fundamentals of Entrepreneurship'.
4. Having passed this course, the student faces a first 'point of no return' as he or she must decide whether to:
   a. become an entrepreneur and go to the next stage;
   b. not become an entrepreneur but seek a job in an area close to entrepreneurship, for instance, a venture capital fund, management consultancy or an intellectual property rights (IPR) bureau. A career as an intrapreneur (internal entrepreneur) in a large corporation is another attractive option for students who have passed the first three stages of the 'technostarter path'.
   c. Forget about entrepreneurship.
5. If the student decides to become an entrepreneur, he (or she) will have to find a subject for his enterprise. This can come from a project of his own (either his Master's or doctoral thesis or something he has developed outside the curriculum) or he has to find the subject elsewhere, for instance from a patent belonging to the university. Having chosen the subject, he enters the design phase as described in section 6.1. He will now have to follow advanced education in parallel to running the design phase. The university will apply a selection process and admit those who pass to a course in 'Writing your Company's Business Plan'.

6. The design phase ends when the student has written a professional business plan that can be presented to investors. He now reaches a second point of no return where he must decide whether to:
   a. proceed with the plan;
   b. start working on another plan if his original business plan was not successful while he continues to wish to become an entrepreneur;
   c. step out.
7. If the student decides to go ahead with the plan, the choice for the subject of the business is final and incubation should start. Formally speaking, the university will have to decide whether or not to let the student benefit from the incubator facilities and the flows of support that are associated with them. If both the student and the university take a positive decision, the development phase has started. During incubation, the development phase must be completed, after which actual production and sales begin.
8. The transition to the start-up phase coincides with a move from the incubator to a facility for shared accommodation where starters can develop their enterprise until they have generated enough scale to rent their own premises. In a shared accommodation facility, young enterprises can rent more space while sharing certain facilities. In the ideal situation, the university has land for setting up a technopark, science park, technopolis, or whatever the name. In such a park, land is leased to shared accommodation facilities, high-tech companies and research facilities of corporations or independent institutes, thus creating the full circle of the know-how carousel of Figure 2.1.

Ideally, the education of students who use their thesis project or other research project as the basis of their enterprise should be synchronised with their development as entrepreneurs and their entrepreneurial education. Figure A2.2 schematically shows the synchronisation of technological education, entrepreneurial education and the development of the new enterprise:

- Undergraduate courses can incorporate early entrepreneurship classes. Students at this age are only beginning to think about becoming an entrepreneur and the subject of their enterprise; this is the introductory phase of the enterprise.
- After his Bachelor's graduation, the student will start thinking about his thesis project and this project may become the base for his enterprise. Having become more serious at this age, the time is ripe for advanced courses in entrepreneurship. The thesis project and the

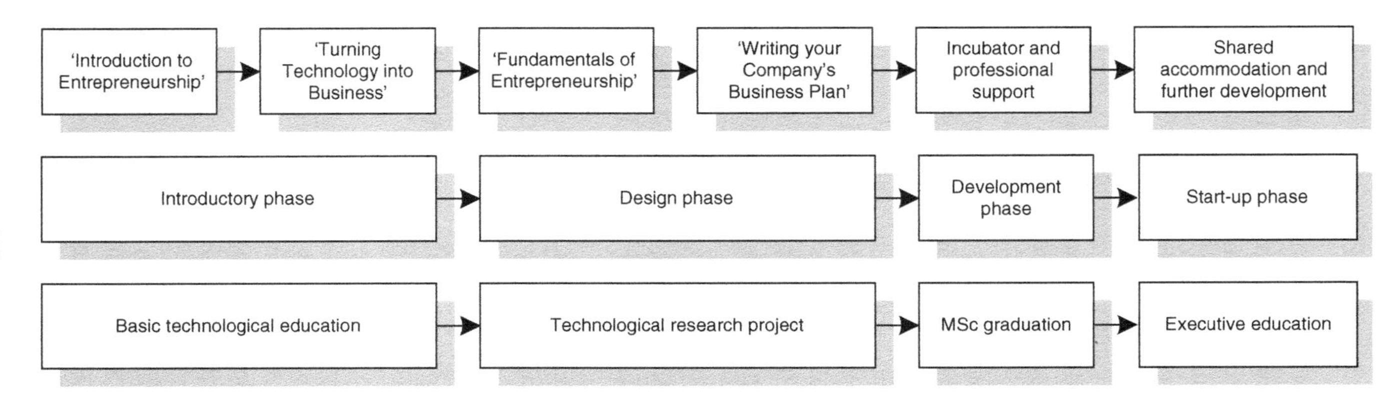

Figure A2.2 Synchronised dual education and development of the enterprise

advanced courses will then coincide with the design phase of the enterprise.
- The development phase of the enterprise usually starts at the moment the student receives his MSc or PhD degree. At this stage, the university can offer assistance with incubator facilities and professional and technical support.
- When the enterprise is well into the start-up phase, the enterprise moves out of the incubator and can relocate to a technopark in order to stay close to the university. For masters, the university can offer post-experience education courses and seminars in which young entrepreneurs exchange experiences.

Although the reality of a student's development as an entrepreneur does not synchronise with technical and entrepreneurship education as nicely as depicted, we strongly believe that it is a powerful method that can give universities of technology and science, agricultural and medical faculties an edge that will allow them to attract the best and most entrepreneurial students from all over the world.[204] As many young enterprises will remain close to the university, this will enhance the role of the university as a creator of high-level employment and a centre of the know-how carousel.

A2.2 IS TEACHING ENTREPRENEURSHIP COMPATIBLE WITH SCIENTIFIC EDUCATION?

Education in entrepreneurship is made up of both scientific education and vocational education. Scientific education aims to create scientists or technologists who can pursue a career in research, even if most graduates choose not to do so. It implies learning how to analyse phenomena, then how to apply and develop theory to arrive at scientifically valid conclusions. Vocational education is about applying theory and learning skills. Entrepreneurship requires:

- knowledge (obtained from scientific education);
- skills (motivating others, communication skills, building trust, choosing the right people, and so on);
- attitudes (courage, ethics, perseverance).

Education in entrepreneurship is a mixture of the three and so is education at business schools. Students will acquire analytical tools, the skills to use them and attitudes to guide them. An investment decision is a skill rather than a science; different people will come to different conclusions.[205]

But the data upon which such a decision is based should have a scientific basis: market analysis according to market research methods, technical data based on scientific methods, cost calculations according to business economics. Writing business plans and learning from case studies and management games are powerful integrative tools; however, they are geared to the use of data, and to applying skills and attitudes rather than the elements of scientific education.[206] In none of them is there a single 'correct' result as there is for, say, a mathematical exercise. Such tools are popular in education but one should not forget to teach the underlying analytical methods: market research, strategy, psychology, financial decision-making, financing, intellectual property and technology. Universities that consider that entrepreneurship courses are not their cup of tea because they are not scientific, should consider the fact that entrepreneurship comprises a mix of educational elements. In addition, they should not forget that no academic education can get by without teaching skills, if only skills in languages, presentation and computer skills. Universities should therefore not be afraid of giving academic credits for courses in entrepreneurship.

Some people suggest that entrepreneurship is a talent and not something that can be learned. There is however some evidence that entrepreneurship can be 'taught'. Vesper and McMullan have demonstrated that students who have taken courses in entrepreneurship made what were seen as better business decisions than did counterparts who did not have an entrepreneurship education.[207] This is not the last word on the subject and the question about the effectiveness of education in entrepreneurship deserves and requires more research.

Most entrepreneurs never went to a business school, and according to Dame Anita Roddick, founder of Body Shop, they should not. Her motto was:

> Don't get a business degree, get angry. Learn from the business school of life . . . The problem with business schools is that they are obsessed with the status quo. They encourage you to go deeper into the world as it is. We need good administration and financial flair, after all, but we need people of imagination too.[208]

Let us now turn to the four educational stages in more detail.

A2.3 TEACHING ENTREPRENEURSHIP

Introduction to Entrepreneurship

Awareness programmes are not usually part of a university curriculum. They are usually informal meetings to which students are attracted by well-known speakers who enthuse about the joy of entrepreneurship and the benefits it brings to founders and society. It is better to ask young alumni-entrepreneurs to talk about their enterprise than to have pep-talks by professors.

Although these kinds of activities can be a good start, they are not powerful as they are extracurricular. Some universities have adopted the approach that all Bachelor's students (that is, students from all faculties) follow a compulsory course in 'Introduction to Entrepreneurship' in their curriculum (usually in the last Bachelor's degree course year). This is a good litmus test for the attitude of the university towards entrepreneurship. Such an introduction can take the form in which teams of four to six students write a business plan for an imaginary company of their own choice. When the teams have been formed and when they have chosen their company, they receive lectures on topics such as strategy and positioning, marketing, production, organisation, financial plan and presentation. The lectures are often given by external experts, preferably entrepreneurs and members of professional service firms. Lectures from alumni-entrepreneurs from the same faculty describing their experiences as entrepreneurs give a good flavour and supplement the more specialised lectures. After each lecture, the student groups have to write the corresponding chapter of their business plan. Towards the end of the exercise, they have to review the entire plan. On the last day, the groups present their results to a jury who decide their marks. Note that, in this case, the writing of a business plan is just a pedagogical tool; the intent is not to really start a business (although programmes like this have produced some start-ups anyway).

'Turning Technology into Business'

Coming to the next stage, students whose interest is captured by the awareness programmes should be given the chance to participate in elementary electives. The objective of such electives is to increase a student's knowledge of enterprising while they are not (yet) committed to become an entrepreneur. A highly successful programme at TU Delft is called 'Turning Technology into Business'. In this programme, students in groups of four are given a yet unused patent of the university. They are then asked to find commercially attractive applications of this know-how. This does not extend to the writing of a full business plan for this application, as that may be the subject of the fourth type of course. Students follow a systematic search approach and they have to collect data as a preliminary check on the feasibility of various applications. The programme covers the following subjects:

- unbundling technology and assessment of the strengths of the technology components;
- diffusion of technology into products and markets;
- the lead-user concept as a vehicle for the successful introduction of a technology into a market;
- strategies to maximise the yield of technology;
- starting the creation of a new high-tech firm.

The Delft course is comprised of seven afternoon sessions while students work in groups in between the sessions. The course is given by the Management Faculty together with KPN Mobile (the leading cell phone operator in the Netherlands), Philips Electronics and an independent research organisation (TNO) that contributes with its own patents and stimulates employees to follow the course.

Let us give some examples. One of our patents concerned a technique by which air is sucked in at critical locations on the wing of an aeroplane; this technique reduces the drag and saves more energy than it costs. Since the approval procedures to apply such technology in aircraft are very long, it was decided to find alternative applications. Students found these by applying the technology to the spoilers of racing cars and to the wings of windmills. Another patent concerned a polymer that binds water through the formation of hydrogen bridges, resulting in a sort of gel. The story goes that this patent was developed to prevent water leaking from hot water bottles, an application for which there was apparently no market. The team's first idea was to mix the polymer with water in the nozzle of a fire hose, thus making the use of water more effective when fighting fires. A quick test however showed that the contact time between the water leaving the nozzle and reaching the fire was too short to form the hydrogen bonds, so it did not work. The next idea was to insert the polymer into the soil under grass, thus reducing the amount of water needed to maintain golf courses in hot countries by about 90 per cent. This seemed feasible and a team is now working on its commercialisation. These examples show how students are taught to find completely new applications for know-how that cannot be used (or is not yet used) for its original intended application. In conclusion, students learn how to proliferate technology and how technology is applied through new enterprises.

'Fundamentals of Entrepreneurship'

Stage three will attract fewer students than the elementary courses of stage two and the contents now become more serious. In an advanced course, students should learn:

- The necessary analytical tools and instruments associated with entrepreneurship (the subjects have been mentioned above). Such subjects can be taught through rigorous lectures with tests to check the learned content.
- To make decisions about real entrepreneurship dilemmas. Business cases are the ideal tool here especially since a wide range of high-quality and recent cases are available.[209]
- To reflect on actual cases as presented by young, successful and unsuccessful entrepreneurs. Such presentations should be turned into true learning experiences rather than interesting topics to conclude the day, by combining them with the previous two methods and making them the subject of examination.
- To reflect on their own ideas of whether to become an entrepreneur.

A good course in the range of 'Fundamentals of Entrepreneurship' is the course with case studies as described by Kuemmerle.[210] This course has the additional advantage that it addresses international entrepreneurship, which is useful as an increasing number of new ventures face the international option much earlier than before. The course relies heavily on the case method and care should be taken that the cases are supplemented by the other elements listed above. Other cases on entrepreneurship can be found in a book by Clarysse and Roure.[211]

Another successful course in 'Fundamentals of Entrepreneurship' is given by Brown University's Division of Engineering.[212] This course aims at creating a new type of engineer, the entrepreneurial engineer, who 'needs a broad range of skills and knowledge, above and beyond a strong science and engineering background'. The two-semester course is open to advanced undergraduate students of all faculties, although graduates and younger undergraduates are admitted. Students are admitted only after careful screening. For this course, the university collaborates with industries in the neighbourhood. These companies provide the technical product seed ideas. These ideas have to be developed into a concrete business plan by teams of students with mixed backgrounds. Together with the faculty, the companies supervise progress and participate in lecturing. Students are strongly stimulated to start a new enterprise with a business relation to the parent company. The intellectual property belongs to the parent company as a default but many companies do not exercise this right, leaving the IPR to the student teams. They do so not because of a lack of interest, rather because 'they feel more comfortable making the donation'. This aligns with the university's policy to discourage the overuse of non-disclosure and confidentiality agreements; the faculty recommends the parent companies not to offer projects that would be subject to secrecy. The course does not result in many start-ups. However:

> the very deep soul-searching that some students went through to decide between continuing their start-up and competing offers speaks to the psychological investment they made by following the course. The problem students faced in continuing with the project as a start-up was that it was generally a multi-body problem – if only one key individual did not continue, generally no one felt that they could continue. The faculty have continually been surprised by the conservatism of the students. The students accept the argument that at their particular stage of life they have little to lose if the start-up fails, but they cannot bring themselves to take the risk.[213]

This conclusion stems from the first time the course was given, and results may be better in subsequent years. In any case one may expect that the experience of following courses like this will give engineering graduates a different attitude in whatever career they choose to pursue.

Whichever way a university organises a course on 'Fundamentals of Entrepreneurship', students who have passed it should have a comprehensive knowledge of all aspects of entrepreneurship. This will make them eligible for careers as entrepreneurs but also as analysts in venture capital firms, partners in professional service firms, or intrapreneurs (internal entrepreneurs in corporations with profit-responsible business units). Courses like this should make the student confront his choice: will he pursue a career as entrepreneur or do something else? Teachers should give opportunities for reflection on this choice and design methodology to do so. At the end of the introductory and elementary courses in entrepreneurship, students must decide whether to continue going along the way of the entrepreneur or stepping out. After the course in fundamentals a similar choice must be made, but a 'yes-decision' now implies commitment to follow the road to the end.

'Writing your Company's Business Plan'

Those students who become so enthusiastic that they want to start their own enterprise can participate in an elective in which they learn how to write a business plan for their own firm. In contrast to the business plan programme described as a tool for creating awareness, this elective is restricted to those who seriously want to start their own new technology-based firm. In other words, students have to pass the test as to whether they are really committed to starting their own enterprise in order to be admitted to this course (at Delft University of Technology we also require their subject to be technology-based, not necessarily high-tech). Students – as individuals or in teams – bring their own concept to start the business. They then get further teaching and exercises in strategy, marketing, production, organisation, intellectual property rights, financial planning and how to proceed after the establishment of the company. After each instruction, the teams write the corresponding chapter of their business plans which are reviewed at the start of the next class.[214] Lectures are given by specialists from professional service firms such as management consultants, auditors, banks, marketing and IPR bureaus. These lecturers also assess the corresponding chapters of the resulting business plans. In addition to the external lecturers, each team is given a coach who acts as stand-by and critical observer throughout the process of writing the plan. Coaches can be management consultants or young entrepreneurs who have been through this before. At the end of the programme, an independent jury, consisting of entrepreneurs, financiers and university professors, should judge the business plans and the presentations. One can give prizes for the best business plans. Such prizes will help the teams in finding publicity, customers and financial support during the next phases.

In Delft, the course in 'Writing a Business Plan' is given by members of the Stichting Netwerk Jonge Ondernemers (Foundation Network for Young Entrepreneurs) in which firms such as Roland Berger Strategy Consultants, Ernst & Young, Rabobank, Arnold & Siedsma (an IPR consultant), Holland van Gijzen (corporate lawyers) and a marketing bureau participate. These partners contribute in kind (time) while some also give a financial donation which the foundation uses for creating publicity for the courses and the maintenance of a website. Consultants from Roland Berger, most of them Delft alumni, coach the teams throughout the course (and often afterwards). They and the other partners give the lectures and assess the resulting business plans. The foundation keeps track of former students and other entrepreneurs and people interested, and all these are invited to join the final presentations of the business plans. This event has become a popular get-together and a major networking event. The course is given twice annually. It has helped create some 30 companies in 15 years. Subjects that are addressed in afternoon workshops are:

- vision, mission and ambition;
- intellectual property;
- business models;
- market analysis;
- strategy and positioning;
- marketing and sales;
- finance;
- taxes and law;

- preliminary presentations;
- final presentations.

After the course, the foundation members offer young entrepreneurs professional assistance, initially, when they are in the early stages of developing their company, free of charge. The foundation actively helps them to find financiers. Last but not least, after the course, they are part of the club.

A2.4 GETTING STARTED

After completing the course on writing the business plan, the (teams of) students or academics have to decide whether to go ahead with the plan and its subject. This is the second point of no return; the commitment is not only to become an entrepreneur but to start this particular enterprise: 'death or the gladioli' as they say in the Tour de France. The university faces a complementary decision: whether or not to open the doors of its facilities to the student or team. Such facilities, as we have seen in section 8.3, can include incubator facilities (cheap accommodation plus broadband IT, administrative and other operational support features), grants or deferred loans from university funds, professional support and technical support from the technical or scientific faculties. Such facilities should help the starters cross the Valley of Death, that dangerous passage where so many promising activities get stranded between a promising business plan and the growth phase in which the company becomes airborne. The facilities not only help start-ups on the way, but they also convey a clear signal to students in the previous stages that: 'Once you get to this stage, we are here to support you with powerful tools'. Such a signal, if clearly communicated during the early stages, will definitely exert a pull-function for those making up their minds about entrepreneurship.

One of the facilities is a platform where start-ups can meet angels, venture capital firms, providers of subsidies, banks and other parties involved in financing or financial assistance. For many start-ups, the financial world is a black box, a world they are not familiar with, and without help it can take them ages before they make the right contacts. Universities represent fertile ground for investors and the universities should use their clout to get them to meet start-ups in an organised way.

During the incubation phase, the pampering will decrease and the venture will increasingly stand on its own feet. Space in the incubator building becomes too small and its availability is usually restricted for a certain period of time. When the venture has to move out of the incubator building, it is often attractive to stay in the surroundings of the university because of the proximity of technical and professional support and, most of all, colleagues. To this end, universities can offer shared accommodation facilities, on a cost or even profit basis. Such proximity offers all kinds of synergy, including the option to ask young entrepreneurs to contribute to the education in the first four stages of the lecture series of figure A2.1.

After the start, new ventures have to deal with changes in markets, technologies and internal factors such as the desire of some founders to step out. In addition, they have to change from financing partners, angels being replaced by venture capital. It is here that post-experience courses can play a useful role. Such courses will often be based on research in entrepreneurship, the results of which need to be transferred to practitioners. Post-experience courses for advanced entrepreneurs can be complemented by courses for scientists or engineers who are considering a buyout of the company in which they work. This situation arises frequently when the founders retire and want to leave their enterprise in safe hands.[215] There is a huge market for such courses and it is relatively little work for a faculty that already gives courses in entrepreneurship to provide for this. And again, such courses may create options for cooperation in the future.

A2.5 MINORS IN ENTREPRENEURSHIP

The dream of many a young technostarter is to graduate in the subject of their enterprise, both in the technical and the business aspects. For those the university can create a minor subject, preferably for the Master phase. A typical minor subject corresponds to 20 weeks of study and can consist of six courses:

- 'Introduction to Entrepreneurship' (equivalent to two weeks study; see section A2.3).
- 'Turning Technology into Business' (equivalent to four weeks study; see section A2.3).
- 'Intellectual Property for Entrepreneurs' (equivalent to two weeks study). This programme includes introductory lectures and cases in intellectual property rights. This subject can be followed only if programmes 1 and 2 have been passed.
- 'Financing for Entrepreneurs' (equivalent to two weeks study). This programme discusses the design of a financial plan for a new or young firm, with examples from practice. It gives the background to financing, the role of informal investors and venture capital funds (with guest speakers) and a visit to a matchmaking meeting between investors and starters.

- 'How To Write a Business Plan' (equivalent to four weeks study; see section A2.3). It can be followed only if programmes 1 to 4 have been passed.
- Mini research project (equivalent to six weeks study), an individual research task, to be followed only if programmes 1–4 have been passed. In this programme, students get a personal tutor, preferably a PhD student who can use the results for his or her thesis and the student of the minor programme as cheap labour.

If this minor subject is given in a two-year Master's degree phase, technology students can study around 1.5 years in a technical faculty in which their thesis project can be devoted to the subject on which the enterprise will be based. At the same time, students follow the minor subject course in which they get a thorough academic education in entrepreneurship while they learn how to write the business plan for their own firm. Students who want to start their own enterprise therefore get the best of both worlds: technical and business knowledge, according to the model of synchronised education.

Students at Delft can follow a two-year MSc course in 'Management of Technology' (MoT), which has a variant in which the time is divided 50/50 between MoT subjects and subjects relating to entrepreneurship. Some universities offer the option of a three-year joint-degree programme in which the equivalent of two years of study is devoted to a technological subject and the equivalent of one year to study of entrepreneurship. A variation of this is an option in which students spent 1.5 years on their technical subject (at the technical university) and 1.5 years on management and entrepreneurship (in a business school). After three years, they then have an MSc as well as an MBA degree.

Figure A2.3 shows the four options described:

- The student can opt for a specialisation in a purely technological subject.
- He or she can choose a shortened Master's programme in the technological specialisation of his choice, supplemented by a minor subject in entrepreneurship
- He can completely skip a specialisation in a technological subject and go for a Master's degree in technology management, with one year's study in entrepreneurship as an option.
- He or she can select a joint degree, consisting of a normal two-year MSc in a technological specialisation and a shortened one-year MSc course in entrepreneurship or a combination of an MSc and an MBA degree.

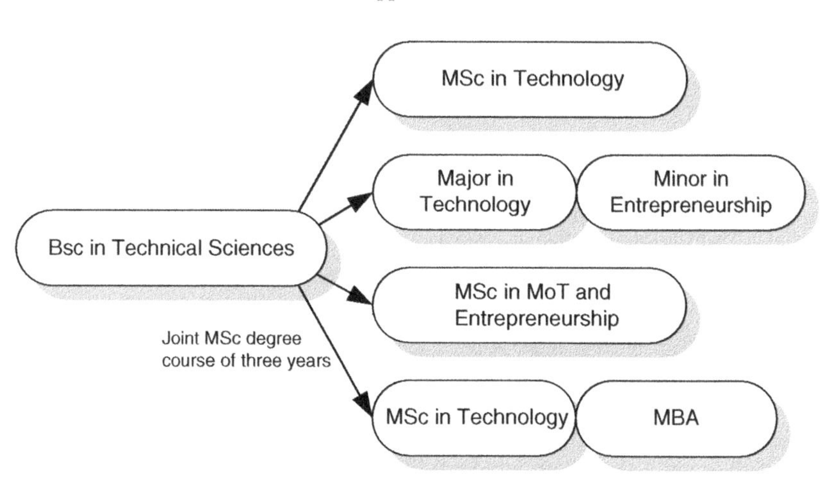

Figure A2.3 A comprehensive education programme with various options for study in entrepreneurship

Note that there are many synergies in this design as lectures can be given simultaneously as electives and part of a minor subject course as well as a one-year programme. The one-year programme for the joint Master's can be the same as the programme of the MSc course in MoT with the entrepreneurship option.

We believe that universities that label themselves as 'entrepreneurial universities' should have a programme as outlined in Figures A2.1 and A2.2. To complement these undergraduate and graduate programmes, it is advisable to give a post-experience course to alumni and others who have had, say, five years of practical experience since their Master's degree. Such a programme could be equivalent to the minor subject course as outlined above, but given in the evenings, weekends and during a few weeks' holiday. The reason why we advocate this option is that students of design faculties (architecture, industrial design and others) rarely start their own enterprise immediately after they complete their Master's degree. Instead, they work for a number of years in an existing bureau in order to learn the trade and to discover a market niche for themselves. Before starting their own niche enterprise, they may want to follow a course in entrepreneurship. A post-experience course could simultaneously address engineers and scientists who want to buy out the firm in which they work. Many technology-based family enterprises face a succession problem and one may expect a large number of buyouts.

For completion, it is advisable to organise workshops on entrepreneurship for university staff. In Chapter 2 we argued that, for technostarter

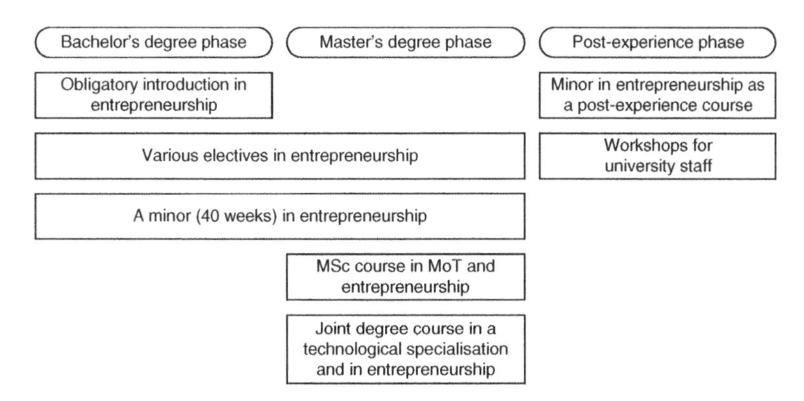

Figure A2.4 Summary of academic entrepreneurship courses

programmes to be successful and for universities to move to the 3GU model, it is mandatory to create a change in culture. Offering workshops to university staff may assist in realising such a change. Figure A2.4 summarises the programme suggested in this paragraph.

Naturally, more variations are possible. The Norwegian School of Management BI in Oslo offers a BSc degree in entrepreneurship with a programme comprised of 50 per cent broad business topics, 40 per cent courses dedicated to entrepreneurship and 10 per cent for an entrepreneurship-oriented thesis project. Their MSc programme in business has a major in 'Innovation and Entrepreneurship' with courses in entrepreneurship, creativity, innovation process management, innovation systems, entrepreneurial finance and global entrepreneurship. The Judge School of Management of the University of Cambridge offers courses in business vision, marketing, business models, finance, building teams, mentoring, communication/presentation/pitching, business plan crafting, self-efficacy, networking skills and entrepreneurship consulting projects. These courses are taught in a wide range of programmes including summer schools, the Enterprisers programme (a one week-programme with Massachusetts Institute of Technology (MIT) Sloan School of Management which created 24 new enterprises as of 2004), MBA modules, postgraduate programmes, undergraduate programmes and bespoke corporate entrepreneurship programmes.

Finally, a word on research in entrepreneurship. In any type of university, research is required to support the educational activities. If it is lacking, the education will have the nature of higher vocational training, which is not the objective of a university. Research in entrepreneurship is therefore a mandatory activity with the aim of gaining academic acceptance of the subject and enhancing educational activities. This is recognised by an increasing number of universities and scientific conferences and periodicals. However, adding the subject of entrepreneurship to a university's research programme is different from adding other new fields of science, as entrepreneurship concerns the mission of the university. Entrepreneurship activities are the only ones in a 3GU that address all three objectives: research, education and commercialisation of know-how. Research also offers good networking opportunities.

During a colloquium at Harvard Business School, sponsored by EFER (European Federation of Entrepreneurship Research) in Boston in 2005, a quick inventory of the research activities of the 31 participating European universities was conducted. There were few systematic research programmes; the subjects appeared to be chosen at random. Subjects such as growth management (scored seven times) and finance-related subjects such as financing, venture capital, angels, women angels, valuation (ten times) scored highest. Next were technology transfer (including the transfer of technology from the scientist to the entrepreneur), university spin-offs and external factors favouring entrepreneurship (each five times). Other research focused on special forms of entrepreneurship such as family enterprises (three times), female entrepreneurship (three times), corporate entrepreneurship/intrapreneurship (three times) and business ethics and conflict situations (three times). Some research focuses on specific branches like the creative sector and the biotech sector. Education in entrepreneurship, historic studies and international entrepreneurship each scored twice, and subjects related to the knowledge economy four times. There were general subjects like success factors in business creation (three times), attitudes towards entrepreneurship and entrepreneurial behaviour (twice), entrepreneurial personalities (once) and leadership (once). Finally, there were some specific investigations concerning user-driven innovation (once) and the development of networks of entrepreneurs after closure of a high-tech corporation (once). This list is by no means comprehensive and it will not be published. Nevertheless, it provides an interesting indication as to what interests entrepreneurship researchers in Europe.

Notes and references

1. This chapter is very much based on the series *A History of the University in Europe*, edited by W. Rüegg and published by Cambridge University Press, Cambridge. In 2008, only the first three volumes had been published.
2. Compayré, Gabriel, *Abelard and the Origin and Early History of Universities*, reprinted from the 1902 edition by the University Press of the Pacific, Honolulu, 2002.
3. *Chartularium Universitaties Parisiensis*, Delalain, Paris, 1889 (quoted from Compayré, op. cit).
4. Compayré, op. cit.
5. Radice, B., Introduction to: *The Letters of Abelard and Heloise*, Penguin Books, London 1974, revised edition 2003.
6. Laurie, S.S., *Lectures on the Rise and Early Constitution of Universities*, Kegan Paul, Trench & Co., London, 1886, quoted from Compayré, op. cit.
7. Rüegg, op. cit.
8. Rüegg, op. cit.
9. Compayré, op. cit.
10. Gieysztor, A., 'Management and resources', Chapter 3 in Rüegg, W. (ed.), *A History of the University in Europe*, Volume 1, Cambridge University Press, Cambridge, 1992.
11. It celebrated its 900th anniversary in 1988.
12. Verger, J., 'Patterns', Chapter 2 in Rüegg, W. (ed.), *A History of the University in Europe*, Volume 1, Cambridge University Press, Cambridge, 1992.
13. Compayré, op. cit.
14. According to Marxism, 'schools and higher educational institutions are founded in order to train the persons who are needed to maintain the ruling class domination'. Rüegg, op. cit.
15. Le Goff, J., *Time, Work and Culture in the Middle Ages*, University of Chicago Press, Chicago, 1980.
16. Much of this paragraph is derived from: Frijhoff, W., 'Patterns', Chapter 2 in Ruegg, W., *A History of the University in Europe*, Volume 2, *Universities in Early Modern Europe (1500–1800)*, Cambridge University Press, Cambridge, 1996.
17. Plato called his philosophical institution the Academia (Academy), after a public garden in the suburbs of Athens.
18. Otterspeer, W., *Group Portrait of a Lady: The Bulwark of Freedom, the University of Leiden 1575–1672*, Bert Bakker Publishers, Amsterdam, 2000 (in Dutch). Part I of a series of four volumes on the history of this university.
19. Jarausch, K.H. (ed), *The Transformation of Higher Learning, 1860–1930, Expansion, Diversification, Social Opening, Professionalism in England, Germany, Russia and the US*, University of Chicago Press, Chicago, 1983.
20. Hammerstein, N., 'Epilogue – universities and war in the twentieth century',

in Rüegg, W. (ed.), *A History of the University in Europe*, Volume 3, Cambridge University Press, Cambridge, 2004.

21. Rüegg, W., 'Themes', Chapter 1 in W. Rüegg (ed.), *A History of the University in Europe*, Volume 3, Cambridge University Press, Cambridge, 2004.
22. Rüegg, op. cit.
23. Hammerstein, op. cit.
24. Rüegg, op. cit.
25. The habits still remain. In a recent case of harassment in a Dutch student association, the police could not take action as the victims did not press charges but relied on the juridical system of the student corporation instead.
26. Israel, J.I., *Enlightenment Contested: Philosophy, Modernity and the Emancipation of Man 1670–1752*, Oxford University Press, Oxford, 2006.
27. Many Frenchmen believed, after the 1870–71 war that the German victory had demonstrated the superiority of the German university system. Hammerstein, op. cit.
28. Mackay, J., *Sounds Out of Silence: A Life of Alexander Graham Bell*, Mainstream Publishing Edinburgh, 1997.
29. A more elaborate discussion of the many changes to the traditional university can be found in: Duderstadt, J.J., *A University for the 21st Century*, The University of Michigan Press, Ann Arbor, 2000. See also: Weber, L.E. and J.J. Duderstadt, *Reinventing the Research University*, Economica, London, Paris and Geneva, 2004.
30. Graham Bowley, 'How Harvard got ahead', *Financial Times Weekend*, 16 October 2004.
31. Kellaway, L., 'Why academics make an unfit subject of management', *Financial Times*, 27 February 2006.
32. Crosier, D., L. Purser and H. Schmidt, *Trends V: Universities Shaping the European Higher Education Area*, European University Association, Brussels, 2007.
33. This view does not necessarily apply to areas outside the domain of technology, natural sciences and medicine. The University of Chicago collected nine Nobel Prizes (the prize for economics dates from 1969) and is associated with several more, due to specialisation, hard work and 'an often brutal debating culture'. Van Overveldt, J., *The Chicago School: How the University of Chicago Assembled the Thinkers who Revolutionized Economics and Business*, Agate Publishing, Beverly Hills, CA, 2007.
34. Lambert, R. and N. Butler, *The Future of European Universities: Renaissance or Decay?*, Centre for European Reform, London, May 2006.
35. S.H.I. Choon Fong, 'State of the university address', National University of Singapore, 13 August 2002, available at http://www.nus.edu.sg/vco/speeches/pdf/State%20of%20the%20University%20Address%202002a.pdf.
36. Nisbet, E.G., 'Earth sciences centre of gravity moves eastward', Letter to the Editor, *Financial Times*, 12 March 2005.
37. The technical component of PA Consultants was created by Gordon Edge and others when they left Cambridge Consultants.
38. 'Business: the new entrepreneurs', *The Economist*, 24 December 1983, pp. 59–71.
39. Pesola, M. 'Cultivated in Silicon's Fen's fertile soil', *Financial Times*, 9 February 2005.
40. 'Clustered cloisters', *The Economist*, 21 February 2004.

41. Vyakarnam, S., *Research Parks and Incubators: Re-defining the Role of the Incubator*, Research Paper, Centre for Entrepreneurial Learning, Judge Institute of Management Studies, University of Cambridge, Cambridge.
42. 'Business: The new entrepreneurs', op. cit.
43. Most universities of technology are handicapped by the fact that they do not have an academic hospital. They build strong links with a suitable hospital in the neighbourhood instead.
44. *The Cambridge Phenomenon* and *The Cambridge Phenomenon Revisited*, published by Segal Quince Wicksteed, Cambridge, 1985 and 2000. Some other data in this paragraph are drawn from these publications as well.
45. *The Cambridge Phenomenon Revisited*, op. cit.
46. *Our Competitive Future: Building the Knowledge Driven Economy*, White Paper, (UK) Department of Trade and Industry, The Stationery Office, London, 16 December 1998.
47. On land given to the college by Henry VIII in 1546.
48. Herriot, W. and T. Minshall, *Cambridge Technopole: An Overview of the UK's Leading High-Technology Business Cluster*, published by St John's Innovation Centre, Cambridge, and updated biannually (we used the spring 2003 version).
49. Herriot and Minshall, op. cit.
50. Carl Schramm, head of the Ewing Marion Kauffman Foundation that fosters entrepreneurship in American universities by giving grants of $70 million a year, is seriously worried that 'universities are becoming too bureaucratic in their approach to intellectual property, creating a new bottleneck in the transfer of technology to start-ups. Several big firms told [him] recently that they are considering switching research to universities in some development countries, because there will be no question over who owns the rights to a breakthrough in those countries', 'Face value: the evangelist of entrepreneurship', *The Economist*, 5 November 2005. Josh Lerner of Harvard Business School ventures similar warnings. Lerner, J., 'The university and the start-up: lessons from the past two decades', *Journal of Technology Transfer*, **30**, pp. 46–56, 2005.
51. www.cue.org.uk.
52. This phenomenon is familiar from the development of the IT industry in Silicon Valley and the Boston area, but it was equally present in the development of the book printing industry, following the first successful book printing with movable type by Johannes Gutenberg in 1454 in Mainz. His financier, Johannes Fust, can probably be regarded as the world's first business angel.
53. Lang, J., 'Creating the climate for innovation', handout, the University of Cambridge, 2003, quoted and edited with permission.
54. The situation in the US was and is different, as private sponsoring, by organisations and individuals, has always played a major role in that country.
55. Quoted from the 'Rector's preface' of the *2004 Annual Report of Oulu University* (by Lauri H.J. Lajunne, Rector).
56. Rebecca Knight, 'How to join audits to autopsies', *Financial Times*, 23 January 2006.
57. H. Etzkowitz of City University New York describes the MIT case as an illustration of what he calls the entrepreneurial university. He gives a consistent framework of such a university and the three stages of its development. His ideas are very consistent with those expressed in this book although the

concept of the third generation university goes a step further than the entrepreneurial university that we would label a transitory phase between the second and third generation universities. Etzkowitz, H., 'The evolution of the entrepreneurial university', *International Journal of Technology and Globalisation*, **1** (1), pp. 64–77, 2004.

58. Niele, F., *Energy: Engine of Evolution*, Elsevier and Shell Global Solutions, 2005.
59. Asked about trends in industrial R&D, the first trend Mr Rick Harwig, CEO of Philips Research, mentions is interdisciplinarity: 'In our research in biochips, the disciplines of biochemistry, IC-technology, electronics, pharmacy and physics merge' (Hanne Obbink in an interview with Rick Harwig, NWO Hypothese, 2005, in Dutch).
60. Wilson, E.O., *Consilience, the Unity of Knowledge*, Knopf, New York, 1998.
61. Wikipedia, 'Consilience'.
62. http://www.stanford.edu/group/dschool/projects/making_a_difference.html.
63. Dyson, J., *Against the Odds: An Autobiography*, Orion Business, Fairacres, 1997.
64. This paragraph is quoted from: 'Higher education and the poor, rebuilding the American dream', *The Economist*, 21 January 2006.
65. In his novel *I Am Charlotte Simmons* (Jonathan Cape/Random House, London, 2004), Tom Wolfe shows, albeit as a caricature, that this applies equally to top US universities. But *The Economist* suggests that: 'Mr Wolfe's satire pales into insignificance compared with the hog-stomping reality that he tries to capture'. *The Economist*, Lexington column, 15 April 2006.
66. 'Is it worth paying all that money?', *Financial Times*, 4 December 2006.
67. Martin Spiewak, 'Im Hörsaal erster Klasse' (in the first-class lecture theatre), *Die Zeit*, 8 September 2005 (in German).
68. Williamson, H., 'Germany's corridors of learning start to chart independent path', *Financial Times*, 25 October 2006.
69. 'French universities: shaking them up', *The Economist*, 7 July 2007.
70. Actually, it was Bill's father. It was part of a complex property deal including the establishment of the Microsoft Research labs next door.
71. 'The father of invention', *The Economist*, 11 July 1998.
72. 'Harvard portfolio asset mix has more foreign equities', *Financial Times*, 20 September 2006.
73. Exceptions prove the rule. University patronage has occurred since the Middle Ages. Immanuel College, Cambridge for example was founded and initially funded by Sir Walter Mildmay (1520–89), Queen Elizabeth I's chancellor. Recently, the Robinson and Wolfson colleges were founded by wealthy individuals who made their money in radio rentals and mail order respectively.
74. 'Jacob's ladder', *The Economist*, 16 December 2006.
75. It has been done before. Harvard College, now Harvard University, was founded in 1636 with a grant from the Massachusetts legislature. It expanded after Mr John Harvard left his library and half his estate to the college that was henceforth named after him. *Harvard and Holland*, N.V. Indivers, Uithoorn, the Netherlands, 1986.
76. This section was written together with Professor Vassil Penchev and Dr Daniel Pavlov of the University of Rousse and Mr Yavor Dimitrov of the Management and Business Development Centre of Rousse, Bulgaria.

77. This chapter was written with Jan Verloop.
78. Interview with Dr K.R. Teer, NRC Handelsblad, 12 June 1985 (in Dutch).
79. Holst invited Einstein and Pauli to his – then small – laboratory.
80. Gupta, A.K. and D. Wilemon, 'Changing patterns in industrial R&D management', *Journal of Product Innovation Management*, **13**, pp. 497–511, 1996. Also see: Giget, M., 'Technology, innovation and strategy: recent developments', *International Journal of Technology Management*, **14** (6/7/8), pp. 613–34, 1997.
81. Burke, D.P., 'Research gets the word: if it doesn't fit – forget it', *Chemical Week*, 28 February 1973, pp. 32–42.
82. The subtitle of Ansoff's groundbreaking book *Corporate Strategy* (McGraw-Hill, New York, 1965) was: *An Analytic Approach to Business Policy for Growth and Expansion*. This subtitle disappeared in later editions.
83. Ansoff, I., *Strategic management*, Macmillan Press, Basingstoke, 1979.
84. Roussel, P.A., K.N. Saad and T.J. Erickson, *Third Generation R&D: Managing the Link to Corporate Strategy*, Harvard Business School Press, Cambridge, MA, and A.D. Little, 1991. Earlier, A.D. Little published *The Strategic Management of Technology*, ADL, Cambridge, MA, 1981.
85. Since the publication of the book it has become a popular game amongst academics to distinguish further phases in the development of industrial research. Liyanage and co-authors for instance discuss research networks as a crucial element of knowledge management and call it fourth generation R&D management (Liyanage, S., P.F. Greenfield and R. Don, 'Towards a fourth generation R&D management model: research networks in knowledge management', *International Journal of Technology Management*, **18** (3–4), pp. 372–93, 1999). See also: W.L. Miller and L. Morris, *4th Generation R&D: Managing Knowledge, Technology and Innovation*, John Wiley & Sons, Hoboken, NJ, 1999.
86. Wissema, J.G., 'The synchronisation of R&D with corporate strategy, objectives, planning and evaluation' (in Dutch), *Bedrijfskunde*, **52** (3), pp. 195–213, 1980.
87. Initially Chemicals was a separate global business, but after a consolidation process became part of Oil Products.
88. http://www.c-fix.com/default.aspx.
89. Veer, J. van der, 'Innovation: from vision to reality', presentation to the Education Without Borders conference, Abu Dhabi, United Arab Emirates, 22 February 2003.
90. Shell Technology Report, Royal Dutch Shell, the Hague, the Netherlands, 2006.
91. 'The rise and fall of corporate R&D', *The Economist*, 3 March 2007, pp. 69–71.
92. *Financial Times*, 11 June 2007, p. 16.
93. Torvalds, L., *Just for Fun: The Story of an Accidental Revolutionary*, HarperCollins, New York, 2001.
94. Verloop, J., *Insight in Innovation: Managing Innovation by Understanding the Laws of Innovation*, Elsevier, Amsterdam, 2004. See also: Davila, D., M.J. Epstein and R. Shelton, *Making Innovation Work: How to Manage It, Measure It, and Profit from It*, Wharton School Publishing, Philadelphia, 2005.
95. Chesbrough, H., *Open Innovation, the New Imperative for Creating and*

Profiting from Technology, Harvard Business School Press, Cambridge, MA, 2003. See also: Vaitheeswaran, V., *Something New Under the Sun*, Supplement to *The Economist*, 13 October 2007.

96. Chesbrough, op. cit.
97. United States Patent and Trademark Office, Annual list of top ten organisations receiving most US patents, www.uspto.gov.
98. Schramm, C.J., *The Entrepreneurial Imperative*, HarperCollins, New York, 2006.
99. Cf. Kuemmerle, W., 'A test for the fainthearted', *Harvard Business Review*, May 2002, pp. 4–8.
100. Doug Richard, 'Start-up secrets, Part II, Creating a team', *Financial Times*, 1 June 2005.
101. Pinchot, G., *Intrapreneuring: Why You Don't Have To Leave the Corporation to Become an Entrepreneur*, Harper & Row, New York, 1985.
102. Jack Lang, University of Cambridge, personal communication.
103. Verloop, J., *Insight in Innovation*, Elsevier/Shell Global Solutions, Amsterdam, 2004.
104. In fact there are more phases in the life of a company, each of which needs a different kind of leadership. Either the leadership has to be replaced or the leaders have to transform themselves, a process of vastly underestimated difficulty. Transfers from one stage to the next are vulnerable moments in the life of an enterprise. In their *Selling the wheel* (Touchstone/Simon & Schuster, New York, 2000), J. Cox and H. Stevens distinguish four phases. The start-up phase requires risk-takers, the early growth phase relationship-builders, the mature phase a captain and crew, while the exit phase requires change managers. In Chapter 4 we will use a model of five stages.
105. Lucy Kellaway, 'And let no highbrow publishing project put us asunder', *Financial Times*, 3 October 2005.
106. Chinese saying.
107. John Ridding, 'Lunch with the FT', *Financial Times*, 5 February 2005, p. W3.
108. *Financial Times*, 13 February 2006.
109. 'A special report: France's troubles – a tale of two Frances', *The Economist*, 1 April 2006.
110. Bennis, W.G. and J. O'Toole, 'How business schools lost their way', *Harvard Business Review*, May 2005.
111. Acs, Z.J. (ed.) *Global Entrepreneurship Monitor 2004*, Babson College and London Business School, 2005, available from http://www.gem consortium.org.
112. Bert Twaalfhoven, 'Choice for life: European entrepreneur', Speech at the Opening of the Academic Year, Vlerick Leuven Gent Management School, 30 September 2002.
113. Economics Department of BankBoston (now Bank of America), *MIT: The impact of Innovation*, Publication of BankBoston, Boston, March 1997 (available from http://web.mit.edu/newsoffice/founders/).
114. Elisabeth Niejahr and Fritz Vorholz, 'Die Politiker machen unrealistische Versprechen' (The politicians make unrealistic promises), interview with Dr Ludolf von Wartenberg, *Die Zeit*, 2 June 2005, p. 25. See also: von Wartenberg, Ludolf and Hans-Joachim Haß, *Investition in die Zukunft*, *Wie Deutschland den Anschluss an die globalisierte Welt findet*, Wiley-VCH, Weinheim, 2005 (both in German).

115. An interesting study linking entrepreneurship and economic growth is to be found in Stel, A. van, *Empirical Analysis of Entrepreneurship and Economic Growth*, in International studies in Entrepreneurship series, Springer, Heidelberg/New York, 2006.
116. In February 2006, EU Commissioners Verheugen (enterprises and industry) and Figel (education) issued a list with recommendations to stimulate entrepreneurship in the EU. Half of Europeans will not start an enterprise if there is risk involved, compared to 30 per cent in the US.
117. For an overview of policies in different countries see: Lundstrom A. and L.A. Stevenson, *Entrepreneurship Policy: Theory and Practice*, International Entrepreneurship series, Springer, Heidelberg/New York, 2005.
118. Stel, A. van, M. Carree and R. Thurik, 'The effect of entrepreneurial activity on national economic growth', Scales paper N200419, EIM Business & Policy Research, Zoetermeer, the Netherlands, and Scientific Analysis of Entrepreneurship and SMEs (Scales), unpublished version of January 2005 (available from www.eim.net).
119. Compare with: Van Osnabrugge, M. and R.J. Robinson, *Angel Investing*, Jossey-Bass, San Francisco, 2000.
120. Note that this is the moment at which the product life cycle with its four phases begins.
121. Note that in the theory of the product life cycle the mature phase is followed by the decline phase when the products are subject to technological substitution or when their market evaporates.
122. The term is in general use. See for instance: Markham, S.K. 'Moving technologies from lab to market', *Research and Technology Management*, Nov–Dec. 2002.
123. One should be careful here as venture capital funds increasingly fund new enterprises at a very early stage, overlapping with the work of angels.
124. Wright, M. and K. Robbie, 'Venture capital and private equity: a review and synthesis', *Journal of Business Finance and Accounting*, **25** (5–6), pp. 521–70, 1998.
125. http://en.wikipedia.org/wiki/Private_equity.
126. Bance, A., *Why and How to Invest in Private Equity*, Special Paper, European Private Equity & Venture Capital Association, Brussels, March 2004.
127. Good cases about deal making can be found in: Lerner, J., F. Hardymon and A. Leamon, *Venture Capital – Private Equity – A Casebook*, John Wiley & Sons, Hoboken, NJ, 3rd edition, 2005.
128. The angel investors in Skype saw a return of 350 times in three years. Some 20 angels refused to invest. *The Economist*, 16 September 2006.
129. http://en.wikipedia.org/wiki/Angel_investing.
130. University of New Hampshire's Centre for Venture Research.
131. Data from: 'Special report: business angels', *The Economist*, 16 September 2006.
132. Wikipedia, op. cit.
133. Begg, D., 'The lessons from a genius', *Financial Times*, 4 December 2006.
134. Lerner, J., F. Hardymon and A. Leamon, *Venture Capital – Private Equity – A Casebook*, John Wiley & Sons, Hoboken, NJ, 3rd edition, 2005.
135. Shane, S., Academic *entrepreneurship: University Spinoffs and Wealth Creation*, Edward Elgar Publishing, Cheltenham, 2004.
136. Thursby, J.G. and M.C. Thursby, 'Pros and cons of faculty participation in licensing', in Libecap, G.D. (ed.), *University Entrepreneurship and Technology*

Transfer, Volume 16 in *Advances in the Study of Entrepreneurship, Innovation and Economic Growth*, Elsevier, Amsterdam, 2005.

137. Mowery, D.C. et al., *Ivory Tower and Industrial Innovation – University–Industry Technology Transfer Before and After the Bayh–Dole Act in the United States*, Stanford Business Books, Stanford University Press, Stanford, CA, 2004. See also: D.C. Mowery, 'The Bayh-Dole Act and high-technology entrepreneurship in US universities: chicken, egg or something else?', in G.D. Libecap (ed), *University entrepreneurship and technology transfer*, Volume 16 in Advances in the Study of Entrepreneurship, Innovation and Economic Growth, Elsevier, Amsterdam, 2005.
138. See various contributions in: Branscomb, L.M., F. Kodama and R. Florida (eds), *Industrialising knowledge – University–Industry linkages in Japan and the United States*, MIT Press, Cambridge, MA, 1999.
139. We try to avoid the term 'postgraduate' as it refers to Master's courses (after Bachelor's graduation) but it is sometimes also used for courses that are given after Master's graduation. In line with common practice, we will use the term 'post-experience courses' for people who have completed their university education (whether with a Bachelor's, Master's or PhD degree) and who return to a university to broaden or upgrade their understanding of a subject, not necessarily the subject they graduated in.
140. Wissema, J.G., *Unit Management: Entrepreneurship and Coordination in the Decentralised Firm*, Pitman Publishing/Financial Times, London, 1992.
141. The European Research Council will spend €12 billion in seven years on open research. The idea is to make Europe more competitive, especially with the US which between 1980 and 2003 received 164 Nobel Prizes in medicine, physics and chemistry against Europe's 68. Europe would need another 700 000 researchers if it were to catch up and bring total R&D spending to 3 per cent of GDP (*The Economist*, 12 November 2005).
142. Leader, 'How Europe fails its young' and 'The brains business: a survey of higher education', *The Economist*, 10 September 2005.
143. Recommended titles are: Wright, M.B. Clarysse, P. Mustar and A. Lockett, *Academic Entrepreneurship in Europe*, Edgar Elgar Publishing, Cheltenham, 2007; Wachman, M. and J.W. Hilty, *Education of a University President*, Temple University Press, Philadelphia, 2005; Bowen, W.G. and H.T. Shapiro, *Universities and their Leadership*, Princeton University Press, Princeton, NJ, 1998; Bright, D.F. and M.P. Richards, *The Academic Deanship: Individual Careers and Institutional Roles*, Jossey-Bass, San Francisco, 2001; Krahenduhl, G.S., *Building the Academic Deanship: Strategies for Success*, ACE/Praeger Series on Higher Education, Greenwood Publishing Group, Westport, CT, 2004; Buller, J.L., *The Essential Academic Dean: A Practical Guide to College Leadership*, JB – Anker series, John Wiley & Sons, Hoboken, NJ, 2007.
144. See for instance: Scott, M.C., *The Professional Service Firm*, John Wiley & Sons, Hoboken, NJ, 1998; Maister, D.H., *Managing the Professional Service Firm*, Simon & Schuster UK, London, 1993, and other books of David Maister; McKenna, P.J. and D.H. Maister, *First Among Equals*, Free Press, New York, 2002.
145. Like hospitals, many modern industrial enterprises are mixtures of enterprises with traditional industrial practices and professional service firms.
146. No one has better described it than Toffler, A., *The Third Wave*, William Collins Sons & Co, Glasgow, 1980.

147. Minzberg, H., *The Structure of Organisations*, Prentice Hall, Englewood Cliffs, NJ, 1979.
148. The sums can be substantial: In 2006, Rensselaer Polytechnic Institute in Connecticut for instance signed a $100 million research agreement with IBM in supercomputing.
149. All data from: 'Academics venture to bring in the money', *The Times Higher Education Supplement*, 21 August 2006.
150. Debackere, K., 'Managing academic R&D as a business at K.U.Leuven: context, structure and process', *R&D Management*, **30** (4), pp. 323–8, 2000.
151. Looy, B. van, J. Callaert and K. Debackere, 'Publication and patent behaviour of academic researchers: conflicting, reinforcing or merely co-existing?', Paper of K.U.Leuven's Research Division INCENTIM, not dated.
152. Jonge, W.M.F and M.T.G. Meulenberg (eds), *Innovation in Agri-Food systems*, Wageningen Academic Publishers, Wageningen, the Netherlands, 2005.
153. In 2003, 30 per cent of the higher educational institutes of the EU used targeting marketing activities to recruit students. The figure in the UK and Ireland was 80 per cent. S. Reichert and C. Tauch, *Trends 2003: Progress towards the European Higher Education Area*, EU Directorate-General for Education and Culture, Brussels, 2003.
154. The (US) National Business Incubation Association (NBIA) publishes interesting reports on this issue. See for instance: Adkins, D., C. Wolfe and H. Sherman, *Best Practices in Action: Guidelines for Implementing First-class Business Incubation*, NBIA, Athens, OH, 2002; and Lewis, D.A., *Does Technology Work? A Critical Review*, NBIA, 2002.
155. For an overview see: Adkins, D., *A Brief History of Business Incubation in the United States*, National Business Incubation Association, Athens, OH, 2002.
156. Johnson, L., 'What's wrong with the right entrepreneurs', *Financial Times*, 19 March 2008.
157. Wissema, J.G., 'Fear of change? A myth!', *Journal of Change Management*, **1** (1), pp. 74–90, 2000 and Wissema, J.G., *Fear of Change? A Myth!* (in Dutch), van Gorcum/Foundation of Management Studies, 1993: 7th edition 1996.
158. Wissema, J.G., 'Offensive change management with the step-by-step method', *Journal of Change Management*, **1** (4), pp. 332–43, 2001.
159. Pinchot, op. cit.
160. An exception to this rule occurs when a product ends up in the decline phase of its life cycle if it is substituted by new technology in most but not all of its applications. In this case only a few firms with relatively modern outfits will remain. An example is rayon, the sales of which started to decline in the 1960s. Many producers abandoned production and a few (including Akzo Nobel) remained with a significantly higher market share than before.
161. Quinn, J.B., *Intelligent Enterprise: A Knowledge and Service Based Paradigm for Industry*, Free Press, New York, 1992.
162. Normann, R., *Service Management, Strategy and Leadership in Service Business*, Wiley, Chicester, 1991. See also: Aa, W. van der, and T. Elfring, 'Realising innovation in services', *Scandinavian Journal of Management*, **18**, pp. 155–71, 2002.
163. Darwin, C., *On the Origin of Species by Means of Natural Selection*, John Murray, London, 1859.
164. Nicolis, G. and I. Prigogine, *Exploring Complexity*, W.H. Freeman & Company, New York, 1989.

165. Adam Smith, *An Inquiry into the Nature and Causes of the Wealth of Nations*, London, 1776.
166. Cf. Nelson, R.R. and S.G. Winter, *An Evolutionary Theory of Economic Change*, Harvard University Press, Cambridge, MA, 1982.
167. Pinchot, op. cit.
168. Buckland, W., A. Hatcher and J. Birkinshaw, *Inventuring: Why Big Companies must Think Small*, McGraw-Hill Professional, Maidenhead, 2003.
169. R.R. Nelson and S.G. Winter, 'In search of useful theory of innovation', *Research Policy*, **6**, pp. 36–76, 1977.
170. *Online Etymology Dictionary*, http://www.etymonline.com/.
171. *Oxford Concise Dictionary*.
172. The term is borrowed from Shell.
173. Waarts, E., Y.M. van Everdingen and J. van Hillegersberg, 'The dynamics of factors affecting the adoption of innovations', *Journal of Product Innovation Management*, **19**, pp. 412–23, 2002.
174. Rogers, E.M., *Diffusion of Innovations*, Free Press, New York, 4th edition, 1995.
175. Fisher, J.C. and R.H. Pry, 'A simple substitution model of technological change', *Technological Forecasting and Social Change*, **3**, pp. 75–88, 1971.
176. http://web.mit.edu/2742/www/sylabus/2_29_ent.pdf.
177. See for instance: H.A. Linstone and D. Sahal (eds), *Technological Substitution*, American Elsevier Publishing Company, New York, 1976.
178. Bright, J.R., *A Brief Introduction to Technology Forecasting*, Permaquid Press, Industrial Management Center, Austin, TX, 1972.
179. After 1900, fuel oil-powered ships started to substitute steamships. A major breakthrough was the decision by Winston Churchill, then Minister of the Navy, to replace steam engines by fuel oil engines during the First World War despite the fact that Britain did not produce petroleum but had an abundance of coal supply. His reason was that the fuel oil-driven ships simply performed better and that the supply of oil could be guaranteed if supply was diversified.
180. http://www.schoonerman.com/.
181. Bright, J.R., op. cit.
182. The expression 'product' is meant to include products, services or the combinations that we used to call 'systems' and that are now often called 'solutions'.
183. A visit to the Gutenberg Museum in Mainz is very instructive as is its website (www.gutenberg.de) from which we took notes for this paragraph.
184. Maurits of Orange started using standard components for guns and he standardised charging procedures for guns, reducing the time between two firings from ten to six minutes. Drilling was thus invented and put to greater use by King Friedrich of Prussia almost two centuries later.
185. Kist, J., *Bibliodynamics*, Otto Cramwinkel Publishers, Amsterdam, 1996 (in Dutch).
186. Rogers, op. cit.
187. Freeman, C. and L. Soete, *The Economics of Industrial Innovation*, 3rd edition, Continuum, London and New York, 1997.
188. Goold, M. and A. Campbell, *Designing Effective Organisations*, Jossey-Bass Publishers, San Francisco, 2002.
189. Vervest, P.H.M., *Innovation in Electronic Mail*, PhD Thesis, Delft University of Technology, Elsevier – North-Holland Publishers, Amsterdam, 1987.

190. See also: Gaule, A., *Open Innovation in Action*, H-I Network, London, 2006.
191. Often misquoted as: 'If you don't know where to go, any road will take you there'.
192. Wissema, J.G., *The Art of Strategic Entrepreneurship: A New look at Strategy* (in Dutch and Russian), Stenfert Kroese, Leiden, the Netherlands, 2001, reprinted 2002 and 2005.
193. Moor, G.A., 'Darwin and the demon: innovating within established enterprises', *Harvard Business Review*, July–August 2004.
194. Wissema, J.G., 'How to assess the strategic value of a capital investment proposal', *Long Range Planning*, **17** (6), p. 25–33, 1984; and Wissema, J.G., *An Introduction to Capital Investment Selection*, Frances Pinter, London and Dover, New Hampshire, February 1985.
195. At TU Delft we created an MSc course to create such managers; www.managementoftechnology.nl.
196. Verloop, J., *Insight in Innovation*, Elsevier and Shell Global Solutions, Amsterdam, 2004; 2nd edition 2006.
197. Wissema, J.G. and L. Euser, 'Successful innovation through inter-company networks', *Long Range Planning*, **24** (6), 1991.
198. Kaufman, A., C.H. Wood and G. Theyel, 'Collaboration and technology linkages: a strategic supplier typology', *Strategic Management Journal*, **21**, pp. 649–63, 2000.
199. Garvin, D.A., 'What every CEO should know about creating new business', *Harvard Business Review*, July–August 2004.
200. Freeman, C., and L. Soete, *The Economics of Industrial Innovation*, 3rd edition, Frances Pinter, London, 1997.
201. Rogers, op. cit.
202. An alternative educational model, designed at Carnegie Mellon, can be found in: Boni, A.A. and S.T. Emerson, 'An integrated model of university technology commercialisation and entrepreneurship education', in G.P. Libecap (ed.), *University Entrepreneurship and Technology Transfer: Process, Design and Intellectual Property*, Advances in the Study of Entrepreneurship, Innovation and Economic Growth series, Volume 16, Elsevier, Amsterdam, 2005.
203. At Harvard Business School the term 'required course' is used.
204. Di Gregorio, D. and S. Shane, 'Why do some universities generate more start-ups than others?', *Research Policy*, **32** (2), pp. 209–27, 2003.
205. According to Tomas Karlsson in an unpublished paper, some 10 million business plans are written every year (in Sweden 10 000 business plans).
206. Christensen, C.R., D.A. Garvin and A. Sweet (eds), *Education for Judgment*, Harvard Business School Press, Cambridge, MA, 1991.
207. Vesper, K, and E.W. McMullan, 'New venture scholarship versus practice: when entrepreneurship academics try the real things as applied research', *Technovation*, **17** (7), pp. 349–58 (1997). See also: Hamilton, C., G.P. Crawford and E.M. Suuberg, 'A technology-based entrepreneurship course', *International Journal of Engineering Education*, **21** (2), pp. 239–56, 2005.
208. Anita Roddick, 'Don't get a business degree, get angry', *Financial Times*, 15 November 2006.
209. There are a number of Harvard and other cases, available at European Case Clearing House (ECCH) Cranfield University, Cranfield, UK. Walter Kuemmerle of Harvard Business School published a book with 29 cases,

organised in five modules: fundamentals and identifying opportunities; valuation and risk assessment; mobilising resources; managing contingencies and changing contexts: growth, harvesting and exit. Kuemmerle, W., *Case Studies in International Entrepreneurship*, McGraw-Hill/Irwin, New York, 2005; and Kuemmerle, W., *Teaching Notes to accompany Case Studies in International Entrepreneurship*, McGraw-Hill/Irwin, New York, 2005.

210. Kuemmerle, op. cit.
211. Clarysse, B. and J. Roure, *Teaching Entrepreneurship: Selected Cases from Gate2Growth Academic Network*, available from the European Institute for Advanced Studies in Management (EIASM) in Brussels (www.eiasm.org), 2007.
212. Creed, C.J., E.M. Suuberg and G.P. Crawford, 'Engineering entrepreneurship: an example of a paradigm shift in engineering education', *Journal of Engineering Education*, April, pp. 185–95, 2002.
213. Creed, op. cit.
214. An excellent text to be used in courses like this is: Lang, J., *The High-Tech Entrepreneur's Handbook*, Pearson Education, London, 2002. An alternative is: Nesheim, J.L., *High Tech Start-up*, Free Press, New York, revised edition 2000.
215. Greiner, L.E., 'Evolution and revolution as organisations grow', *Harvard Business Review*, July–August 1972, pp. 64–73. See also: Penrose, E.T., *The Theory of the Growth of the Firm*, John Wiley, Hoboken, NJ, 1959; and Kor, Y.Y. and J.T. Mahoney, 'Penrose's resource-based approach: the process and product of research creativity', *Journal of Management Studies*, January, pp. 109–39, 2000, and the literature cited there.

Bibliography

ON FUTURES RESEARCH

Bright, J.R. and M.E.F. Schoeman (eds), A Guide to Practical Technological Forecasting, Prentice Hall, Englewood Cliffs, NJ. 1973.

Polak, F.L., *Prognostics: A Science in the Making Surveys and Creates the Future*, Elsevier, Amsterdam, 1971.

Toffler, A., *The Third Wave*, William Collins Sons & Co, Glasgow, 1980.

ON HISTORY OF UNIVERSITIES

Compayré, Gabriel, *Abelard and the Origin and Early History of Universities*, reprinted from the 1902 edition by the University Press of the Pacific, Honolulu, HI, 2002.

Le Goff, J., *Time, Work andCulture in the Middle Ages*, University of Chicago Press, Chicago, IL, 1980.

Otterspeer, W., *Group Portrait of a Lady: The Bulwark of Freedom, the University of Leiden 1575–1672*, Bert Bakker Publishers, Amsterdam, 2000 (4 volumes, in Dutch).

Rüegg, W. (ed.), *A History of the University in Europe*, Cambridge University Press, Cambridge (3 volumes).

ON CHANGING UNIVERSITIES

Crosier, D., L. Purser and H. Schmidt, *Trends V: Universities shaping the European Higher Education Area*, European University Association, Brussels, 2007.

Duderstadt, J.J., *A University for the 21st Century*, University of Michigan Press, Ann Arbar, 2000.

Lambert, R. and N. Butler, *The Future of European Universities: Renaissance or Decay?*, Centre for European Reform, London, 2006.

The Cambridge Phenomenon and *The Cambridge Phenomenon Revisited*, published by Segal Quince Wicksteed, Cambridge 1985 and 2000.

Weber, L.E., and J.J. Duderstadt, *Reinventing the Research University*, Economica, London, Paris and Geneva, 2004.

ON CORPORATE R&D/INNOVATION MANAGEMENT

Chesbrough, H., *Open Innovation: The New Imperative for Creating and Profiting from Technology*, Harvard Business School Press, Cambridge, MA, 2003.
Davila, D., M.J. Epstein and R. Shelton, *Making Innovation Work: How to Manage It, Measure It, and Profit from It*, Wharton School Publishing, Philadelphia, 2005.
Miller, W.L. and L. Morris, *Fourth Generation R&D*, John Wiley & Sons, Hoboken, NJ, 1999.
Quinn, J.B., *Intelligent Enterprise: A Knowledge and Service Based Paradigm for Industry*, Free Press, New York, 1992.
Rogers, E.M., *Diffusion of Innovations*, 4th edition, Free Press, New York, 1995.
Roussel, P.A., K.N. Saad and T.J. Erickson, *Third Generation R&D: Managing the Link to Corporate Strategy*, Harvard Business School Press, Cambridge, MA, and A.D. Little, 1991.
Tidd, J., J. Bessant and K. Pavitt, Managing Innovation, John Wiley & Sons, Hoboken, NJ, 2001.
Torvalds, L., *Just for Fun: The Story of an Accidental Revolutionary*, HarperCollins, New York, 2001.
Verloop, J., *Insight in Innovation: Managing Innovation by Understanding the Laws of Innovation*, Elsevier, Amsterdam, 2004.

ON (ACADEMIC) ENTREPRENEURSHIP AND VENTURE CAPITAL

Adkins, D., *A Brief History of Business Incubation in the United States*, National Business Incubation Association, Athens, OH, 2002.
Adkins, D., C. Wolfe and H. Sherman, *Best Practices in Action: Guidelines for Implementing First-Class Business Incubation*, National Business Incubation Association, Athens, OH, 2002.
BankBoston (now Bank of America), *MIT: The Impact of Innovation*, Publication of BankBoston, March 1997 (available from the MIT website).
Bhidé, A.V., *The Origin and Evolution of New Businesses*, Oxford University Press, Oxford, 2000.

Boni, A.A., and S.T. Emerson, 'An integrated model of university technology commercialisation and entrepreneurship education', in G.P. Libecap (ed.), *University Entrepreneurship and Technology Transfer: Process, Design and Intellectual Property*, Advances in the Study of Entrepreneurship, Innovation and Economic Growth series, Volume 16, Elsevier, Amsterdam, 2005.

Branscomb, L.M., F. Kodama and R. Florida (eds), *Industrialising Knowledge: University–Industry Linkages in Japan and the United States*, MIT Press, Cambridge, MA, 1999.

Dorf, R.C. and T.H. Byers, Technology Ventures: From Idea to Enterprise, McGraw-Hill, New York, 2005.

Drucker, P., *Innovation and Entrepreneurship*, Butterworth/Heinemann, Oxford, 1985.

Fayolle, A., P. Kyrö and J. Ulijn, *Entrepreneurship Research in Europe*, Edward Elgar Publishing, Cheltenham, 2005.

Lang, J., *The High-Tech Entrepreneur's Handbook*, Pearson Education, London, 2002.

Lerner, J., F. Hardymon and A. Leamon, *Venture Capital – Private Equity – A Casebook*, John Wiley & Sons, Hoboken, NJ, 3rd edition, 2005.

Lewis, D.A., *Does Technology Work? A Critical Review*, National Business Incubation Association, Athens, OH, 2002.

Lundstrom, A. and L.A. Stevenson, *Entrepreneurship Policy: Theory and Practice*, International Entrepreneurship series, Springer, Heidelberg and New york, 2005.

Nesheim, J.L., *High Tech Start-up*, Free Press, New York, revised edition 2000.

Pinchot, G., *Intrapreneuring: Why You Don't Have To Leave the Corporation to Become an Entrepreneur*, Harper & Row, New York, 1985.

Schramm, C.J., *The Entrepreneurial Imperative*, HarperCollins, New York, 2006.

Shane, S., *Academic Entrepreneurship: University Spinoffs and Wealth Creation*, Edward Elgar Publishing, Cheltenham, 2004.

Stel, A. van, *Empirical Analysis of Entrepreneurship and Economic Growth*, International Studies in Entrepreneurship series, Springer, Heidelberg and New York, 2006.

Van Osnabrugge, M. and R.J. Robinson, *Angel Investing*, Jossey-Bass, San Francisco, CA, 2000.

Wright, M., B. Clarysse, P. Mustar and A. Lockett, *Academic Entrepreneurship in Europe*, Edgar Elgar Publishing, Cheltenham, 2007.

ON CORPORATE STRUCTURE

Birkinshaw, J. and G. Piramal (eds), *Sumantra Goshal on Management*, *Financial Times*, London and Prentice Hall, Englewood Cliffs, NJ, 2005.

Goold, M. and A. Campbell, *Designing Effective Organisations*, Jossey-Bass, San Francisco, CA, 2002.

Minzberg, H., *The Structure of Organisations*, Prentice Hall, Englewood Cliffs, NJ, 1979.

Wissema, J.G., *Unit Management: Entrepreneurship and Coordination in the Decentralised Firm*, Pitman Publishing/*Financial Times*, London, 1992.

ON MANAGEMENT OF PROFESSIONAL SERVICES FIRMS

Holbeche, L., *The High Performance Organisation*, Elsevier, Amsterdam, 2005.

Maister, D.H., *Managing the Professional Service Firm*, Simon & Schuster UK, London, 1993.

Maister, D.H., *First Among Equals*, Free Press, New York, 2002.

Nicolis, G. and I. Prigogine, *Exploring Complexity*, W.H. Freeman & Company, New York, 1989.

Normann, R., *Service Management, Strategy and Leadership in Service Business*, Wiley, Chichester, 1991.

Scott, M.C., *The Professional Service Firm*, John Wiley & Sons, Hoboken, NJ, 1998.

ON MANAGEMENT OF UNIVERSITIES

Buller, J.L., *The Essential Academic Dean: A Practical Guide to College Leadership*, JB – Anker series, John Wiley & Sons, Hoboken, NJ, 2007.

Krahenduhl, G.S., *Building the Academic Deanship: Strategies for Success*, Series on Higher Education, ACE/Praeger, Greenwood Publishing Group, Westport, CT, 2004.

Richards, M.P., *The Academic Deanship: Individual Careers and Institutional Roles*, Jossey-Bass, San Francisco, CA, 2001.

Glossary

Note: Words in *italics* refer to other definitions in this list.

Academic: member of the scientific staff of a university. Also used for scientists and technologists working for other *know-how institutes*.

Accelerator: see *incubator*.

Angels: see *business angels*.

Appellation system (in the context of this book): from the French *appellation d' origine contrôlée* – certified name of the origin (of wines). Using a hierarchy of names, the *appellation* statement indicates the quality of the wine as assessed by independent experts.

Applied science: the use of existing theory to develop original new technology, adding applied knowledge without developing new theories in the domain of *pure science*. Also called technological development.

Basic or fundamental research: the search for new scientific discoveries using mainly purely scientific methods. Only the scientific disciplines are defined; the direction is indicated but without specific objectives or applications. Mainly used in enterprises.

Business angels (or, for short, **angels**; synonym for informal investors): individual investors who, alone or together with other angels, invest in young enterprises at the *development phase* or *start-up phase*. Such investments are usually high risk. Angels not only provide money, they also coach the founders or *CEO* of the enterprise and they make their networks available to the starter. In this way, they create a win–win relationship with the investment while they reduce the risk. Angels usually invest only in companies in product or service areas in which they have experience. Informal investment leads to a form of private equity (as does venture capital and other investments that are realised outside stock exchanges).

Business plan: a plan for a new venture describing the business model, the products and/or services to be delivered, the expected client base, details of the development activities needed, the production facilities, the organisation and staffing of the enterprise together with a forecast of the financial development and investment funds required at certain stages. The preparation of a business plan forces the *founders* to agree what they want to do and to consider all aspects of the new venture. The business plan should demonstrate the economic viability of the new venture and, as such, it is an important communication tool with investors and other stake holders.

Cambridge Phenomenon: the emergence and creation of a high-tech industry in the rural area around Cambridge since about 1970 and in connection with the University of Cambridge.

Carried value or **carry**: the value of an investment at the moment of *exit*, less the original investment which is increased by the *hurdle rate*.

Cascade model of education in entrepreneurship: see *funnel model*.

CEO: chief executive officer, the president or managing director of a company, the highest-ranking person in the executive management. In companies set up by *technostarters*, one of the *founders* is often the CEO but this is not necessarily so.

CFO: chief financial officer, the director or board member in an enterprise responsible for finance and administration.

Chancellor: head of the first generation university and still the head in some universities today (for instance in the UK, where the chancellor is the formal head of the university and the vice-chancellor is the acting head). In some countries the *rector* is head of the university whilst in others countries the president, usually a non-academic, heads a board of management.

Collaboration and the commercialisation of know-how: relatively new activities of universities regarded as of equal importance to the traditional tasks of research and education. Collaboration refers to cooperation in *R&D*, on a commercial basis or not, with industry or other partners. See also *commercialisation of know-how*.

Commercial spinouts of scientific projects: one of the ways in which a university can commercialise *know-how*. In this case, the primary aim of the research is to advance science, and commercialisation is an often unintended spinout. *Technostarters* who use their thesis project as the base of their enterprise fall into this category.

Commercialisation of know-how (also named *valorisation of know-how*): the way in which a *know-how institute* transfers knowledge to the market, either via existing companies or via new enterprises. Commercialisation implies that the institute receives a reward; in the case of valorisation this may or may not be the case. We often use the term commercialisation as short for *collaboration and the commercialisation of know-how*.

Consilience: the unity of knowledge; literally the 'bringing together' of knowledge of different disciplines; unified learning; the idea that there are no distinct border lines between the various scientific disciplines; the idea also that these disciplines converge towards a common result. The opposite is reductionism, the fragmentation of, and specialisation in science. See also *transdisciplinary* research and development.

Corporate culture (or just **culture**): the attitudes and informal aspects that govern the behaviour of those working in the firm. Norms and values guide behaviour and habits. The culture is often formed from the personal and business norms and values of the entrepreneur who started the firm. The culture is reinforced by the selection of personnel who should 'fit' the culture, and by 'stories' (the myths and sagas of the firm, the heroes and the failures) that people tell each other. Through culture the people working in the firm distinguish themselves from those working in other firms. *Structure* is the formal element that supplements culture in creating attitudes of people in a firm.

Course: the total of all the activities to be carried out in order to obtain a Bachelor's or master degree; hence the terms Bachelor's or undergraduate course and Master's or graduate course. Other courses are doctoral courses to assist those who work on a doctorate degree and post-experience courses, aimed at participants with a completed university education and practical experience. Typical day courses take 1–4 years to complete. Also: a series of *lectures* on a specific subject.

Cross-faculty teams: teams consisting of members from different faculties and often from different universities and increasingly including non-university members as well. Forerunners of *university institutes*.

Deal-making (or **closing of a deal**): reaching an agreement between investors and the *founders* of a (new) venture. This may include an agreement about the distribution of the *carry*. *Venture capital* firms use the term deal flow to describe the number of deals they have closed and their size.

Dean (in the context of this book): head of a *faculty* of a university. This is often a job that is rotated between the professors of the faculty and then it is typically taken for a period of four years. Increasingly, universities are appointing non-academic managers as deans.

Decline phase: phase in the life of a product or service in which the market becomes smaller as the product becomes substituted by a new product, based on superior technology, or when it simply becomes obsolete (men's hats for instance). See *product life cycle* and *mature phase*.

Deductive learning: learning in which the laws of a discipline are explained after which they can be used to solve problems. The opposite is *inductive learning*.

Design or pre-seed phase of an enterprise: phase in which the product and/or concept of the enterprise are being developed. To be followed by the *development phase*. See Figure 6.1.

Development: applying existing science and technology to solve a problem without adding to the domains of *pure science* and *technology*. Also: the search for improvements to existing products and processes with the aim of improving the quality–cost ratio. Both the target and the road are well defined. Although often viewed otherwise, development work has mainly a defensive nature as it can easily be copied by competitors and does not lead to lasting competitive advantage.

Development or seed phase: phase of an enterprise in which the product and/or concept of a new enterprise, as designed in the preceding phase *(design phase)*, is developed into a prototype. To be followed by the *start-up phase*. See Figure 6.1.

Disruptive innovation: an *innovation* that substantially changes social practices, the way we work and live (examples: the steam engine, electricity, telephone, mobile phone, email).

Elite (in the context of this book): selected, highly talented students and academics.

Embedded research: a construction whereby a team of researchers from an industrial firm co-locate with researchers of the university. This is usually a form of *pre-competitive research*. See Figure 8.2.

Entrepreneurs: we prefer the definition: 'dreamers who do, who take hands-on responsibility for creating new business. The entrepreneur may be the creator or inventor but it is always the dreamer who figures out how to turn an idea into a profitable reality' (G. Pinchot, *Intrapreneuring: Why You Don't Have to Leave the Corporation to Become an Entrepreneur*, Harper & Row, New York, 1985).

Executive directors (or **executive managers**): managers who lead the enterprise on a full-time base (or almost full-time). The opposite is *non-executive directors*.

Exit: the moment an investment is sold or cancelled.

Exploratory research: the search for entirely new products or processes, or superior new technologies that can substitute existing technologies by the process of technological substitution. In industrial exploratory research, the technology domain and the business objectives are defined but they can be adjusted depending on the emerging results of the research. In other words, there is a well-defined technological and business target but the road towards it is uncertain. Exploratory research stems from offensive strategies; the work is optimistic in nature.

Facilities: departments in a university responsible for all non-academic activities.

Faculty (in the context of this book): a group of academics who pursue the same branch of science or technology.

First flow of finance: money allocated to universities by the government department for science and education as a basic fee to cover costs of education and 'free research'. This is usually a lump sum and a form of input financing. See also *second*, *third* and *fourth flow of finance*.

First generation R&D: see *technology-push R&D*.

First generation university (also called **medieval** or **scholastic university**): the term denotes universities from their origins in the twelfth century until the Renaissance when the first transition period set in.

Founder: the (techno)starter(s) who create(s) a new enterprise. One of the founders is often the *CEO* but this is not necessarily so, or only so for a short period.

Fourth flow of finance: money received by universities as endowments. Endowments can be given for a specific project or they can be given as a general supplement to the university's funds. They can or cannot carry an obligation, for instance to name a building after the donator. See also *first*, *second* and *third flow of finance*.

Fourth generation R&D management: see *open innovation*.

Fund: used in this book as an *Investment Fund for Starters (IFS)*.

Fund Management Company (FMC): company that manages the investments of a Fund.

Fundamental research: see *basic research*.

Funnel model: a model for an educational programme in entrepreneurship which includes a number of stages in which the entrepreneurial intent increases after each stage while the number of students decreases. The principle is that, from all students that enter the university, eventually only the real entrepreneurs are left at the end of the process, while the 'dropouts' have had a comprehensive or more serious introduction to entrepreneurship and management in general. Also called the cascade model.

Graduate course: educational activities for those who already have a Bachelor's degree and leading to a Master's degree.

Graduation: The award of a Bachelor's degree.

Grande école: French for 'great school' meaning *elite* universities with a role comparable to that of *university colleges*. An example is the Ecole Nationale d' Administration (ENA, a post-graduate college).

Growth phase: phase of a new enterprise that follows the *start-up phase*. In the growth phase the business activities are growing fast. To be followed by the *mature phase*. See Figure 6.1.

Humboldt university: *see second generation university*.

Hurdle rate (or **hurdle**): percentage by which an investment is cumulatively increased in order to calculate the *carried value*.

Incapability to change: fundamental attitude against any changes of people involved in change processes. No matter how many good reasons for change are given or how many guarantees against personal setbacks, the worker or manager will resist or sabotage the changes. See also *inclination to change* and *willingness to change*.

Inclination to change: active, anticipatory and self-adjusting attitude of people involved in change processes. This term can be defined as the perceptible endeavour to be constantly examining one's own performance and that of one's department, and adapting it to meet the demands emanating from the dynamics of the company's 'environment' or from changed ambitions of the organisation. See also *incapability to change* and *willingness to change*.

Incubator: building in which *start-ups* can develop their enterprise under guidance. The conditions of renting space in an incubator are usually very favourable and below market rates. Depending on the situation, the incubator offers services from administrative services to professional coaching and technological support. If such services are widely available, the incubator can also be called an accelerator, but there is no common use of these terms. Residence time in an incubator or accelerator is usually limited. After this time has expired, the young enterprise may move to a *shared accommodation* facility.

Inductive learning: learning to apply the rules of a discipline by carrying out practical exercises, rather than by having the rules explained or by consciously deducing the rules.

Informal investors: see *business angels*.

Innovation: the successful introduction of something new; successful as shown by acceptance in the market or other use. An innovation is often based on an *invention*. If the innovation substantially changes social practices it is called *disruptive innovation*.

Inside-the-box innovation: incremental innovation aimed at the improvement of what already exists using established technology. Inside-the-box innovation creates new value propositions for customers. See also *outside-the-box innovation* and *substitutive innovation*.

Interactive research: the cooperation between *spinouts* or *technostarters* in their early stages, and the university. It is often an informal, non-structured cooperation with Master's degree students having a placement in the firm and academics offering unpaid advice, walking in, walking out.

Interdisciplinary R&D: research and development activities comprising various and integrated scientific, technological and/or design disciplines. See also *monodisciplinary R&D*, *multidisciplinary R&D* and *transdisciplinary R&D*.

Intrapreneur: combination of 'internal' and 'entrepreneur', meaning a manager of a distinctive unit of a larger enterprise who is profit-responsible and has a wide authority to take decisions, approaching a real *entrepreneur*. Often used in large enterprises to create flexibility and a quick response to the market.

Intrinsic quality factors (of a university): factors such as vision and strategy, organisational structure and culture, quality and attitudes of staff and students, possession of land, buildings and funds which to a large degree define the university and which cannot be changed easily.

Introductory phase: very early stage in the development of an enterprise in which the founders basically play with ideas. Once a subject for the enterprise has been chosen, the *design phase* begins.

Invention: a new (hitherto unknown) device, process or algorithm that has been demonstrated to work. Not all inventions are based on scientific work; many are ideas developed by trial and error. An invention may come from a technical idea, an observation of a need or problem for which a solution can be found, or from combinations of these. When an invention has been put to use, it becomes an *innovation*.

Investment Fund for Starters (IFS): in the context of this book, a fund in which investors put money in order to invest in *technostarters* and university *spinouts*.

IPO (initial public offering): shares of the company are offered to shareholders via a stock exchange for the first time.

IPR (intellectual property rights): general term for rights of ownership of original creative material. Patents, trademarks and copyrights are examples of IPR.

Know-how: see *technology*.

Know-how carousel (also called **know-how hub**): the synergistic combination of traditional academic research and education, *R&D* institutes of enterprises, independent (often specialised) *R&D* centres, facilities for *technostarters*, financiers of many kinds and professional services of many kinds (accountants, management consultants, marketing consultants, intellectual property specialists and so on) that collaborate in the creation and exploitation of know-how, preferably on the grounds of the university or near it. A know-how carousel is internationally regarded as a front-runner in knowledge creation in specific fields; a centre no researcher and no enterprise, active in the field, can ignore. In other words, it is a place where 'things are happening', where you have to be if you want to be in the front line of developments, whether you are an existing enterprise, a technostarter, an academic or a student.

Know-how hub: see *know-how carousel*.

Know-how infrastructure (or **innovation infrastructure**) of a nation or region: the way technology and market needs diffuse in a network of various participants, with each participant playing a vital role. These models have been elaborated into the concept of a national (or regional) innovation system (NIS) by which the innovation capabilities of a nation or region can be analysed, monitored and subsequently improved.

Know-how institute: organisation that creates new knowledge such as a university, a private *R&D* institute or department, an academy of science and other public or private institutes.

Lecture: element of an academic *course*. A typical lecture can take between one hour and one day.

Lingua franca (in the context of this book): language used on a large scale by people with different mother tongues. In the Middle Ages Latin was used as the lingua franca of Europe, and Chinese in South and East Asia. Today,

English is the lingua franca all over the world, in academic as well as business life.

Mandatory course: course that all students following a certain programme are required to take. The US name is required course.

Matchmaking: bringing investors (often *business angels*) and *start-ups* together in order to assess possibilities for participation.

Mature phase: phase of an enterprise in which it has become an established company. Follows the *growth phase*. In the mature phase, an enterprise usually starts developing other products or services but it can also do this earlier. See Figure 6.1. According to the theory of the *product life cycle*, the mature phase is followed by the *decline phase* in which the product or service is being substituted by a product based on new technology, or the product simply becomes obsolete. Note that it may take centuries before the decline phase sets in.

Monodisciplinary R&D: research and development activities based on only one scientific, technological or design discipline. See also *multidisciplinary R&D*, *interdisciplinary R&D* and *transdisciplinary R&D*.

Multidisciplinary R&D: research and development activities based on two or more scientific, technological or design disciplines working together in a complementary way. See also *monodisciplinary R&D*, *interdisciplinary R&D* and *transdisciplinary R&D*.

National Innovation System (NIS): see *know-how infrastructure*.

Nationes: institutions comprised of students and academics from the same region in the *first generation university*. They live on in an informal way in certain students' associations.

New technology-based firm (NTBF): newly created enterprise that is based on new science or technology or new applications of science and technology. There are two kinds of NTBFs: university spinouts (known as *spinouts*) and *technostarters*. In our terminology this is identical to *start-ups*.

Non-executive directors: part-time members of the board of management of an enterprise who have a supervising and advising role to the *executive directors*.

NTBF: see new technology-based firm.

Open Innovation: method of managing innovation by making the *R&D* department a profit centre rather than a cost or service centre. Open innovation suggests sharing knowledge with other parties. The concept of *fourth generation R&D management* broadly covers open innovation.

Outside-the-box innovation: the employment of new technology to cover new markets. Outside-the-box innovation creates new business. It is a form of diversification. See also *inside-the-box innovation* and *substitutive innovation*.

Participation: in the context of this book, buying or having shares in a company. As in: 'We participate for 20 per cent in company X', meaning that we own 20 per cent of the shares of company X.

Patent: Copyright to an invention; exclusive right (monopoly) to use an invention, nowadays a temporary monopoly. See IPR.

Post-experience course: educational activities following a certain amount of work experience (typically varying from two to ten years). Post-experience courses may have a certain level of prior education as an entrance requirement (for example Bachelor's or Master's level) or not.

Postgraduate course: educational activities immediately following the award of a Master's degree.

Potential for change: the extent, at the beginning of a change process, to which there is trust and order in the organisation, thereby allowing it to enter successfully into a change process. If the potential for change is small, it is better to improve it before going into the change process directly.

Pre-competitive research: one of the ways in which a university can commercialise *know-how*, usually for large enterprises. This type of research often has an explorative nature and focuses on the development of basic technologies that are to be turned into applications by the sponsors themselves. The research is limited in scope, in the sense that it allows the participants to use the basic research to develop competing applications. The client can be a single sponsor or a group of companies and possibly other institutions, often organised as a foundation. The subject of the research is decided by the sponsors and the university researchers together. The collaboration can have the form of *embedded research* (one client only) or simply be a research project. The latter may or may not incorporate cooperation by researchers from the sponsoring organisation; if they are involved, each researcher works from his own location. See Figure 8.2.

Private equity (PE): capital that is directly invested in enterprises or start-ups, that is, without the involvement of stock exchanges. *Business angels* and *venture capital* funds are examples of private equity. The term 'private equity funds' is also used for investments that can take substantial enterprises out of the stock market (buyout capital).

Product life cycle: model that describes the various phases in the life of a product or service. Usually four phases are defined: the *start-up phase* (or pioneering phase), the *growth phase*, the *mature phase* and the *decline phase*. The start-up phase is preceded by the design phase and the *development phase*, which are usually not included in the product life cycle concept. See Figure 6.1.

Professional support (in the context of this book): specialised advice to *technostarters* and university *start-ups* on topics such as marketing and market research, intellectual property rights, finance, administration and reporting, quality management, logistics, procurement and others.

Programme (in the sense of educational programme): all *courses* a *faculty* or university provides.

Pure science: widening scientific knowledge by new descriptions of phenomena and forming and testing fundamentally new theories.

R&D: research and development.

Rector (or **rector magnificus**): highest academic in a university, in the *second generation university* often also the head of the university but not always so (see *chancellor*). In the *first generation university* the rector was not always the highest academic, the function then being merely symbolic but highly respected.

Reductionism: see *consilience*.

Required course: US term for *mandatory course*.

Research-on-demand: one of the ways in which a university can commercialise *know-how*. The objectives and terms of reference of the research are well defined. The client pays for the research, in full or in part, and concludes a contract with the university similar to a contract with an engineering bureau. Research-on-demand can be requested by corporations, small and medium-sized enterprises *(SMEs)*, consortia of companies, governments or government agencies (for example NASA in the US), branch organisations, other research organisations and perhaps other clients.

Right of first refusal: right of a supplier of goods or services to offer a contract to the buyer. Only if, after a certain period of time, no agreement has been reached, can the buyer contact other suppliers. In the context of this book: right of an *Investment Fund for Starters* that is linked to a university to offer investment to a university *spinout*.

Second flow of finance: money received by a university to carry out research with specific objectives. This finance is usually provided by the state through independent foundations that invite competing proposals for the research to be carried out and weighing them by peer review. The second flow of finance is a form of output financing. See also *first*, *third* and *fourth flow of finance*.

Second generation university (also called **Humboldt university**): science-based universities with a research objective (and education in its slip stream) that started after Napoleonic times in Germany and rapidly took over the other models in the nineteenth century. Lasted until, in the 1960s, the second transition period set in. The second generation university is the substitute for the *first generation university* and the first transition period. In this book we speculate that it will eventually be taken over by the *third generation university*.

Serendipity: the effect by which one accidentally discovers something fortunate, especially while looking for something else entirely. The word derives from an old Persian fairy tale and was coined by Horace Walpole on 28 January 1754 in a letter he wrote to his friend Horace Mann, an Englishman then living in Florence (not the famed American educator). The letter read:

> I once read a silly fairy tale, called The Three Princes of Serendip. As their highnesses travelled, they were always making discoveries, by accidents and sagacity, of things which they were not in quest of: for instance, one of them discovered that a mule blind of the right eye had travelled the same road lately, because the grass was eaten only on the left side, where it was worse than on the right – now do you understand serendipity? One of the most remarkable instances of this accidental sagacity (for you must observe that no discovery of a thing you are looking for, comes under this description) was of my Lord Shaftsbury, who happening to dine at Lord Chancellor Clarendon's, found out the marriage of the Duke of York and Mrs. Hyde, by the respect with which her mother treated her at table. (*Wikipedia*)

Shared accommodation: facilities in what is usually called a science park or technology park, where relatively young enterprises (not necessarily starters) can rent accommodation at a commercial price. Many young enterprises move from an *incubator* to shared accommodation, where they can stay, in principle, as long as they wish.

SMEs: small and medium-sized enterprises.

Spinout (short for **university spinout**): *new technology-based firm* in which the university owns the *know-how* (or shares the ownership with the sponsor of the research that led to the know-how). Spinouts can be the result of initiatives by the researchers or of a systematic identification process by the university. See also *technostarters*. In our terminology, spinouts are a subcategory of *start-ups*.

Standardisation: the development, implementation and successful acceptance of common rules for performing specific tasks.

Start-up: new company created by an individual or group of individuals. In this book: equivalent to *new technology-based firms*, that is, *spinouts* and *technostarters*.

Start-up phase: phase of a new enterprise, after the *development phase*, in which production and commercialisation begin. To be followed by the *growth phase*. See Figure 6.1.

Strategy-driven technology management: a way of managing *R&D* in which R&D is synchronised with corporate and business unit or divisional strategy. Also named third generation R&D.

Structure: the totality of formal arrangements within the company that divide and coordinate the work of all those working for and associated with the firm. Structure comprises the definition of the tasks of individuals, groups and departments, their mutual relationships and their communication, coordination and supervision. Organisational schemes, responsibilities and formal competences of the departments and individuals, reporting systems and formats, in short all elements that can be written down and that can subsequently be enforced are part of the structure. Structure is commonly divided into corporate governance and internal governance. Corporate governance is that part of the structure that deals with the responsibilities and competences of the executive directors (board of management in Europe), the non-executive directors (supervisory council) and the shareholders and possibly other stakeholders as well as the mutual relations between these groups and individuals. Internal governance relates to the responsibilities of executive directors vis-à-vis the internal organisation and the division of the workers of the company into groups and departments and their arrangement. Both subdivisions of structure are relevant to innovation. *Corporate Culture* is the non-formal element that supplements structure in creating attitudes of people in a firm.

Subject (in the sense of education): element of a *course*. A subject is made up of *lectures*, tutorials, practical work and other elements. The time required for a typical subject can vary from one week to half a year of study.

Substitutive innovation: innovation aimed at the substitution of old technologies by new ones with a significantly higher quality–cost ratio. The market remains more or less the same. See also *inside-the-box innovation* and *outside-the-box innovation*.

Synchronised education: synchronised technological education, entrepreneurial education and the development of the enterprise of *technostarters*.

Technical sciences: equivalent to *technology*.

Technician: person skilled in the technique of a particular art or craft. This does not include scientific knowledge of the art or craft. See also *technology*.

Technological escalation: the development of the quality–cost indicator of a new *technology* as a function of time. This usually follows an S-shaped curve, meaning that initially the indicator grows exponentially but turns into decelerating growth after a point of inflexion.

Technological proliferation: the process by which existing *technology* is applied to different uses.

Technological stretch: the incremental improvement of existing *technology*.

Technological substitution (or **technological succession**): the use of new *technology* to replace old and inferior technology in existing applications.

Technological succession: see *technological substitution*. Also: the range of technological substitutions in an application.

Technological surprise: the creation of a totally new *technology* that is used to satisfy an as yet undiscovered or unknown need.

Technology: has two meanings:

- A body of knowledge, synonym for *know-how*, as in: 'Shell is leading in LPG technology'.
- The totality of applied sciences. It tries to understand phenomena and to design processes with the aim of doing something with this knowledge, by putting it to practical use. Its opposite, *pure science*, aims at understanding natural phenomena for their own sake, *la science pour la science*, to know why.

Technology-push R&D: way of managing *R&D* by which much initiative is left to the researchers, creating an almost academic atmosphere in corporate R&D laboratories. Also named first generation R&D management.

Technopreneurs: the Indonesian word for *technostarters* and young enterprises.

Technostarters: students or academics who want to establish their own science or technology-based firm. Technostarters own the *know-how* on which the new enterprise is based. They are the shareholders and they often form the management of the company. A subcategory of *start-ups*. See also *spinouts*.

Transdisciplinary R&D: research and development activities focused on a solution that involves scientists, engineers and designers from many disciplines, where the disciplines are no longer one-to-one related to individuals. Predecessors are *monodisciplinary R&D*, *multidisciplinary R&D* and *interdisciplinary R&D*. See also *consilience*.

Third flow of finance: money earned by a university from commercial contracts. This concerns a form of output financing. See also *first*, *second* and *fourth flow of finance*.

Third generation university or 3GU: speculative model described in this book of the university as it is going to be. The third generation university is characterised the centre of a *know-how hub*, with an emphasis on *transdisciplinary R&D*, collaboration with enterprises and other external partners and an active policy for the creation of *spinouts* and *technostarters*.

Third Generation R&D management: see *strategy-driven technology management*.

Third university objective: the exploitation or commercialisation of the university's *know-how* and collaboration with industry and other partners in creating *know-how*.

Type 1 universities: mainly teaching institutes, often but not always on the level of higher professional education. In that case they are strictly speaking not universities but higher professional schools. Some provide for sound scientific education. The research activities of these universities are limited or not present at all. Type 1 universities are unlikely to have systematic collaboration with industry or facilities for technostarters. They may migrate to *Type 2 universities*.

Type 2 universities: Type 2 universities have an average scientific base. In practice this means they will have some outstanding scientists while the average level of science is medium. Education is linked to their research efforts. These are 'true' universities, not higher professional schools that are only universities in name. They may migrate to *Type 3* or *Type 4 universities*.

Type 3 universities: *Type 2 universities* that in addition are active in collaboration with industry and other partners, in the commercialisation of know-how and while having extensive educational and operational facilities for technostarters. Type 3 universities may migrate to *Type 4* or *Type 5 universities*; the route is usually towards *Type 4 universities*.

Type 4 universities: universities that create cutting-edge science or technology and that provide excellent education. The older universities of this type are the ones that collect the Nobel Prizes. Type 4 universities are inherently unstable, as they have to migrate to *Type 5 universities* in order to maintain their scientific front position.

Type 5 universities: *Type 4 universities* that in addition are active in collaboration with industry and other partners, in the commercialisation of know-how and while having extensive educational and operational facilities for technostarters. Type 5 universities are the leading universities in this world and there are only a few.

Undergraduate course: educational activities leading to the Bachelor's degree.

University colleges (Latin: *domus scholarium*): set up as accommodation for poor students in the early Middle Ages, the university colleges developed into elite groups of academics and students who shared accommodation while the students received extra tuition. This model still exists, for example in Oxford and Cambridge. While most academics and students are housed outside the colleges, students receive tuition from academics in the college. Such colleges can have considerable funds from endowments and with these, they play a stimulating role. The role of the colleges is complementary to the 'normal' faculty organisation; colleges do not award diplomas. In the EU there is a trend to organise courses for selected, highly intelligent students (and ask extra fees for this) and the name 'university college' is sometimes adopted for such activities. The French have created so-called *grandes écoles* as separate academic institutions to the universities where selected students receive premium education.

University institutes: main organisational element of the third generation university. Organisations that are part of a university and report directly to the board of management that carry out *transdisciplinary R&D* on focused subjects. They consist of specialists from different faculties, often from different universities or from industry and independent *R&D* organisations. They are the institutionalised version of *cross-faculty teams*.

Valley of Death: the stage in the development of a young enterprise when financing by *founders*, friends and family is no longer sufficient while it is still too early to use *venture capital* funding or the use of bank loans. The Valley of Death can be overcome by *business angels* or university funds.

Valorisation of know-how: see *commercialisation of know-how*.

Venture capital: a form of private equity for investment in the later early stages of new enterprises. Venture capital often follows *business angel* financing. Venture capital firms handle larger sums than angels, while offering less or no coaching. Venture capital is still considered high risk. Like angels, venture capital firms are temporary investors. Venture capital is usually replaced by an *IPO* or money from an investment fund.

Willingness to change: attitude of people involved in change processes of willingness to go along with changes that arise from the demands made on the organisation by the dynamics of the 'environment' or by changed ambitions. This term is closely related to passive willingness, not objecting and being prepared to do something if someone else takes the initiative. See also: *incapability to change* and *inclination to change*.

Index

Printed and bound by CPI Group (UK) Ltd, Croydon, CR0 4YY

23/04/2025

14660986-0004